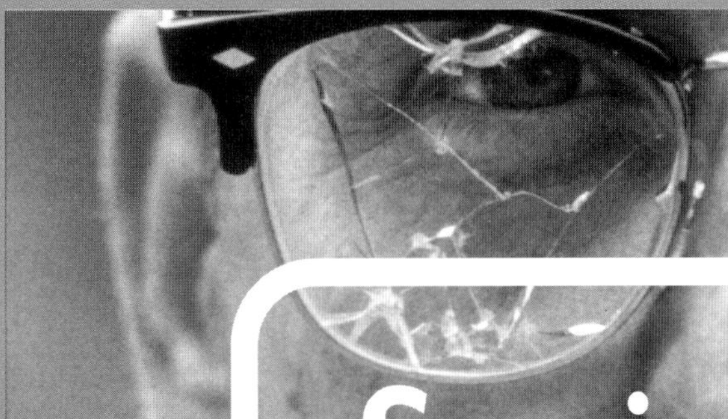
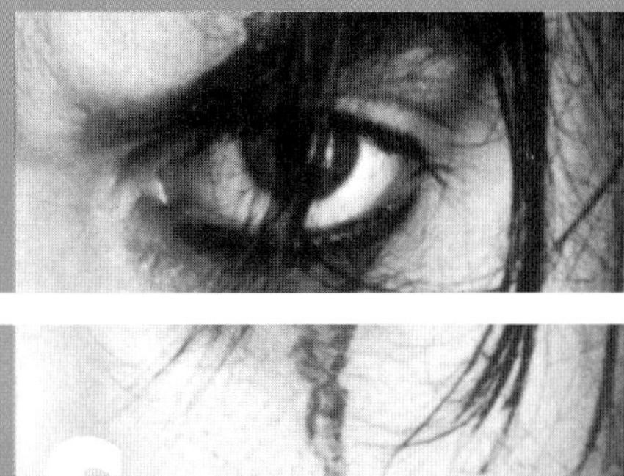

Seeing Sense

on Film Analysis

Leon van Nierop

with
Norman Galloway
Tascoe Luc de Reuck

J.L. van Schaik
ACADEMIC

Published by J.L. van Schaik Publishers
1064 Arcadia Street, Hatfield, Pretoria

First edition 1998
ISBN 0 627 02325 8

Cover design by Iaan Bekker
Typesetting in 10½ on 12½ pt Palatino by Pace-Setting & Graphics, Pretoria
Printed and bound by National Book Printers, Drukkery Street, Goodwood, Western Cape

Cover photographs:

Falling Down (Warner Bros.)
The Crow II: City of Angels (Miramax)
Three Colours: Blue (MK 2 Diffusion)
Breaking the Waves (October Films)

Dedicated to the second-year students of 1995, 1996 and 1997 at the Cinema and Television School, Technikon Pretoria, whose enthusiasm and commitment inspired me to write this book.

The author, Leon van Nierop, is a well-known film analyst and critic who lectures part-time at the Cinema and Television School, Technikon Pretoria. Two of his senior students, Norman Galloway and Tascoe Luc de Reuck, have contributed case studies throughout to enhance the student-driven approach of this publication.

PREFACE

The introduction of film study or analysis into the school curriculum along with the presentation of courses on the art of cinema at several technikons and universities has led to more and more students becoming cinema literate at an early age.

Cinema literacy means studying and understanding the relationship between the different elements that make up a film: photography, the script, editing, music, subtext, sound, etcetera. It means examining each element separately and understanding how it contributes and relates to the whole. It also means having a general background to a particular director's films and knowing where each film fits into his/her and the film industry's overall development. Above all, though, cinema literacy also means *enjoying* a film while taking it apart. It is that very passion and thirst for more knowledge which enhances our enjoyment of what we are trying to do, which provides us with a better understanding of the director's intentions.

We should become familiar with all the elements a director uses to get his or her message across and should be able to examine their effectiveness. As Joseph M. Boggs (1996: 8) said in *The art of watching films:* "Analysis shouldn't explain everything about a movie, it should fine-tune our tastes." To do this we have to put our senses into first gear when watching a film. Our attention should be totally devoted to the film and we should watch it as if it's the first time that we are seeing a film. We must be alert to any clue the director puts on our way that may lead to the eventual understanding of the film's motives.

It could happen that a mediocre, glossy film may appeal to our senses and seduce us into thinking that it is a great piece of cinema, but upon analysing the different elements and the director's intentions, we may see right through this disguise.

Movies can inspire us to understand the world we live in better and to broaden our horizons. The more we understand, the more we appreciate. The purpose of analysis, then, is to break down into fragments those scenes within a film which we do not understand and to discover their meaning. This will then allow us to understand the film as a whole, as well as the context in which the director was making it. Roger Ebert, the well-known critic for *The Chicago Sun-Times* remarked: "It is said that the human brain divides its functions. The right brain is devoted to *sensory* impressions, emotions, colours and music. The left brain deals with *abstract* thought, logic, philosophy and analysis. My definition of a great movie: while you're watching it, it engages your right brain. When it's over, it engages your left brain" (Ebert, 1996).

It was repeated queries from students on film study assignments that finally persuaded me to attempt this book as a guideline to discovering or rediscovering the joys of cinema. From my discussions with these students I realised that many of them had no idea how important elements such as editing, subtext, directing and irony are in a film. As a matter of fact, some scarcely understood what these words meant in this context. When they did understand these terms, they did not know how to apply them. Therefore I decided to write this book with the help of two final-year Cinema and Television School students who were given the same assignments that scholars or students usually get. They were specifically asked to make their contributions easily accessible and to write economically, just as they would for an assignment in class. Their individual contributions have been indicated in the text and two full-length essays and an example of a review are included in Chapter 11.

My notes (and the students' contributions) were based on my lectures for Film Appreciation and Development 1 and 2 at the Cinema and Television School at the Technikon Pretoria, and I must thank all the second-year students since 1995 who have helped me to shape and polish these lectures.

In this book I have attempted to introduce scholars and students to the joys of analysing films, of discovering how to take a film apart and then of fitting all the pieces together again. The book is definitely not aimed at established film critics, who already possess this knowledge, nor does it try to be a formal theoretical document on film analysis. It simply tries to answer the questions put by scholars and students who are beginning their courses on film analysis or film appreciation.

The examples were chosen from mainly contemporary, but also classic films. They are readily available in video stores and are thus accessible to students, with the exception of *The Cabinet of Dr Caligari* and *Camera Buff*. Many of the examples are from more recent films, as I have discovered that quoting examples from classic films by masters like Fritz Lang and Sergei Eisenstein often leaves students in the dark because they have no access to these films and the examples therefore mean nothing to them. References to classics have therefore been kept to a minimum. However, I still hope that through these examples students will be inspired to discover films they may not have chosen had they gone to their local video store.

Finally, the book is meant to be enjoyed. It sets out to prove that cinema is the most powerful, and perhaps most exciting, art form of the twentieth century and beyond, but that one needs certain easy-to-follow and simple guidelines (without getting entangled in theoretical intricacy) to appreciate films fully.

Special thanks to the following people: Helen Kuun, Pieter Geldenhuys and Driki van Zyl from Ster Kinekor, Halima Khan from UIP, John Ferreira from Nu Metro and Laetitia Pople from *Beeld* who went to great trouble to obtain the press released photographs used in this book; Greg Landman from *Ster Kinekor Video,* Henni Erasmus and Gustav Singer from *Absolutely Fabulous Video* in Rivonia for giving us access to video released films; Darryl Accone, editor of *Star Tonight;* Mike Rix; the personnel of the Cinema and Television School and the library of the Technikon Pretoria.

Special thanks to the publishing team of J.L. van Schaik – especially Magdaleen du Toit who supervised the editing process, René Snyman who patiently pursued publishing rights for the photographs and Francis Galloway, the publisher, who commissioned the manuscript, believed in the project and never gave up looking for ways to put an affordable book on the market.

Happy movie going!

LEON VAN NIEROP
December 1997

A note from the publisher

The publication of this book was delayed for several months while we were negotiating the publication rights of photographs. This proved to be a daunting task! We extend a warm word of appreciation to the national and international studios and producers who backed our educational goal. We believe that the investment in this social and educational project will benefit the film industry in South Africa. Film Studies is a newcomer to courses offered at secondary and tertiary educational level in the country and there is a general need for an affordable and locally produced textbook, based on contemporary and available films, on which courses can be based. The main aim of *Seeing Sense* is to guide a developing new audience in the science and art of film watching and therefore to enhance the growth of cinema literacy in the country.

DR FRANCIS GALLOWAY
Head: Academic Division

△ **A** Ralph Fiennes is never dwarfed by the overpowering, majestic desert landscape in Antony Minghella's *The English Patient*. (Miramax)

▽ **B** A wounded Brad Pitt as a young detective is being led away by Morgan Freeman as an experienced police officer on his final and most gruesome case in a misty, dark, ominous scene from David Fincher's masterpiece *Seven*. (New Line)

△ C

D ▽

△ **E** Comedies usually use high-key lighting, as in this scene from *Fierce Creatures*. (Copyright © 1996 by Universal Studios, Inc. Courtesy of MCA Publishing Rights, a division of Universal Studios, Inc. All rights reserved.)

◁ **C** The house explodes, first realistically, and then in backwards motion, in David Lynch's surrealistic *Lost Highway*. (Courtesy of Ciby 2000)

◁ **D** Note the effective use of lighting to create an other-worldly atmosphere in *The Arrival* by David Twohy. Also note that Charlie Sheen's red clothes form a striking contrast to the darkness and spots of light which surround him. (Copyright © 1996, Courtesy of LIVE International)

△ F

G ▽

△ **H** Grotesque make-up effects were actually the real superstars in Robert Rodriquez's *From Dusk till Dawn*. (Miramax)

△ **I**

J ▽

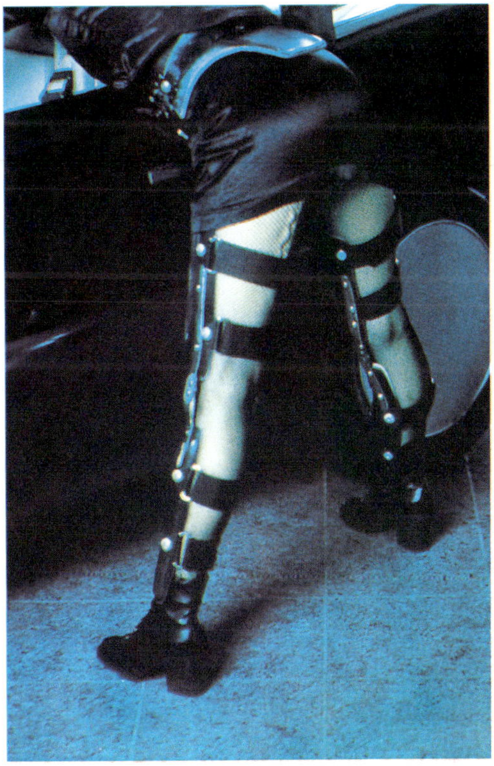

▷ **I J** Realistic make-up contributed to the gruesome realism of David Cronenberg's *Crash*. Note in (I) the wounds of the photographer Vaughan played by Elias Koteas and in (J), the injuries of the accident victim Gabrielle, played by Rosanna Arquette, which are used by her and her lovers to achieve sadomasochistic pleasure. (Courtesy of MDP Worldwide)

◁ **F** Note the luscious colours used in this lyrical scene from Darrell James Roodt's *Cry the Beloved Country*. (Courtesy of Anant Singh and Videovision Entertainment)

◁ **G** The hostility, yet at the same time barren beauty, of Rechi in Dagestan (standing in for Chechnya), is radiantly captured in Pavel Lebesher's realistic photography in *Prisoner of the Mountains*, directed by Serguei Bodrov. (Courtesy of Fortissimo Films)

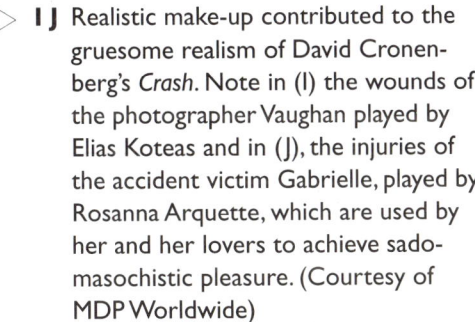

△ **K**

L ▽

△ **M** Alan Parker used actual locations for his lavish, though realistic version of *Evita*. (Buena Vista International)

◁ **K** The spectacle never dominates the human elements in Kenneth Branagh's version of *Hamlet*. (Courtesy of Castle rock; Photographer: Rolf Konow)

◁ **L** The audience-friendly spaceship in George Lucas's spectacular *Star Wars*, here featuring Harrison Ford as Han Solo, Alec Guinness as Obi-Wan Kenobi, Mark Hamill as Luke Skywalker and Peter Mayhew as Chewbacca. (20th Century Fox)

△ **N** Brenda Blethyn as Cynthia and Marianne Jean-Baptiste as Hortense discover that they are related in Mike Leigh's gritty *Secrets and Lies*. (Courtesy of Ciby 2000)

△ **P** Alan Parker directs Madonna in a scene from *Evita*. (Buena Vista International)

◁ **O** Tim Robbins's performance in Frank Darabont's *The Shawshank Redemption* demonstrates that although his body is imprisoned, his soul remains free. (Courtesy of Castle Rock; Photographer: Michael Weinstein)

▽ **Q** A group of destitute Irish mothers whose sons are on hunger strike, in a scene from Terry George's *Some Mother's Son*. (Courtesy of Castle Rock)

CONTENTS

1

Why should we analyse films?

The aim of film analysis is to help us gain a better understanding of a director's intentions. Either by writing about it or discussing it, we may help other viewers to understand the film better and to enjoy a film more.

The English Patient by Anthony Minghella is an excellent example of a film that is so complex that it needs careful analysis because it frequently makes huge jumps in time as it flashes back to previous occurrences. The student could piece many of the scenes together by finding a narrative structure which runs through the film and explains the reasons for the fractured style to the audience.

1. Ralph Fiennes and Kristin Scott Thomas as the doomed lovers in Anthony Minghella's Oscar-winning film *The English Patient*. (Miramax)

CHAPTER

1

Why analyse

When writing about film (for a class assignment for instance), one of your first considerations should be whether it will appeal to an audience's particular tastes or not.

The hard truth is that Hollywood is business orientated, therefore the producer of studio films usually has a particular audience in mind when investing his money. He certainly wants to make a profit, and he often does not really care for the artistic contribution a film will make to the cinema scene. He gives his audience what they want, be they action junkies, karate kids or romance addicts.

This, unfortunately, leads to the "hamburger syndrome": if one feeds audiences hamburgers only, like happens with films such as *Con Air, Face/Off* and *Speed 2: Cruise Control,* they will never appreciate anything else! Recently, however, with the strong emergence of so-called "art" and independent films which require more from viewers than merely looking at pictures, a new culture is taking shape.

We must judge whether the film makes contact with that intended audience, or if it has a universal message which is accessible to any audience.

The film *Seven* (also written as *Se7en*) may be a good example. Audiences who flock to see this film usually want to be "terrorised". After the film they may ask: did this film succeed in scaring me? Or did it fail in its purpose? How did it scare me and why? Films like *Seven,* Stanley Kubrick's *The Shining* and Ridley Scott's *Alien* frighten audiences because they create the very real fear that such events could actually happen to them. These directors have succeeded in making their audience believe in the impossible.

2. John Travolta and Nicolas Cage, as two men wearing each other's faces, fight for their lives in John Woo's exaggerated thriller *Face/Off.* (Buena Vista International)

3.
Whoopi Goldberg, here pictured in *The Associate*, switches from comedy to intense drama with the greatest of ease. (Courtesy of PolyGram)

Seven is about a serial killer who selects his victims according to the seven deadly sins (pride, greed, lust, wrath, gluttony, envy and sloth). The director, David Fincher, has made the story so real and the terror so vivid that we become completely engrossed in and convinced by it. It can therefore be said that *Seven* succeeds in its purpose, because the director has created a real fear for the unknown and has perhaps tapped into our subconscious fears. This does not mean that we should judge a film only by the expectations it creates. We should always leave ourselves open to any experience or interpretation and then react to the influence it has on us.

When evaluating a film like *The Rock* by Michael Bay and *Con Air* by Simon West, one may feel that it will appeal to teenagers and action junkies, but not necessarily to cinema-goers who prefer the more subdued quality of films like *The Saint* or *Night falls on Manhattan*. The effects are like those in a video game – way over the top, but the characters revert to stereotypes and the climax is implausible even for an action film.

Above all, we should understand the different relationships between all the elements in a film to understand the director's intentions.

In Robert Altman's *Short Cuts* the director shows a number of scenarios which seemingly have no relationship to each other. They are simply fragments of a whole, with one common thread linking them all: fate. In the end, he brings them all together, showing and explaining the relationship that each of the stories and characters has with the others. Without analysing the scenes within the film as separate entities, we would be unable to understand the film as a whole.

–TLdR

In *Strictly Ballroom* Baz Luhrmann, the director, has constructed his film meticulously. Every shot has been carefully directed, orchestrated and timed to fit into a rhythmic whole. It is like a brilliantly written symphony in which every note matters. The film resembles a whirlwind dance, moving continuously to a grand climax with other, less dramatic scenes supporting and balancing the narrative. It concentrates on the human face behind the glitz, tradition and facade that make up ballroom dancing. It deals with the unglamorous truth behind the peacock appearances, and the bizarre which is traditionally part of this culture.

Baz Luhrmann presents this organised chaos with more than just a hint of madness – his tongue is firmly in his cheek. His style is perfectly reflected in his main actor, Paul Mercurio's, fiery eyes tinted with insan-

4. Paul Mercurio as the temperamentally driven ballroom dancer who, to his mother's horror, introduces new steps at the glittering championship in *Strictly Ballroom*. (Courtesy of M & A Film Corporation)

ity. Luhrmann also makes filmic sense out of the flashy temperaments, and the contrast between the drab, industrialised world outside and the elaborate pomp and splendour inside the ballroom. We laugh at the characters but with a kind of melancholy sympathy for their extravagant, single-minded dreams.

GUIDELINES

Some guidelines which could be useful when analysing a film are discussed below:

Be objective Of course it is not always possible to be completely objective! But prejudices should never influence our analysis. Don't make up your mind about a film on, for example, alcoholism *(Leaving Las Vegas)* or drug abuse *(Trainspotting)* before seeing it, even if you have specific views on the subject or have read negative reports about the film. It is usually more helpful for a student to read reviews *after* he has seen a film and written about it, as reviews tend to influence one's perceptions.

You may have had some unpleasant experiences with a particular subject yourself, but you should look at the way the director presents his subject matter and his reasons for doing so. Does he merely exploit the subject? Or does he help an audience to gain insight into a character's dilemma?

Philadelphia is a great example of this. Director Jonathan Demme confronts the controversial issue of Aids and prejudice with a high degree of sympathy for the victims. He certainly does not exploit the subject matter and shows a side to Aids which many may not have seen before. He confronts our prejudices and our ignorance, allowing us to develop a deeper understanding of both the subject matter and ourselves as human beings.

One may not agree with what the director is trying to say, but at least a film of this nature can inspire debate, and this is effectively what analysis is all about. It allows us the opportunity to look into and understand another side, a different side of an issue that we may not have fully understood before.

Another good example is Danny Boyle's *Trainspotting*. This film explores the lives of drug addicts in Scotland. It is an important landmark in film because for the first time it not only points out the dangers of drug abuse, but attempts to explore why people use drugs. In his own subtle way, the director succeeds in not only showing his audience why people find it "cool" to get involved in drugs, but also what dangers arrive on their doorstep as a result of their decisions. He is saying that although we have the freedom of choice, we do not have the freedom of consequence.

Boyle doesn't preach. He simply invites a predominantly young audience to make up their own minds about the subject and its harmful effects, hopefully by appealing to their sense of responsibility. His film is all the more accessible in that he speaks a modern, street smart, almost "music video" kind of language and therefore makes direct contact with the audience for which the film was intended.

As Leon van Nierop said in *Beeld*, it is almost as if Boyle injects his audience into the bloodstream of a junkie, using brilliant visual imagery in an attempt to make sense out of the chaos which surrounds them.

–TLdR

Form your own opinion

Pre-publicity or "hype" should not influence your perception at all, difficult though this may be.

With a film like Alan Parker's *Evita,* awards, a very seductive trailer, scores of interviews, television coverage, articles and raving reviews may have prescribed to us that we were supposed to hail the film as a masterpiece. This may explain why some people left the cinema disappointed. As far as musicals are concerned, it is a brilliant film. But *Evita* also became its own worst enemy. It was almost impossible for the film to live up to its massive publicity campaign, although many critics felt that it did.

The film and its characters must be convincing

Given a particular situation, we must be able to believe in the people and the situations in which they find themselves. Even if the film is pure fantasy like *E.T.: The Extra-Terrestrial* or *Babe,* the premise and material should still be convincing in that particular context.

If a film takes place against a certain background, ask whether the

5. Ewan McGregor is completely convincing as the drug addict, Renton, trying to go cold turkey in *Trainspotting.* (Courtesy of Film Four International)

director has manipulated the characters and situations just for effect, as Jonathan Lynn did with *Sgt. Bilko,* where a clownish sergeant (Steve Martin) abuses his authority in a farcical manner to get his own way. Or does the director stay true to his milieu, the motivations of his characters and, in this case, military ethics? In *Sgt. Bilko,* one got the impression that the director simply exploited the subject matter for a few cheap laughs. The same applies to a very American exploitation of the civil war in Ireland in Alan J. Pakula's *The Devil's Own,* turning it into a violent commercial thriller which had little to do with the real subject matter at hand. One even got the impression that he was trying to say that Americans (as represented by the actor Harrison Ford) would be able to save the hopeless situation!

6.
The casting of Brad Pitt in the role of an Irish terrorist swings the audience's sympathy towards the superstar instead of the character in *The Devil's Own* by Alan J. Pakula. (Columbia Tristar)

Although *Chariots of Fire* takes place during the 1920s and the characters may seem foreign to our modern way of thinking, Hugh Hudson's film is convincing and even elicits feelings of elation. It is a purifying experience in its portrayal of good old-fashioned patriotism symbolised in the fervour of a Scottish Christian and a Jew for their country, Great Britain. It also celebrates good sportsmanship, unity, pride, religion and the glory of winning for reasons other than money.

The two athletes, Eric Liddell (Ian Charleson) and Harold Abrahams (Ben Cross) are convincing as people, even though their behaviour and motivation seem a bit strange compared with today's money-driven society. They firmly believe in themselves and are bent on winning, each for his own reasons. Liddell runs for the glory of his Creator; Abrahams wants to win for his university, his coach and his country. Both characters are brilliantly portrayed.

If a story takes place on the streets (as in John Singleton's *Boyz N the Hood* or Larry Clark's *Kids*) do the characters, the language they use and the way they behave ring true, or has the director "sanitised" the subject matter and language to appeal to certain tastes?

Everything should be functional

When a film uses lavish photography in which every detail is meant to be visible, such as in *Sense and Sensibility* by Ang Lee, or has a sweeping score like *Legends of the Fall* by Edward Zwick, are these techniques used

7. In Berit Nesheim's *The Other Side of Sunday*, with Hildegun Riise and Marie Thiesen, conservatism and religious indoctrination are symbolised by the dark shadows which haunt the victims of emotional abuse, while the young girl's spiritual and sexual awakening is reflected in glowing light. (Courtesy of the Swedish Film Institute)

to manipulate us or do they have a specific function? Are they integrated into the overall statement of the film and do they gently underline the emotion evoked? Or do they drown us in their excessiveness, as was the case with Zwick's film?

In David Fincher's *Seven* and Richard Donner's *The Omen,* the often overbearing music has a dark, oppressive, macabre quality. This is used by the directors to highlight the atmosphere of evil and illustrate domination, suffering, diabolical phenomena and degradation. On the other hand, in many horror films (cf. the *Friday the 13th, Scream* and *A Nightmare on Elm Street* series), music is deliberately used to shock the audience when they least expect it, often creating a cheap, sensational, undesirable and even comical effect.

The classic Hitchcock thriller, *Psycho,* is perhaps the best example of functional music, composed by Bernard Herrmann. As Janet Leigh is murdered in the shower, the spine-chilling violin music, with its high-pitched tone actually imitating the stabbing motion of the knife, heightens our shock. We become the victim as the music attacks our senses!

However, in Alan Parker's *Come see the Paradise,* Richard Attenborough's *In Love and War* and Roland Joffe's *The Scarlet Letter* the often sweeping, hummable "audience-friendly" music has been used to glamorise the proceedings and carry these films through their weak spots and cover an empty core.

The film *In Love and War* has no story or plot to speak of (not even in the subtext), and the music sounds as if it was specifically composed for the dialogue. When Chris O'Donnell (as the young Ernest Hemingway) proclaims his love for the character played by Sandra Bullock – or vice

8.
Matt Dillon plays against type as the weak and selfish husband of a flamboyant songwriter in Allison Anders's *Grace of my Heart.* (Copyright © 1996 by Universal Studios, Inc. Courtesy of MCA Publishing Rights, a division of Universal Studios, Inc. All rights reserved.)

9.
Linus Roache gives a touching performance as a priest who is victimised for his beliefs and sexual orientation in *Priest* by Antonia Bird. (Courtesy of Film Four International)

versa – the music swells as the announcement is being made. This is, of course, a technique typical of melodramas but here it is taken to the extreme and becomes a cheap, clichéd trick.

Conversely, Nicholas Hytner's *The Crucible* also has sweeping, impressive photography and music, but the beautiful pictures are quickly eroded by the religious fanaticism and mass hysteria which sweep through the town, quietly accompanied by the unobtrusive score. In film, less is often more. We notice the chilling effect of hypocrisy, adultery and conservatism in the bleak exterior scenes (often reflecting the characters' desolate, cold inner lives) and the darkness which surrounds them. The coldness of the light seeps through the edges and alienates the characters rather than warming them.

Changing a cinema-goer's mood or perception

Is the person who leaves the cinema different from the one who entered it? For example, one may be in a pessimistic mood before walking into *Mrs. Doubtfire* or *Panic Mechanic,* but upon leaving the cinema one may feel a changed person.

In the case of *Panic Mechanic,* one gains the impression that South Africans are looking at their own country through different eyes. The film tries to help them laugh at themselves. Its central message is not to take life and oneself so seriously. That is often the only way to survive! Leon Schuster's film succeeds on that level, even though some of the situations are excessively crude and overdone and as such do not always convey the message successfully.

Schuster's film also tries to comment on a society riddled with fear, paranoia, prejudice and racism. Yet some cinema-goers leave the cinema unchanged, feeling that the hysterical slapstick scenes and predictable jokes damage the film's good intentions.

A film could give new insight into a situation, as with *William Shakespeare's Romeo and Juliet.* Director Baz Luhrmann's "cool", high-tech presentation makes Shakespeare's immortal love story more accessible to teenagers, bored by reading the original tragedy at school. Thus it creates a new awareness, even though it may offend the sensibilities of traditional scholars of Shakespeare.

10. Claire Danes as an angelic Juliet in Baz Luhrmann's contemporary adaptation of *William Shakespeare's Romeo and Juliet.* (20th Century Fox)

Withstanding the test of time

Another question you may ask is whether a film has withstood the test of time. Has it aged gracefully or is it dated?

Many people feel that *Doctor Zhivago,* that sweeping and richly textured David Lean melodrama based on Boris Pasternak's novel, is now far too slow and self-indulgent, even boring. (Remember, "boring" means different things to different people!) Conversely, the same director's *Lawrence of Arabia* and *Brief Encounter,* with their timeless messages and appeal, are as fresh today as when they were originally released.

The same applies to what many critics regard as the best film ever made, namely *Citizen Kane* by Orson Welles, as well as to *Psycho* by Alfred Hitchcock, *2001: A Space Odyssey* by Stanley Kubrick and *Schindler's List* by Steven Spielberg. Twenty years from now these films will still have a forceful impact because of the timelessness of their style and the way they present their universal messages.

Making a statement or having a message

There is usually a reason why a writer decides on the particular subject matter as the theme for his film. Often he or the director wants to convey a message to the audience. Does he indeed communicate this message, or does it become inaccessible?

> Peter Weir's *Dead Poets Society* makes a number of timeless statements about human behaviour. The director shows young people that they should follow their dreams, explore the questions that lie within their souls, and then use their knowledge to make the world a better place.
>
> It shows parents too that they should be aware of their children's dreams. They should look past their own ambitions and encourage their children to excel at what they love. The message is that every one of us needs to "seize the day": *Carpe Diem!,* because our time could be running out. This appeal is certainly relevant today, and probably always will be.
>
> *Dead Poets Society* can also be seen as an attack on an archaic school system which no longer inspires students to learn, but simply feeds them with information that they are unable to use. It exposes a form of traditionalism that does nothing but stifle the imaginations of those that pass through it.
>
> –TLdR

The purpose of the film

When analysing a film, one should always ask: *why* did the director make this film and *who* is its audience? One should then analyse it accordingly.

A director's sole purpose may be to entertain. That is why Rob Cohen never intended his *Daylight* to be in the same league as, for example, an Ingmar Bergman film.

The director's purpose could be to create a greater awareness of certain issues. Excellent examples are Steven Spielberg's *Schindler's List* and

Bruce Beresford's *Paradise Road*. These films remind us that we should never forget the suffering that many people needlessly endured, nor the humanity which saved their lives.

In *Paradise Road* a group of Australian, Dutch and British women are captured and imprisoned in a prisoner-of-war camp in Sumatra. Beresford pays tribute to their will to survive in a civilised manner under inhuman conditions. There is no glamour here. The actresses like Glen Close and Pauline Collins are mostly without make-up to expose the truth and illustrate their suffering realistically and without gimmicks. The humour, horror and compassion for the characters in the film are perfectly captured in the New World Symphony which they hum. This moving piece of music is, of course, also symbolic of their dreams and hopes. Ironically, not everybody survives to see the "new world" which emerged after the world war in 1945. This is an example of a multi-textured film which centres around every possible human condition and emotion.

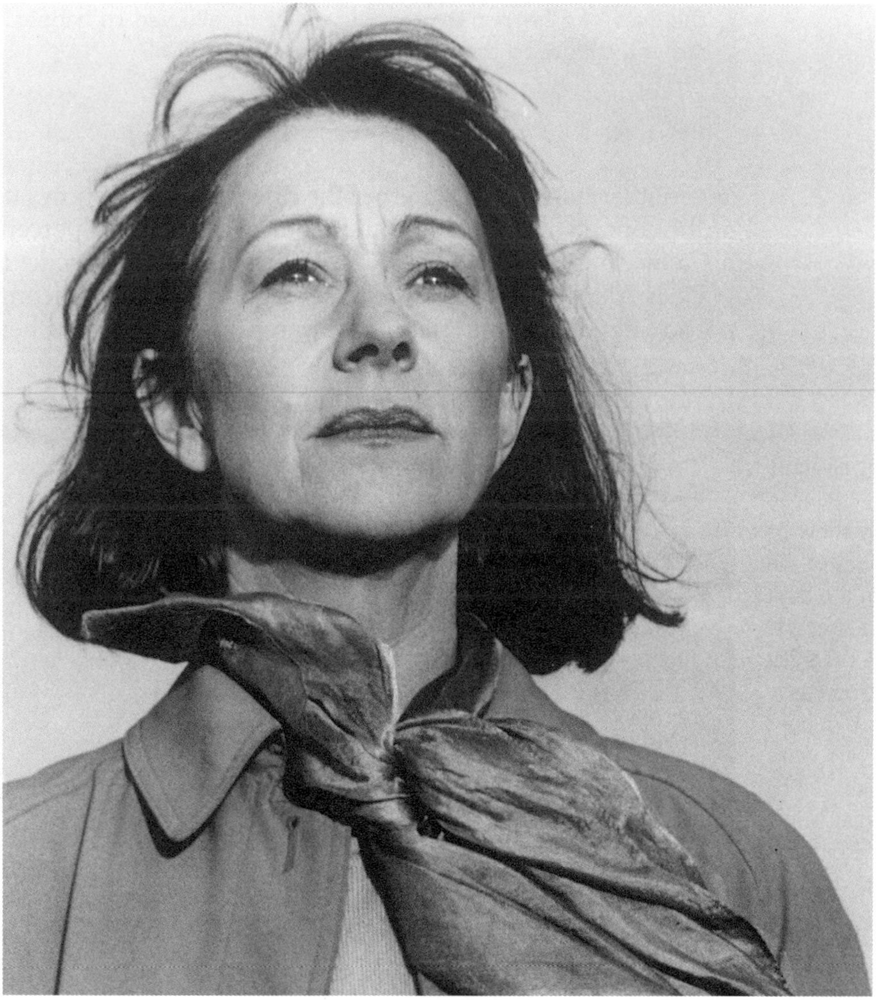

11.
Helen Mirren gives a realistic and sympathetic portrayal of an unglamorous mother who battles to save the life of her son in Terry George's *Some Mother's Son.* (Courtesy of Castle Rock; Photographer: Denis Mortell)

Alternatively, a film may try to give a different perspective of a person's life, such as Oliver Stone's *Nixon*. The question is, do these directors succeed in their objective?

In *Nixon*, Oliver Stone successfully shows another side to a man that many people hated. He shows a compassion and understanding which many thought alien to the late president. By doing this, he proves to many of us that there are always two sides to a story. Stone forces the audience to look at the president from different angles, personal and political, allowing us to decide for ourselves how he should be recorded in the annals of history. He therefore succeeds in his objective of giving a new insight into the life of Nixon, the man *and* the president, as well as the reasons for his actions.

The same can be said for Spielberg's *Schindler's List*. Spielberg vividly portrays the pain and the suffering that millions of people were exposed to as a result of the Holocaust. He forces many indifferent viewers, who were not concerned with the atrocities of the war, to look straight into the eyes of a horror that should never be allowed to happen again. The film is a tribute to the human spirit and to survival.

– TLdR

Yet another question is whether the director indeed shows us both sides of the coin or does he manipulate our emotions and perceptions about his subject, as Stone did in *JFK* or Roland Joffe in *The Scarlet Letter?*

Does Alan Parker show *Evita* as a goddess and an icon, or does he portray her as a manipulator who carefully orchestrated her way to the

12. Does director Barry Levinson really show us both sides of the coin in the dark drama *Sleepers?* Here Brad Pitt and Jason Patric star as two boys who were abused by guards in a reformatory and take revenge as adults. (Courtesy of PolyGram)

top? In fact, Parker concentrates on both sides of Evita's fame. Remember the sequence where she locks the bedroom door on her new husband? That single scene says it all: she had got what she had wanted, but was not going to pay the price any more.

Does watching a film like Larry Clark's *Kids* alert parents and children to the negatives of promiscuous behaviour? Or is *Kids* an indulgent, dangerous film in which a director lingers too long on the beauty of young bodies under the pretext of trying to convey an important message?

> *Kids* is a film that is supposedly aimed at the youth. It tries to show them the dangers of promiscuous sexual behaviour, often under the influence of drugs, as well as the consequences. Whether it is suitable viewing for kids, the very audience it addresses, is debatable, but the fact that it makes a social statement is unquestionable. The film serves as a definite wake-up call to all concerned, whether it be the youngsters involved or the parents who live their lives blissfully unaware of the dangers around them.
>
> Many people feel that *Kids* is really aimed at the parents, warning them to pay more attention to the lives of their children. It is therefore questionable whether the director's objectives are achieved. Is the audience for whom the film is intended capable of grasping the meaning of the film and therefore heeding its warning? Or will they simply shrug their shoulders and carry on as usual?
>
> –TLdR

Minor technical details should not detract from the overall enjoyment of a film

Small continuity errors, like a glass which is nearly empty in one shot and almost full in another, or a barely discernible boom shadow should not play a major part in one's critical enjoyment of a film. A microphone which is visible on the top right corner of the screen could be the result of the projectionist's framing in the cinema! Of course one could note the mistake, but if a film has a shattering impact, why concentrate on the contents of a glass?

Repetition should serve a purpose

If something is repeated, you may also ask whether there is a purpose to it. Does it serve as a symbol or does it show sloppiness on the director's side?

In *The Shawshank Redemption,* director Frank Darabont frequently draws our attention to the Bible, which the prison authorities hide behind. They use it to their own benefit, yet commit the most repulsive atrocities in the name of religion. In other words, they do not practise what they preach. In the end, that very Bible serves as the downfall of the corrupt prison system when the character played by Tim Robbins uses it, also indirectly, to expose prison brutality and corruption.

13. Frank Darabont frequently stresses the lifegiving friendship and intense relationship between two convicts, played by Morgan Freeman and Tim Robbins, by placing them closely together in scenes from *The Shawshank Redemption*. (Courtesy of Castle Rock; Photographer: Michael Weinstein)

In *Chariots of Fire* the character Harold Abrahams repeatedly relives the moment Eric Liddell beat him. At first we get an objective view of the race run in real time; then we see it repeated in slow motion on several occasions, which could convey Abrahams's shock at losing to Liddell. It is also as if he is examining his every move in the slow motion scenes that follow. During this sequence a man lifts up the spectator seats and the sound resembles a heart beating anxiously, or even a person clapping his hands in a derogatory way. The repeated slow motion images of the race and the lifting of the seats pound like a headache in the athlete's head. This prompts Abrahams to contact a coach to help him prepare for the next race.

EXERCISES

1. Discuss whether films like *The Chamber* and *Ghosts From the Past* really make contact with their intended audiences and change their perceptions of a certain situation? If so, why? If not, what are the shortcomings?
2. Do you think Spike Lee is ever really objective in his films? Write an essay on his approach to subjects such as racism, specifically with regard to *Get on the Bus*.
3. Are the characters in the following films convincing as human beings, or are they merely plot devices or mouthpieces for the director's and writer's statements?

3.1 *Seven*

3.2 *The Last Supper*

3.3 *Higher Learning*

3.4 *Do the Right Thing*

4. Write a short essay on the sweeping music score of *The English Patient*. Could the film have had the same impact without it?
5. "If you feed an audience on hamburgers alone, they won't ever appreciate the finer and more delicate tastes in life." Does this statement also apply to our local directors and producers?
6. Compare the different styles of directors Bruce Beresford and Steven Spielberg and their portrayal of survival in *Paradise Road* and *Schindler's List*.

2

How do we analyse a film?

Where do we begin to take apart the jigsaw puzzle? And what do we then do with all the different pieces? How do we discover the relationship between all the elements?

THEME

Look at the story

A good starting point is to establish what the film (story) is about. Once you have more or less decided on this – you may change or expand your ideas as you go along – you can use it as a base to judge the effectiveness or contribution which the other elements make to your overall impression of the film.

Dead Poets Society concerns a teacher who is hired to teach English at a traditional school. He attempts to inspire his students to think for themselves and use their knowledge to live fruitful, successful lives. They take his advice and re-establish a society he established years before which promotes free, inspired thinking. Eventually the teacher, Mr Keating, is blamed for the suicide of a young student whose parents would not allow him to achieve his dreams. He is banished from the school.

On delving deeper into the subject matter, it becomes clear that director Peter Weir is really trying to tell us to "seize the day", and to use every living moment to strive towards our dreams and towards excellence. No dream is too great or impossible to realise if you believe in yourself.

Many of the incidents in the film are simply metaphors, in other words, events which occur in order to imply a resemblance to the central theme and to illustrate it further. These incidents warn us about the tragedy that can result when young people are denied the opportunity to follow their dreams and have their imaginations stifled.

–TLdR

14. Young minds in turmoil in Peter Weir's *Dead Poets Society*. (Warner Bros.)

You should also study the subplots of a particular film, and decide whether they support the main story line or are simply used to fill the time.

Quentin Tarantino's *Pulp Fiction* has numerous subplots, which include the dangerous relationship between Vincent (John Travolta) and Mia (Uma Thurman). We can see how things are poised to go horribly wrong when Vincent has a discussion with himself about the moral implications of what he is contemplating. Fortunately, as it turns out, all thoughts of an illicit relationship go out the window when Mia accidentally overdoses herself. Vincent saves her life. This establishes a bond (which is never explored in detail) between him and Mia. Vincent's death then becomes a form of poetic, if somewhat random, justice.

Another subplot involves Vincent's partner, Jules. After what may or may not have been a miraculous escape, Jules becomes convinced that he has been favoured by some higher power. Ultimately he becomes the only character who undergoes a radical change in the film. This subplot serves to strengthen Jules's character. He is a killer, but he is willing to change. This contributes to our ability to identify with his character.

The humanity of the characters stems from the fact that they are flawed. They are not perfect and often make careless mistakes. Since we share this characteristic, we are able to suspend our disbelief.

Within the various episodes the characters change roles, shifting between being heroes and being villains. Ultimately there is no distinction between good and bad, and it is this factor which probably contributes to the freshness and originality of the film.

– NG

Establish how the director communicates his message (the theme) to the audience

The director *structures* a film in a particular order to get the maximum effect from each scene, especially in relation to the next.

"Structure" means the way scenes are put together and follow each other to form a whole. Structuring a film is like having an architect draw up a plan and having the builders start at a particular place: the foundation. We all know you cannot build a house without a proper foundation; you cannot build the top storey without something to support it.

Does this then mean that a film should always have the classic three-act structure? For example, in *Dead Poets Society* the acts would be as follows: (1) A beginning: Mr Keating arrives at the school; (2) the development: he changes the boys' lives; and (3) the resolution of the conflict: the conservative school system wins on the surface when they kick him out, but actually the boys' lives are the richer for his teachings. Luckily this is not the case. It would be extremely boring if every film started at the beginning ("once upon a time ..."), developed the story and ended with "and they lived happily ever after"! Film structure is far more flexible.

Some directors deliberately challenge us to a new awareness by mixing up time, story and space, as Quentin Tarantino does with *Reservoir Dogs* and *Pulp Fiction*. Many people argue that he confuses his audiences. But *why* does he ignore the classic three-act structure and what purpose does it serve? Tarantino catches us off guard with his postmodernist structure, because we never know what to expect. He challenges us to orientate ourselves with every scene by mixing up the time frame. Therefore he also forces us to ask questions and not merely to be spoon-fed.

As you watch the events in *Pulp Fiction* unfold in a disjointed order, you actively become involved in the film. You try to answer certain questions (such as what are Vincent and Jules doing in shorts and T-shirts?). Later the answers become apparent, and everything slots into place.

Another advantage of this structure is that we are privy to information which makes much of the characters' dialogue ironic (such as the conversation between Vincent and Jules in the coffee shop, when we already know that Vincent is going to die).

– NG

Establish why the director presents his material in a particular way

A director often starts a film in the middle of a story, or even at the end, such as in *The English Patient*. Sometimes he chooses to give us certain information, while at other times he withholds that information from us, as Hitchcock often did in his thrillers. What does the director leave in and what is left out? And why?

The suicide scene from Peter Weir's *Dead Poets Society* is presented in a very understated manner. There are no histrionics and manipulating music or swirling camera movements. Weir does not show us the external blood and violence of the scene (for instance, we do not see the actual pulling of the trigger and blood oozing from the boy's head). He attempts to make us focus on the inner tragedy of the situation. The picture we conjure up in our imaginations when the parents hear the shot may be worse than anything Weir could explicitly have shown us. Thus the effect and impact are sensitively heightened.

In *Strictly Ballroom* the director Baz Luhrmann uses a flashy, flamboyant style to tell his story. His technique is almost as dazzling and exciting as a peacock strutting its colourful feathers because, in this film, Luhrmann is dealing with a glamorous world in which false appearances, overstated hairdos and shining costumes rule.

Strictly Ballroom is about a fiery young dancer, Paul Mercurio as Scott, who wants to invent new, spontaneous steps for a ballroom competition. However, traditionalists, among them his mother and the president of the dance federation, oppose him. Against impossible odds, and with the appropriate flair, he succeeds in realising his dream and turning his Cinderella girlfriend into a princess. Luhrmann underlines his theme and subtext with breathtaking adeptness and uses every technique to support the story and its structure – from the emphasis on artificiality (the toupees, excessive make-up and costumes) to the sweeping rhythm of his camera, the kitschiness and use of the music, to his unpredictable editing techniques. There is reason in the madness.

The different story elements must relate to each other

The elements must relate to each other in a particular way and must form a unified whole as far as the theme is concerned. There is usually a single theme running through the entire film, and each segment must support and contribute to that theme. If one can cut out a scene or dia-

15. Tara Morice changes from wallflower to princess of the ballroom floor in *Strictly Ballroom*. (Courtesy of M & A Film Corporation)

logue without it harming the film, it usually means that that scene or dialogue has no function and should not have been there in the first place.

Everything must be motivated. Too many coincidences or the hero literally dropping out of the sky like a god to save those in peril, as often happens in Arnold Schwarzenegger's films, could harm a film thematically. Since this "miraculous saviour" has not been hinted at earlier, this element is not completely motivated and therefore does not always convince. One can only suspend disbelief to a certain degree!

In *The Scarlet Letter,* the character played by Demi Moore is unexpectedly saved by the Indians. This takes us by complete surprise as there has been no build-up to this rescue action or even a hint that the Indians have a reason to save her in the first place. We scarcely know that they were lurking behind the bushes and were watching the proceedings. Therefore the sudden rescue is completely unconvincing.

Conversely, a seemingly insignificant scene like two of the boys talking to each other in *Dead Poets Society* is relevant to the whole, because the scene may allow us to experience the feelings of those particular characters – feelings of inspiration which could relate to something that takes place later in the film, like the boys discussing the forming of a poetry society. Here we already notice the positive influence the teacher has on them, but we realise that because the rest of the school does not understand them, it could lead to problems.

– TLdR

DIALOGUE

The dialogue must be convincing

Dialogue is vitally important if the message of the film is to be successfully conveyed. We need to be convinced that what the characters are saying is not only true, but also believable. The same ideas should not be repeated too often in the dialogue. Words should be used sparingly and economically.

Too much dialogue can distract. If a film is based on a stage play, the dialogue should be adapted to the visual medium. For example, characters will not necessarily say what they see. The camera, which also serves as a narrator, communicates this aspect to us in pictures. In the dialogue Mr Keating uses in *Dead Poets Society,* you may ask whether he inspires his students through his use of language and by talking in their particular vernacular.

The dialogue in *Pulp Fiction* seems almost to be orchestrated around a musical rhythm. This rhythm can be compared to popular *rap* music, which is associated with gritty street life. The dialogue follows a beat which is born of the cruel realities of life. The characters always have a quick comeback, or snappy remark.

The dialogue, however, remains realistic. This is because the characters often engage in conversations which have absolutely no real meaning (such as the conversation between Jules and Vincent about unclean animals). This is quite true to everyday life – we don't always say significant and important things. Tarantino realises this, and by including this "meaningless" conversation he is able to create a kind of understanding between the audience and the characters. Tarantino's achievement lies in the fact that he makes killers seem just like ordinary people with everyday jobs. Everything is done in "good fun" and "humour" from beginning to end.

– NG

CHARACTERS

Characters usually develop or change

The schoolboy characters in *Dead Poets Society* develop from the first scenes. As a result of the influences around them, especially the jump start Mr Keating gives their imaginations, they undergo both emotional and psychological changes in the process of acquiring insight into themselves.

One of the main characters, portrayed by Robert Sean Leonard, develops from a loyal, reliable son (his parents' view) to an individual inspired through self-discovery to follow his dream of becoming an actor. However, in the end he reaches the point where, unable to follow this ideal, he tragically resorts to suicide rather than pursue the dream his parents have for him. This is an example of a character changing completely during a film.

– TLdR

The most significant change in character in *Howards End* is the change which Mr Wilcox, played by Anthony Hopkins, undergoes. He is unable to let go of the guilt associated with the house at Howards End. He goes to extraordinary lengths to ensure that the rightful owners of the house never claim it. Mr Wilcox wishes to preserve the memory of his wife, as well as to keep his scandalous affair with another woman secret. By the end of the film, however, he accepts that he is flawed, and reveals his secret. He is also prepared to reveal the fact that the house at Howards End does not rightfully belong to him. This shows that he has somehow managed to tear himself away from the past and to continue with his own life. It is ironic, however, that someone had to die for him to realise this.

– NG

In *Strictly Ballroom* almost all the characters change: Scott learns to accept his parents with all their shortcomings because he has now learnt to understand their bizarre behaviour. His girlfriend, Fran, not only blossoms into the princess of the dance floor, but discovers love and achieves freedom from her overbearing grandparents. A life lived in fear is a life half-lived.

TITLE

A film's title usually relates to its theme

When you see the title, *Dead Poets Society,* think of what it says to you. Also think of *Chariots of Fire, Witness* and especially *Strictly Ballroom.* A film's title can say much about its content. It can be an important key to what the film is all about. The latter implies rigidity and unbending rules in a flamboyant culture. *Chariots of Fire* refers not only to the athletes' bodies, but also to their classic artistic and emotional battles. It also has a religious reference.

The Shawshank Redemption by Frank Darabont hints at the prisoner (Tim Robbins) repossessing his own life, which has been taken away from him, and reinstating his honour and humanity. The corrupt authorities could imprison his body, but not his mind. Hope and friendship keep him alive. He recovers from captivity by, in a way, paying for a sin he has not committed, and brings about change in the process. It is only right at the end that we understand the "redemption" of the title, while "Shawshank" is quite obviously the jail in which the prisoner is kept.

A more complex title is *The Unbearable Lightness of Being,* based on Milan Kundera's novel and directed by Philip Kaufman. During the Prague Spring of 1968, a doctor, Tomas (played by Daniel Day-Lewis), marries a photographer (Juliette Binoche) but continues to see other women, especially Sabina (Lena Olin). Tomas and his wife leave for Geneva at the time of the arrival of the Russian tanks.

Tomas's philandering goes on and his young wife decides to leave him. Sabina is also in Geneva and has taken on a lover but keeps up the contact with her two friends. In the end Tomas accepts his love for his wife and his country and returns to work as a farmer. He is reunited with her. After spending a night at an inn, they are killed in an accident. Sabina gets the sad news.

But what does the title mean? Part of the answer can be found in the letter which Tereza leaves Tomas when she decides to return to Prague. She says: "Instead of being your support, I am your weight. Life is also very heavy to me, while it is so light to you. I can't bear this lightness, this freedom."

As Pauline Kael (1985–89: 428) put it: "We go through life only once – it's like going on stage unrehearsed. It's the suspended state of a person in an occupied country – especially if the person, like Tomas (Daniel Day-Lewis), is part of an advanced society under the domination of a backward society. (It's also the floating state of exile.)" The two women in Tomas's life, Sabina (Lena Olin) and Tereza (Juliette Binoche) represent lightness or no responsibility and the weight of responsibility respectively. Kael (1985–89: 429) suggests that "Tomas's commitment to Tereza [is] his redemption – his gaining the weight that saves him from the unbearable lightness of being".

CREDITS

Even the way the credits are presented could contribute to the film's overall feel or theme

Remember those extremely disturbing, fragmented, scratched titles of David Fincher's *Seven* or even *Mimic?* What purpose do they serve?

They create a particular mood in the viewer, a mood which can support the emotion the director is trying to achieve. They put our minds into reverse gear as if we are experiencing everything in a distorted way, almost from back to front. Right from the beginning, by watching these shuddering, bizarre titles, we know that we are entering a warped world inhabited by evil. The credits already destabilise us and put us "in the mood" to expect the worst. In the end they roll backwards, further distorting any sense of reality still left in us.

The opening of a film is always extremely important. Unfortunately, many people tend to talk during the beginning of a film or rush out to buy popcorn while the credits are rolling. One has to ask oneself why a film starts the way it does. (Alfred Hitchcock demanded that no one should enter the cinema after *Psycho* had started and cinema managers in those days had to adhere to his demands!) In many ways, the beginning of the film sets its tone. The start can show us where the film is leading, along with the situation of the characters.

Chariots of Fire by Hugh Hudson has a classic, formal credit sequence which supports the film's traditional structure. The actors' names are not mentioned, but we see them running along the beach to the sound of Vangelis's stirring and underscored theme. The camera glides over the main characters' faces, and here already we can see the difference between them. One is enthusiastic and open, the other motivated and carefree, another solemn and determined. The technical titles appear unobtrusively over the scene where the men glide like a massive white boat "with wings on its heels" through the shallow water. Every image favours tradition, simplicity and supreme formality.

RELATION TO OTHER FILMS

Place the film in thematic context relative to a particular director's work

When judging an Oliver Stone film, for example, one should bear in mind that he usually has a leftist, moralistic view of American society, strongly influenced by the shattering of the "American dream" when Vietnam exploded in America's face. He makes social comments and often gives his own interpretation of American history *(cf. JFK, Nixon).* He often turns people into symbols (as in *Natural Born Killers)* and his films are like rapid machine-gunfire on his audiences. Each new Stone film must be judged against this background, otherwise finer points and subtext could get lost in the process.

Katinka Heyns's *Paljas* forms a perfect companion piece to *Die Storie van Klara Viljee,* in which she paints a vivid picture of rural South Africa. Unlike several other Afrikaans films, such as Koos Roets's *Kaalgat tussen die Daisies,* which exploits the more naive members of the South African community, Heyns's films are never condescending. She does not belittle the characters by turning them into stereotypes.

Paljas (meaning "to perform magic") tells the tale of a simple family whose lives are changed when a circus train pulls in next to their house at a deserted siding in the Karoo. The innocence of the characters is never corrupted, only their perceptions change. The circus also serves as a metaphor for the changes which are taking place in the South African nation's psyche as people adapt to a new political dispensation. The characters gain a better understanding of the bigger world which has passed them by, symbolised by the trains which never stop at the station. It shows their cautious rebirth into a new dispensation which, although still alien, provides liberation from the old ways.

Compare how a film's subject or theme relates to other similar treatments

The charming film about a group of out-of-work men who decide to strip for a living, *The Full Monty* (meaning "going full frontal"), is even more significant when compared to other films on the same subject, like *Striptease*. Unlike these films, *The Full Monty* gives a human face to strippers – the kind the average person can identify with. In this film the soul is important, not the body.

Here there are no designer bodies or Chippendale pectorals. These are ordinary, overweight men who are so desperate for work that they will do anything to survive. They do not sell their souls, though. They stay true to themselves and their friends, and taking off their clothes literally means gaining acceptance as part of a community that discarded them when they were unemployed, and accepting themselves for who they are, and not who other people would like them to be.

If the director focuses on Aids (as in *Philadelphia, Jeffrey* or *And the Band Played on*), how does he treat this problem in relation to other directors? How does Richard Attenborough's treatment of the apartheid struggle in *Cry Freedom* compare with South African born Darrell James Roodt's treatment of a similar theme in *Cry, the Beloved Country?*

Attenborough's treatment clearly shows a foreign perspective. Essentially what we see on screen is the way in which South Africa was portrayed in the international press at that time. He is concerned with the greater concept of apartheid, and as a result only the system is examined with little regard for the human factor. He relies essentially on a stereotype portrayal of certain characters (such as policemen and white housewives).

On the other hand, a local director like Roodt through his treatment of Alan Paton's *Cry, the Beloved Country*, shows an understanding for the human side. By examining apartheid through Paton's work, Roodt shows an understanding of how people are influenced within a corrupt system. His message becomes universal, rather than applicable exclusively to South Africa. Although most of the film addresses the racial separation in South Africa, Roodt also chooses to address universal concepts such as forgiveness and friendship. *Cry, the Beloved Country* does not generalise, it does not say that all whites were evil. Instead we are given a balanced picture, and as a result it is a film which examines both sides of the story.

– NG

Examine the mood the director creates and how it relates to the overall theme

In *Picnic at Hanging Rock,* Peter Weir creates a disturbing, uneasy atmosphere with the underlying tensions of fear, sexual repression, frustration and evil which he presents in an eerie, "beautiful" way. Why does he do this?

Picnic at Hanging Rock portrays a supposedly true event at the turn of the century when three Australian schoolgirls and a teacher disappeared without a trace. This causes the destruction of a strict order and leads to the eventual suicide of the headmistress. The mystery of the disappearance is never solved.

Weir presents the girls as holy virgins from a Raphaelite era, dominated by an uneasiness and a prehistoric evil presence: the volcanic rocks, a rumbling sound, ants and snakes. By using silence and unobtrusive noises in nature, he also creates an atmosphere of expectation. Fate is literally a character in the film, waiting to pounce on the innocence and beauty of the girls.

Slow motion often gives a dream-like quality to the scenes (one of the characters says: "What we see and what we seem are but a dream. A dream within a dream.") By using slow motion and strange sounds, even heavily loaded silences, Weir underlines this supernatural theme. He almost presents evil as exquisite, without underestimating its destructive power. It is as if Hanging Rock (the primitive and prehistoric) unleashes the girls' (primitive?) sexual impulses in an almost esoteric way, presented in a visually elegant style of fragile Victorian innocence corrupted by unearthly forces.

EXERCISES

1. Describe exactly how one should analyse a film without overexplaining the director's intentions and the style in which the film was made.
2. Analyse the various plots and subplots of a film like *Short Cuts*. How do they each contribute to the overall effect of the film? Is every story really necessary?

3. A film often has a good story or plot, as is the case with *The Devil's Own*. Upon analysing that story's structure and the way it is presented by Alan J. Pakula, do you think he does justice to the story, especially as far as the casting is concerned? Is it really a good plot or has it been done before? And, does the story convince?
4. Describe what is meant by the structure of a film. Illustrate your answer with examples from recent films, explaining what a good, solid structure is and why some films have loose structures.
5. Take a careful look at the following characters, and say whether you think they change during the course of the film, or not. Give reasons for your answers.
   - 5.1 Count de Almasy in *The English Patient*
   - 5.2 The three women in the *Three Colours* trilogy
   - 5.3 Bess (Emily Watson) in *Breaking the Waves*
   - 5.4 Jean Michel Basquiat in *Basquiat*
   - 5.5 Renton (Ewan McGregor) in *Trainspotting*
   - 5.6 The husband in *Once Were Warriors*
   - 5.7 Alex in *A Clockwork Orange*
   - 5.8 Ellie (Jodie Foster) in *Contact*.

3 Cinematography

Just as a painter uses his brush or an author uses words to communicate or tell his story, so the film director uses the camera as his narrator. By using his camera, he decides how the audience should see a certain object or character, and so influences our mood and perception.

He can do this in an objective way where the camera is simply a recording device, as in John Ford's films or comedies like *Fierce Creatures* or the straightforward no nonsense *Ghosts From the Past* by Rob Reiner. He can also do this in a subjective way in which he manipulates our viewpoint as Danny Boyle does in *Trainspotting* or Baz Luhrmann in *William Shakespeare's Romeo and Juliet*.

Joseph M. Boggs (1996: 110, 111) describes the importance of the image, and therefore the use of the camera, as follows:

> Film speaks a language of the senses. Its flowing and sparkling stream of images, its compelling pace and natural rhythms and its pictorial style are all part of this non-verbal language. So it follows naturally that the aesthetic quality and dramatic power of the image are extremely important to the overall quality of a film.
>
> The continuous and simultaneous interplay of image, sound and motion on the screen sets up varied, complex and subtle rhythms.

A director should never become overtly conscious of his film's "look", therefore literally falling in love with the picture's appearance. This tendency, as in Franco Zeffirelli's *Brother Sun, Sister Moon* or *The Sparrow,* or Carroll Ballard's *Fly Away Home,* could result in a chocolate-box appearance where the image is simply used to decorate the film.

16.
Zdenek Sverak learns to befriend a Russian boy Kolya (Andrej Chalimon) in Jan Sverak's masterpiece *Kolya,* which deals with friendship and toleration. (Courtesy of Pandora)

The director should also refrain from using every trick in the book, from tilting and zooming to crane shots and hand-held shots, merely to impress his audience. He may appear to be trying to show off all he has learned in film school in one film, without the story requiring such elaborate treatment. He should not incorporate techniques which have nothing to do with his narrative style or the message he is trying to convey.

In *Breaking the Waves* Lars von Trier's excessive use of an unstable hand-held camera detracts from rather than complements the film's message. One would expect all kinds of cinematic tricks in a science fiction picture like *Star Wars* or *Independence Day,* but not in a tightly constructed family drama (like *Marvin's Room*), which revolves around inner conflicts.

When evaluating the "look" or visual style of a film, you should ask yourself:

- Why does the director make you see a scene from a certain angle or perspective?
- Is that particular shot objective or subjective?
- Does it fit into the overall tone of the film?

In *Witness,* Peter Weir makes extensive use of manipulative camera angles in the witness scene in the bathroom. All the shots are from an angle which matches the eye-level of the Amish boy, Samuel, played by Lukas Haas. Everything towers above him, adding to the menace created by being in an unfamiliar environment. Samuel enters a toilet stall, but he does not close the door completely.

When the murder takes place, Samuel watches the events unfold through this gap. At one stage, the camera takes on a subjective point of view. We as the audience become Samuel as we see events from his perspective. Likewise, when the villain is searching the stalls to find Samuel, the angle is subjective from the child's perspective. We see through his eyes as he desperately struggles to close the cumbersome lock with his small hands. This heightens the tension experienced by the audience.

– NG

DEVICES TO INFLUENCE THE AUDIENCE'S PERCEPTION

The director uses several devices to influence his audience's perception of the images he presents to them:

- Cinematic composition
- Camera angles
- Movement
- Special filters
- Special lenses
- Focus
- The use of certain elements and omission of others

Cinematic composition

Composition can be summed up in the French term *"mise en scène"*. This means the arrangement of images and movements within a certain space. The frame "encloses" the images. *Mise en scène* literally means to stage the action and photograph it in a certain way. Like an artist with a painting, a director may balance the objects in the frames to convey a specific atmosphere or relationship between them.

Also note the cold, hostile, desolate nature in *Breaking the Waves*. Whereas Ireland is often presented as a picture-postcard country, Von Trier concentrates on the bleakness within the beauty and the starkness which surrounds Bess. In this way he reflects the coldness of society against a woman who is desperately longing for warmth and consolation, but finds herself emotionally frozen, especially by the prejudice of the almost heartless clergy in the town.

In *Strictly Ballroom* Scott and Fran dance in front of a huge illuminated Coca Cola sign on top of a building. They are isolated from the industrial city in their own glamorous, commercially orientated world. They dance for money or for fame, but fail to realise that it is the emotion in the dance which really matters. Their true rhythms come from the streets below, a fact they still have to discover or they themselves may turn into little commercial billboards erected by other people.

In *The Searchers,* John Ford emphasises the insignificance of man against the overwhelming and timeless scope of the Wild West, specifi-

17. Lars von Trier emphasises the cold desolation of nature in a small town where a woman (Emily Watson) suffers from a lack of love. Here a priest (Jonathan Hackett) discovers her after she has collapsed from emotional exhaustion. The bleakness of the surroundings also reflects the hostility of the town and its people towards her in *Breaking the Waves*. (Courtesy of October Films)

cally Monument Valley. The horsemen and farmers are small against the grand majestic setting, emphasising the fact that they are intruders.

Also remember how lonely, almost funny, the disillusioned soldier (Kevin Costner) looks against the vast landscape surrounding him in *Dances with Wolves*. Here is a landscape relatively free of humans and kept in an unspoilt state by its rightful inhabitants, the Indians. The white man has no place there, and the soldier realises his insignificance.

The massive rock formations in John Ford's *Stagecoach* also have the appearance of tombstones or symbols of a great, unseen power.

The same applies to the formidable and threatening rock mountain in *Picnic at Hanging Rock*. When the angelic girls clad in white approach it, we sense its destructive, primitive and dominating power. Peter Weir often depicts the rock formations from the point of view of the characters, which is why they appear to be so threatening and overpowering. They dominate the screen.

However, the particular scene or image should blend in with the rest of the sequence, so as not to distract our attention too much. It must form part of a whole, and not be like some scenes in *The Ghost and the Darkness*, where Africa serves merely as a decoration, creating a kind of "travelogue". Compare the train journey and the abundance of tourist-friendly animals. Every shot must be designed with certain goals in mind:

- To direct attention to the object of the greatest significance. A standing character usually has more prominence than a sitting one, seen in context of course.
- To keep an image in constant motion. A good example is John G. Avildsen's original *Rocky*. In the training montage, Sylvester Stallone as the boxer is in constant motion, but the attention and focus always stay with him, his emotions and what is happening to him. The background is not important. The world passes by and he scarcely notices.
- To create an illusion of depth.

> David Lean is a master at creating depth in his cinematic compositions. In his film, *Doctor Zhivago*, he successfully creates an illusion of depth in order to show us how the two sides of a possible confrontation are about to march towards each other. He creates anticipation by keeping both the strikers and the army in focus.
>
> –TLdR

In *In Love and War,* the hospital is in constant focus as the young, restless Ernest Hemingway character looks at his fellow patients and tries to make friends with them. Every person and object there are important to him, and most of these are constantly in focus.

18.
In *johns* David Arquette and Lukas Haas are convincing as two Los Angeles street hustlers who sell their bodies in order to survive. (Courtesy of Overseas Film Group)

Also compare the use of focus in two other scenes in the same film. In the first, the nurse who saves the life of the main character is lost in thought as she contemplates the horrors of war and the futility of bloodshed. Therefore her surroundings are out of focus. We are aware only of her inner pain and conflict. In a later scene she is admiring the beauty of Venice as the horrors of war have now slowly started to fade. The director, Richard Attenborough, therefore keeps the surroundings in perfect focus because they are important to her.

"Composition" refers to the harmonious arrangement of the parts of a work in relation to one another. A director often "balances" his images on screen so that one half of the screen does not carry more weight than the other, unless he wants to make a specific point by means of creating an uneven feeling. There is, of course, no clear rule in this regard, but the screen usually has some kind of balance.

Clint Eastwood's *Unforgiven* starts with a perfectly balanced image. The scene is vertically divided into three sections: on the left-hand side a part of a house with a verandah is visible; on the right, a solitary figure is digging a grave; in the centre is a single pole connected to the house (it is probably a clothes line). Horizontally, the screen is split into two equal parts. The top part is dimly lit by a cold, desolate sunset without any warmth whatsoever. The bottom part of the screen, closest to the camera, is dark and forbidding. The screen is therefore perfectly balanced and tells its own story about loneliness, depression and failure without a single word being spoken. Over this image, Eastwood rolls words which serve as a background to the story.

A few seconds later, a woman's face is disfigured by a thug and a man saves her life by apprehending the attacker. In this particular scene, the saviour's arm and the gun dominate the screen. His face is in the top right-hand corner, his arm connects his face to the gun in the top left-hand corner. The gun is slightly out of focus and thus even more threatening, while the attacker's arm fills the rest of the screen. The screen is literally divided into a threatening triangle.

Also note the haunting empty space between the two characters in *Cry, the Beloved Country* which may suggest an emotional distance or sadness between them. The man on the horse (Richard Harris) is physically elevated above the reverend Kumalo (James Earl Jones), but his head is bowed as if the grief he is carrying is almost too much to bear. The reverend, on the other hand, stands upright in spite of his age, and looks the white man straight in the eye. Kumalo is therefore the white man's spiritual equal, in spite of the superior position afforded the latter by the apartheid system.

Camera angles

The director may use a certain camera angle to make a statement.

Low angle

When an object is seen from a low angle, it usually dominates the screen. This technique is often applied in films to give a child's perspec-

19. A white farmer (Richard Harris) still seems to have a position of superiority in this scene from *Cry, the Beloved Country* because he looks down upon the priest from his horse. In reality the priest (James Earl Jones) is in a far more favourable position because of his proud, upright manner as opposed to the farmer's slouched shoulders in this film. (Courtesy of Anant Singh and Videovision)

tive, such as in *E.T.: The Extra-Terrestrial* by Steven Spielberg, *Kolya* by Jan Sverak or Peter Weir's *Witness.* The image can also become threatening if photographed from a low angle, or conversely, it can indicate that a character (often a child) feels protected.

In *Unforgiven's* first scenes, a woman is viciously attacked. We are often in her position as the assailant "attacks" the viewer (the camera). We see him as a menacing, larger-than-life monster from a low, threatening angle.

In *Witness,* Samuel wanders through a train station. Everything is shot from a low angle, suggesting a subjective point of view through Samuel's eyes. Things appear threatening. However, when the boy stands in front of a towering statue depicting what seems to be a protective angel, this low-angle perspective changes from being threatening to suggesting a sense of protection or safety. The statue symbolises a father figure (which Samuel is missing), and instead of becoming a new menace in an already terrifying environment, it stands out as a symbol of protection. Later this symbol manifests itself in the father-like figure of John, the policeman who eventually saves the family.

– NG

20.
A young Lukas Haas witnesses a murder in Peter Weir's *Witness*. (Courtesy of Paramount)

In *Strictly Ballroom* three selfish women try to prevent the innocent Fran from dancing. We see their grotesquely made-up faces from a low angle with unflattering lighting, making them appear even more threatening. Luhrmann puts us in Fran's position, and we are intimidated, along with her, by their condescending attitude.

High angle

When an object is seen from a high angle, the director usually tries to give an overall view of a situation. He may show how a character is led into a trap, or that he is threatened.

A good example of this are the driving scenes in Stanley Kubrick's horror film, *The Shining*. Here we see an overhead shot of Jack Torrance's car driving through the countryside to its final destination. The high angle gives us the feeling that the character is being led into a dangerous situation, one that could threaten his life and those of his family. The overhead angle also gives the impression that the situation is being watched by a higher power, and that everything is now beyond the control of the characters.

– TLdR

An extreme high angle, on the other hand, could be used to shock us by suddenly reversing our perspective.

21.
Jack Nicholson as a deranged writer who goes on a killing spree in a desolate hotel in Stanley Kubrick's magnificent exercise in horror, *The Shining*. (Warner Bros.)

In *Psycho,* Hitchcock suddenly switches camera angles and gives us a bird's-eye view of Milton Arbogast (Martin Balsam) being attacked by the murderer at the top of the stairs. Suddenly the camera switches to yet another overhead position as the victim appears to hover in the air for a few seconds before plunging to his death.

In *The Shining,* Stanley Kubrick gives an overall high-angle view of the plant maze while the mother (Shelley Duvall) and the young boy (Danny Lloyd) wander through it. As with the driving shots discussed earlier, he does this to show that the characters are trapped in a hostile, claustrophobic environment which could also be symbolical of the maze of madness in which they later find themselves. It seems as if a higher kind of power, perhaps an evil force, is actually watching them, ready to pounce on or entrap them. It is also as if the mad Jack Torrance (Jack Nicholson) is spying on them, suggesting that an evil power has taken possession of his senses. Subsequently the maze serves to exaggerate their sense of confusion and desperation.

Extreme close-ups

Extreme close-ups may also signify entrapment, as in *The Shawshank Redemption,* where there are frequent extreme close-ups of the faces of Tim Robbins, as well as those of the warder and the Morgan Freeman character. The same technique is applied to Hannibal Lecter (Anthony Hopkins) in *The Silence of the Lambs* in the scene in which Clarice (Jodie Foster) meets him for the first time.

Extreme close-ups furthermore draw our attention to an important, life-changing moment in the lives of the characters, as happens to Meryl Streep and Leonardo DiCaprio in *Marvin's Room* when they make peace without verbally addressing the issue at hand. DiCaprio, as the rebellious son, has left the house; his mother has discovered the note in which he explains his action to his beloved aunt (Diane Keaton), not his unfeeling mother. The boy does not know about his mother's discovery until this moment, when he realises that his mother really cares for him. She just cannot express it in words.

Here extreme close-ups literally confront us with these thought processes racing through the characters' minds, their realisations and their coming to terms with each other's failings. They now understand that they love each other in spite of previous mistakes.

Often extreme close-ups also focus on intimacy between two characters. When Tita and Pedro in *Like Water for Chocolate* make love, the world around them ceases to matter, hence the soft lighting and focus on the physical relationship between the lovers. Nothing is allowed to intrude.

Even in *The Graduate*, when Elaine Robinson (Katharine Ross) has to choose between the husband favoured by her parents and the man she loves (Dustin Hoffman), the director (Mike Nichols) uses extreme close-ups of her parents' talking faces. Although we do not hear what they are saying, we can imagine the conversation. In this way, they appear

22. Although society tries to separate the two boys, they never succeed in creating an emotional distance between Ste (Scott Neal) and Jamie (Glen Berry) in this honest depiction of love in *Beautiful Thing* by Hettie Macdonald. (Courtesy of Film Four International)

23. An extreme close-up emphasises the passion and power which finally overcome the obstacles in the courtship between Tita (Lumi Cavazos) and Pedro (Marco Leonardi) in Alfonso Arau's *Like Water for Chocolate*. (Courtesy of Pandora)

grotesquely unfeeling and rude. They are just talking, selfish faces that say the same meaningless things over and over again without any consideration for their daughter's happiness.

Through extreme close-ups, a director like Ingmar Bergman also tries literally to gain access to a character's soul.

> Near the beginning of Krzysztof Kieślowski's *Three Colours: Blue* we see an extreme close-up of Juliette Binoche's eye when she is told that her husband and child (her entire family) have been killed in a car accident. The pain that we can see in her eyes intimately and clearly depicts her feelings. Since the eye is the window of the soul, the director successfully manages to penetrate her thought processes by this extreme and unsettling close-up.
>
> –TLdR

Movement An image is usually kept in constant motion by using several camera movements to keep the scene "alive". The movements can be divided into a number of categories, as discussed below.

Panning

"Pan" is short for "panorama", and such a shot consists of a continuous horizontal movement from one side of the frame to the other. This tech-

24.
Juliette Binoche loses her husband and beloved daughter in Krzysztof Kiešlowski's *Three Colours: Blue*. (Courtesy of MK2 Diffusion)

nique can be associated with a certain character's point of view. It imitates our own vision and directs our eyes to a specific point, whether we want to move in that direction or not. In this way, a director follows the action directly.

Panning is usually applied during fast moving action sequences like the car chase in *Metro* or the boat heading for a town in *Speed 2: Cruise Control*, where the spectator has to follow a chase or an ambush in order to establish exactly what is going on. In several of the boat sequences in this film Jan De Bont pans along with the action in order to place the viewer in the same situation as the characters and so heighten the dramatic tension.

The movement may be slow and leisurely, as in *Unforgiven* where two rain-drenched figures walk through the streets of an evil town after a prostitute has been maimed, and the camera follows their movements from a verandah until they reach their destination close to the camera.

A slow panning movement can create tension, as in *Picnic at Hanging Rock* where the camera does a 360° pan so that we can have an overall view of what is happening around that particular character who is walking through unfamiliar, hostile territory.

It can also be used to signify confusion, as happens to the Leonardo DiCaprio character in *The Basketball Diaries* when he goes cold turkey and the room starts spinning around him. The circular camera movement, with its distortions, takes us into the mind of the drug addict and shows us what he is going through. It imitates his hallucinatory state and unbalances us to reproduce the unsettling, nauseating feeling that he is experiencing.

Nowadays the modern action film seems to have lost all sense of direction, as it merely serves to highlight American patriotism, as is the case in *Air Force One, Con Air* and *Men in Black*. Although they are excellent action films, often using flamboyant panning movements to allow the audience to experience the roller-coaster ride in all its glory, these films seem to have lost touch with reality. They have become action rides with stories lacking convincing characters. People are killed for no reason, as is emphasised by flashy camera movements which seem to celebrate murder and mayhem, instead of registering the horror of senseless killings.

Even James Cameron's technically brilliant *Titanic* suffers from visual overkill and lack of compassion for its characters. *A Night to Remember*, made about the same disaster in 1958, is a more touching and compassionate film, mainly because the director did not invent a lightweight love story to support the main tragedy. There were enough tales of bravery to keep the audience riveted and none had to be invented. *Titanic* reaches a low point when the Leonardo DiCaprio character elbows a distressed man out of the way who is reciting Psalm 23 by urging him to get a move on through the valley of death!

In the opening sequence of *Shallow Grave*, the camera seems to be rushing at a frantic pace into the very heart of the city. This is accompanied by a fast-paced music score, and the director Danny Boyle is able to hurtle us into his film from the start, whether we like it or not. These quick-moving images are countered with slow-moving shots through the forest in which the bodies are eventually buried.

The fast-paced opening draws us into the film, as well as suggesting the breakneck pace at which the characters in the film live their lives. *Shallow Grave* tells a universal story of friendship and betrayal, and the use of this particular technique in the opening succeeds both in demanding and keeping our attention for the duration of the film.

– NG

Tilting

Here the camera moves in a vertical line. It often starts at a character's feet and moves upwards to emphasise his or her beauty, strength or height. The same may be done with an object, for example, a high building or the steep face of a cliff.

In *The Quick and the Dead,* the camera tilts down from the Sharon Stone character, across a bar room's floor, picks up the perpetrator's shadow, and tilts up towards the arrogant card-player's face as he disdainfully looks at her. It emphasises the difference and space between the characters and the cautious, hostile and scornful way they view each other.

One of the best examples of tilting is from *The Crying Game*. One of the characters, played by Jaye Davidson, is supposedly a beautiful woman. Later on, when we least expect it, the director (Neil Jordan) reveals the fact that "she" is actually a man by slowly tilting downwards to expose the character's true gender.

–TLdR

25.
Jaye Davidson is not what he appears to be in Neil Jordan's *The Crying Game*. (Miramax)

Zoom

By using a zoom shot, a director can focus on a specific object in one continuous movement. This technique literally thrusts the viewer's attention onto a character or object of great importance. The camera appears to glide towards something (although the camera itself does not move).

Here is an example: In *When a Stranger Calls* a frightened girl gets calls from a psychopath while she is babysitting in a large house. She is terrorised by his continuous phone calls. After the umpteenth call, he calls her one last time. The zoom lens moves in on the telephone as it rings and rings and no one answers, reflecting the importance of the object to the character and the degree of terror it evokes.

Hand-held camera

This technique is usually employed in documentary films, like *Hoop Dreams* and *The Battle of Algiers,* to give a sense of immediacy and realism.

It can also be used to suggest instability, as is done with the many hand-held shots in *Breaking the Waves* by Lars von Trier. This (at first seemingly unmotivated) instability obviously foretells the state in which the main character, played by Emily Watson, will find herself. She is going to lose the only anchor in her life, her husband and their sexual relationship. In several unsteady scenes, Von Trier reflects upon the instability of Emily's life and future. (Many people confessed that this high degree of visual instability made them quite seasick upon seeing it on the big screen.)

26. Emily Watson in *Breaking the Waves.* (Courtesy of October Films)

Hand-held shots can also heighten tension in a horror movie. In most of the *Friday the 13th* films one finds a helpless teenager being chased through the woods by the maniac, Jason. We literally follow in the monster's footsteps as we stalk the girl through the dense undergrowth, the unstable camera movements simulating his point of view. His madness and the fact that he turns into an unstable "animal" as he pursues her are clearly portrayed by the instability of the shots. The same applies to *Scream* by Wes Craven.

The same technique is used in *Don't Look Now* by Nicolas Roeg, where the character played by Donald Sutherland chases what he perceives to be a child in a red raincoat through Venice. We see the chase from his unsteady point of view, and this suggests anguish, fear and danger.

Dolly or crane shots

A dolly or trucking (also called "tracking") shot is taken from a moving vehicle, or an object on tracks to permit a smooth movement. In this way, the viewer has a sense of becoming part of the action. It creates a feeling of movement.

In *Strictly Ballroom,* when Scott makes his triumphant entry onto the stage on his knees, the camera dollies along with him to emphasise the elegant, smooth movement. The same applies to Scott and Fran's excitement as they strut around the ballroom for their Pan-Pacific dance, giving us a feeling of being part of the dance and the rhythm.

A Clockwork Orange features an opening sequence which consists of an extended dolly. The camera starts with a close-up of the protagonist, Alex, as he narrates the opening. This serves to establish Alex as the central character, and creates a bond between this antisocial misfit and the audience. The camera then dollies backwards to reveal the club in which Alex and his friends are enjoying their drug-laced drinks.

Gradually, the alien surroundings are revealed to the audience. Although the decor is quite explicit, the slow camera movement ensures that the audience is not distanced from the film. (If cutting had been used instead, the audience may have reacted with revulsion.) This movement also suggests that Alex is central to this story, placing the focus on the character rather than on his social surroundings. This further supports the bond between audience and character.

Danny Boyle pays homage to this technique in *Trainspotting,* although the movement is reversed. The characters sit in surroundings resembling those seen in *A Clockwork Orange*, but this time, instead of starting close, the camera starts at a distance and moves slowly into the close-up.

– NG

27. Ewan McGregor is Renton who experiences the highs and lows of drug abuse in *Trainspotting*. (Courtesy of Film Four International)

Steadicam

A steadicam is a portable camera which is carried by the cameraman. It steadies itself so that there are no jerky movements.

This camera is often used during realistic chase sequences where the action is supposed to run "smoothly" as the camera operator follows a murderer and cuts back to the cop chasing him through the streets of a city. This time the director prefers smooth transitions without jerky or unstable movements. He simply wants to record the action as economically and excitingly as possible, as in some of the action scenes in *Speed* and its sequel, and *Con Air* and *Dante's Peak*.

Slow motion

Slow motion is brought about when a scene is filmed at a faster rate than 24 frames per second, but is played back at the standard rate.

It is usually used to create a dream-like impression (as in the opening scenes of *Blue Velvet,* when the fireman waves to us from the moving vehicle). It can also be used to emphasise the beauty and triumph of a winning moment (as in *Chariots of Fire*) or to create an intense emotional feeling, as in *Strictly Ballroom* when Scott and Fran finally triumph with their own individual steps at the championships.

Slow motion scenes can also convey a feeling of unexpected shock or horror, as in *Don't Look Now* by Nicolas Roeg, when Laura Baxter (Julie Christie) loses consciousness in a restaurant. It takes us by complete surprise as she starts falling and pulling the table cloth, the plates, jams and

28. Through the use of slow motion Hugh Hudson stresses the glory of the magnificent moment when an athlete (Ben Cross) breaks the ribbon in *Chariots of Fire*. (20th Century Fox)

cutlery down onto her. Many people have said that, upon losing consciousness, one sees the world in slow motion. Roeg here imitates what is actually happening to Laura, but also influences our perception of it.

The final sequence of *Shallow Grave* depicts the three friends laughing together as a group. The sequence is shot in slow motion, creating a feeling of warmth, happiness and companionship. However, the scene is loaded with irony – we know that each of them have betrayed the other in some way. The result is a sequence in which the following message is emphasised: If you cannot trust your friends, then look out for yourself. In a case such as this where slow motion usually promotes an intense and positive emotional response, Boyle succeeds in loading this normally clichéd technique with bitter and tragic irony.
– NG

Slow motion often draws our attention to a character of great significance. A beautiful woman (Patricia Arquette) gets out of a car in David Lynch's *Lost Highway*. Because she may be evil and may have a profound impact on the main character's life (in this case the actor

29.
Christopher Eccleston, Kerry Fox and Ewan McGregor as the friends from hell in Danny Boyle's darkly satirical comedy about friendship gone wrong in *Shallow Grave*. (Courtesy of Film Four International)

Balthazar Getty's), Lynch slows down the speed of the shot to force us to look at her in closer detail, as if to suggest that there is something sinister about her.

We also notice that she looks familiar and discover that she resembles a woman who has just been brutally murdered, also played by Arquette. Thus the slow motion is used to draw our attention to the fact that there is a resemblance between her and her alter ego, that she is dangerous

30.
Patricia Arquette plays dual roles in David Lynch's brooding surrealistic nightmare *Lost Highway*. (Courtesy of Ciby 2000)

and significant to the plot, and it suggests that the Getty character may be threatened by her in some way.

Sam Peckinpah often uses slow motion during his "death ballets" in films such as *The Wild Bunch* when the bodies of characters fly through the air in a slow movement, sometimes glorifying the moment of death or even prolonging it. Slow motion can also signify defeat or failure.

In *Face/Off* John Woo takes slow motion to ridiculous extremes. Every motion and movement in scenes requiring the actors to shudder at the loss of a loved one is slowed down to make the motion as over the top as the special effects are, drawing our attention to the absurdity of the improbable plot.

Fast motion

Fast motion occurs when a subject is photographed at a slower rate than 24 frames per second and then is played back at the usual rate. The movement appears to be jerky and stocky.

This technique is usually used in comedy scenes (compare many Charlie Chaplin classics), or to give the impression of mechanical, exaggerated movements, as in the sex scene in *A Clockwork Orange* which involves Alex and the two girls he has picked up. Fast, jerky movements are also achieved through a series of fast jump cuts. These jerky movements emphasise the fact that sex is a mechanical action for Alex and that he goes through it like a well-oiled machine simply bent on completing the action and starting over again. There is no emotion involved. This also hints at the title of the film.

Freeze-frame

With this technique a frame is reprinted several times to give the impression that we are looking at a photograph. In *Days of Heaven* by Terence Malick, the film starts with several still photographs superimposed over one another to sketch a short history of the characters and their environment.

In *Strictly Ballroom* Baz Luhrmann brings the seductive rhythm of the dance to an abrupt end with a freeze-frame, thereby jerking us back to reality and forcing us to listen to the dialogue which exposes the complicated politics behind the scenes.

In *Thelma and Louise,* the image freezes in the final scenes as the two women drive off a cliff while holding hands. They are "immortalised" as this image is etched into our minds. Ridley Scott may also be implying that they have defeated death and that their friendship can be seen as a triumph.

Thawed frame

Here a still image or freeze-frame is "defrosted" and comes to life.

31.
A defiant Louise (Susan Sarandon) and Thelma (Geena Davis) take on a world ruled by chauvinists and bigots. They win by being united in death. (MGM)

In *Trainspotting,* Begbie is telling his friends a story in a bar. When he reaches the conclusion, he casually throws his empty glass over his shoulder. Here the image is frozen, letting the audience share the shock of the other characters as we realise that the glass is going to hurtle down onto someone below.

At this stage, the narrator reveals the truth behind Begbie's story, and we see a sequence in which Begbie's lies are exposed. When the film returns to the present, the frame thaws and the glass falls to the floor. In this case, the frozen and subsequent thawed frames act like a set of photographic parentheses. Effectively, the frozen and thawed frames become brackets, within which is inserted an additional element to characterise Begbie's brutal nature more effectively.

– NG

Special filters A filter controls the amount of light allowed through the camera lens. It can also distort an image through manipulation of the light. Sometimes a director will even pull a nylon stocking over a lens to soften the lines around a character's face or make her appear younger.

Certain lenses emphasise or suppress light. A blue filter can create either a sombre or serene picture, while a yellow one can create a feeling of warmth or sensuality. Other filters can be used to create a feeling of alienation or coldness. Directors often use the day-for-night filter in which images filmed during the day appear darker, as if shot at night.

Special lenses *Telephoto lens*

A telephoto lens can bring objects to an extreme close-up from a great distance. This lens is often used to pick out an important character in a crowd (like Dustin Hoffman in his *Tootsie* drag as he walks unnoticed and unrecognised among a New York crowd), or to draw our attention to an object of great importance. It also diminishes the distance between two objects in a long shot.

Wide-angle lens

A wide-angle lens is usually used to give the impression of wide, unexplored, virgin country and to explore its vastness for visual impact. Compare the broad landscapes in films like *Far and Away, Lawrence of Arabia, The English Patient* and *Unforgiven* in this regard.

Fish-eye lens

By using a fish-eye lens, images are often distorted.

A great example of this occurs in *The Basketball Diaries.* Leonardo DiCaprio's character is experiencing withdrawal symptoms and is anxiously trying to find some money for drugs in the study. The camera with the fish-eye lens moves in circles around the room. Each time it reaches the character, we get another distorted view of him in another position. The distorted picture successfully depicts his state of mind, reflecting his anxiety, hallucination and restlessness.

In *The Ghost and the Darkness,* the director (Stephen Hopkins) gives us a lion's point of view as the predator approaches the baboon tied to a pole and the hunter (Val Kilmer) sitting on top of a self-made construction. By using the fish-eye lens, we not only see things the way the marauding lion (who kills for pleasure, not food) is supposed to see them, but the distortion of the images also evokes terror in the hearts of viewers, because the baboon and hunter are reduced to mere objects waiting to be slaughtered. They have no meaning beyond being bait for a killing machine.

Focus Through sharp focus, a director makes an object stand out more sharply in relation to other objects. For instance, the director may focus on one face in the foreground, while the others are slightly out of focus. In this way, he gives more prominence to a certain character and places special emphasis on him.

This happens in *Ghosts From the Past,* where Bobby DeLaughter (Alec Baldwin) is talking on the phone and accepts the case of a widow, Myrlie Evers (Whoopi Goldberg), who wants the racist killer of her husband to stand trial once again after he has already got off in two previous trials almost thirty years before.

We first see Bobby in focus and then realise that his wife (Virginia Madsen) is listening to him in the background. She is out of focus, but we know she is overhearing the conversation. Her body language in the out-of-focus shot already discloses how she feels about her husband's plight. As she talks to him and he realises that she has heard what he said, she comes into focus.

Here we understand that she is against his accepting the case (she proves to be racist) and that this is the beginning of the end of their marriage. It also emphasises the great emotional distance between them which we would not necessarily have noticed had the director, Rob Reiner, simply cut from one face to the next. It also heightens the dramatic tension as we become aware of her presence before Bobby does.

Ingmar Bergman uses this technique in *Persona* where most of the (inner) drama revolves around the relationship between two women. Their faces often almost become one and are only distinguished by focus.

On the other hand, soft focus can be used to evoke a feeling of romanticism, warmth and romance.

> In the scene where a group of girls visits the mysterious Hanging Rock mountain in *Picnic at Hanging Rock* by Peter Weir, the director employs a soft-focus technique. With the bright light and the white clothes that the girls are wearing, the scene takes on a dream-like quality. The girls seem to be transformed into angels. The soft focus also creates an atmosphere of mystery and purity, as well as suggesting suppressed sexuality.
>
> – NG

In *To Gillian on her 37th Birthday,* Gillian (Michelle Pfeiffer) who is supposed to be a ghost or a figment of the main character's imagination, is also seen through a soft lens, giving an almost angelic, unreal glow to her face and features. By using this lens, the camera is able to portray her to us as her husband fondly remembers her.

Depth of focus

With depth of focus, so often found in *Citizen Kane,* a director focuses on all the subjects or characters simultaneously. We see more deeply and clearly into the picture without the director drawing our attention to one specific object or person. We take in the whole picture and have to select objects of importance for ourselves.

The same applies to the highly realistic world where the Bruce Willis character views the chaos (cars travelling through the air) in *The Fifth Element* by Luc Besson.

Blurring of the background

By blurring the background, a director deliberately blurs or dims images which are not important, either to focus our attention more sharply on a specific action or character or to create a sense of confusion in the background. A character could be in deep conversation close to the viewer, while (unimportant) traffic passes by in the background. To avoid distracting our attention from the important dialogue in a street scene, for example, the background is blurred.

In *Alien* characters such as the one played by John Hurt, often take close-up views of strange objects (during the discovery of a derelict spaceship, the space jockey and subsequently the eggs). As Hurt's head moves closer, the background is blurred, while the director concentrates only on the strange round shape of the astronaut's helmet and the frightened face lit by the search lamp on top of his head. The blurred background could also suggest that something is hiding there.

Distorting or breaking up the images

This usually occurs when a character is in visual contact with another in a strange environment. By blurring the action, or even interrupting the images (as happens when a television signal breaks up), the viewer is unsettled because he does not have a clear view of what is happening. This implies danger or even that a character who cannot be reached is dying, as happens to Ellie during her trip in *Contact*.

In *Alien,* the astronauts on the spaceship often lose contact with their colleagues who are investigating the surface of the planet outside. The frequent interference and distortion of the television images on the screens inside the spaceship suggest danger, even an unseen force which is disrupting the communication. One often finds these images in films about aliens or space creatures who are causing havoc with earth's electronic signals.

What is included and what is omitted

A director often deliberately omits information or does not concentrate on a particularly gruesome action, preferring to allow us to fill in the details for ourselves. Hitchcock often uses this technique. He rarely shows a murder in explicit detail as in *Psycho,* but chose rather to give free reign to our imagination to fill in the picture.

In the original *Alien* we seldom see the monster in its entirety in a clear shot or in the kind of detail Steven Spielberg uses to portray his monsters in the later scenes in *Jurassic Park* and its sequel. This makes the alien of Ridley Scott and the designer H.R. Giger even more frightening, because we only get glimpses of him. We seldom see the creature in all his glory in the first *Alien*. In the three sequels though, the creatures' grotesque shapes and features are fully explored to evoke even more terror.

Even in *Jurassic Park's* initial monster scenes we are only permitted a glimpse of a giant claw or the sounds of its thunderous approach. However, once Spielberg has established the dangers, he shows us his computer-generated monsters in full.

The final sequence of David Fincher's *Seven* involves a gruesome discovery by one of the characters: a human head is delivered in a box. Although we never actually see the head, we can easily imagine the macabre details. This is possible since Fincher has already shown us, with alarming realism on numerous occasions earlier in the film, the demented manner in which the killer sets about performing his deeds. It is therefore not necessary to show the head in the box. In fact, what we are able to imagine by that stage is much more shocking than what any special effects artist could have put together.

– NG

Another good example of omission comes from *Shanghai Triad* by Zhang Yimou. An innocent young boy, played by Wang Xiao Xiao, enters the shadowy world of the Chinese Mafia. When gang battles rage or people are killed, he often looks the other way, or watches from afar, only seeing the shadows of men in hats with guns moving like ghosts through the darkness.

This emphasises the fact that the boy is so terrified by what is happening and that the gruesome reality is so alien to him, that the action takes place on an almost surrealistic level. It is outside his frame of reference and he does not exactly realise how brutal the slayings are. Yimou is not as preoccupied with the explicit details in the way Quentin Tarantino may be, but more with the way the boy experiences the events.

EXERCISES

1. A good director often uses his camera as narrator. Do you agree? Discuss with examples.
2. When watching *Lost Highway* by David Lynch, it becomes evident that we are now entering "Lynchland". Explain what is meant by this term, concentrating on the strange visual look of the film. Is it successful, or do you find it to be too self-conscious and inaccessible?
3. Explain what is meant by "cinematic composition" by referring to at least five scenes from recent films.
4. Camera movements can be divided into ten categories. Name them and give an example in each case.
5. Name and discuss at least two films in which directors use depth of focus.

4

Visual design

THE ROLE OF THE ART DIRECTOR AND PRODUCTION DESIGNER

The art director is responsible for designing the sets for a film. He is often directly involved in the construction of the set and studies particular thematic designs in collaboration with the director, the cinematographer and even the editor.

He sketches the set for a film, whether it be the office of a sleazy car salesman in *Fargo,* the romantic, though cluttered, bedroom where De Almasy and Katherine make love in *The English Patient,* the crowded streets of a futuristic Los Angeles in *Blade Runner* or the grim room where a tycoon's son is imprisoned after his kidnapping in *Ransom.*

He must ensure that sets look "used" or "lived in". The house that Frances Lacey (Kathy Bates) and her children try to turn into a home in *A Home of Our Own* reflects the personalities of the family. It is clearly a house that is used, where people live, and which does not have the brand new plastic look so often associated with the sets of soap operas or situation comedies.

Compare the sensual, "erotic-friendly" designer bedrooms in a Zalman King film with the realistic bedroom Marge Gunderson (Frances McDormand) and her husband occupy in *Fargo.* The latter is a comfortable middle-class bedroom where a couple live their day-to-day lives and talk about their work. One can see that this rundown bedroom is "lived in", while the glossy bedrooms of any Zalman King film or *One Fine Day* appear to have been constructed the previous day without anybody having slept in the carefully designed bed, let alone having lived in the room.

A set is often used for sheer visual delight and effect, like the 1950s restaurant where John Travolta and Uma Thurman dined in *Pulp Fiction*. This keeps it in perfect sync with the overall elaborate, darkly funny tone of the rest of the film which also pays homage to the pulp novels of the 1950s.

The art director and production designer must also be fully aware of the atmosphere the director is trying to create. Their designs must be functional and must fit the film's mood, as in *Lost Highway* where the bedroom the two main characters occupy is dark, ominous and gloomy. It looks more like a funeral parlour (which it eventually becomes) than a bedroom. The same applies to the wooden house which explodes in reverse as in a dream. (Colour photo C, page x)

LIGHTING

A director and the lighting cameraman control the amount of light allowed into the picture. In this way, with special lighting, an object can take on an ominous appearance, can be bathed in angelic light, or can take on a whole new meaning. When judging the effective use of lighting in a film, you have to determine certain factors, as discussed below.

Although the film will never reach classical status, David Twohy's *The Arrival* uses highly effective lighting in the scenes in which Zane Ziminski (Charlie Sheen) discovers some unearthly activity in the Omni Tech Plant. Hiro Narita's imaginative contrast between light and shadow and the interplay between bright colours (as shown in colour photo D, page x) demonstrate the feeling of fear, uncertainty and eerie excitement so prevalent in these scenes.

The time of day

If a scene takes place during the day, one expects it to have a certain bright look and cheerful feel to it. (Compare the comic and chaotic sequences in the zoo in *Fierce Creatures* by Roger Young and Fred Schepisi.) The light source is usually the sun. If the scene takes place inside a building, like in John Cleese's office, the light source can be the sun coming in through a window or door or, of course, from an electric fixture in the ceiling. These are obvious examples. (Colour photo E, page xi)

Often, however, a director uses artificial light, or gives an impressionistic view of a scene through his use of light and its source. It is important to note how the director uses the realistic light to create mood or atmosphere. The same applies to a night scene. How effectively does a director use the available light in a scene and why is it presented in a certain way?

One of the best examples of effective lighting can be found in the first half-hour of *When a Stranger Calls* by Fred Walton. A babysitter (Carol Kane) is alone in a rich couple's house looking after the children. As she studies, the director cuts to different views of the house. The lounge is dark and gloomy, the corridor has an empty, menacing feel about it and the light behind a half-open door is decidedly eerie. Through the clever use of lighting and the absence of bright colour, Walton creates an uneasy, uncanny atmosphere without using gimmicks or foreboding music. Wes Craven pays tribute to this sequence in the opening scenes of *Scream*.

When Laszlo de Almasy and his beloved Katherine walk through a market in Cairo in *The English Patient*, it appears as if they are lit by an invisible, radiant light. Compared to the other people who almost disappear into the background, they stand out. These two characters are discovering love – a love that is so great they will later die for (or from) it – hence the bright lighting which illuminates them.

Lighting as an element of style

The use of lighting is usually integrated into the director's style. Lighting tells its own story.

In *Batman*, Tim Burton employs a Gothic visual style. There are towering buildings, grey mist and huddling crowds. It seems as if the entire city is shrouded in darkness. But the lighting technique extends beyond this: the hero is also constantly shrouded in darkness, suggesting that Batman (Michael Keaton) is an extension of the city. It adds dimension to his character, indicating a darker side to the hero.

In direct contrast is the way in which the villain, the Joker (Jack Nicholson), is lit. His insane grimace becomes even wider as Burton exposes him in full light. The Joker is always well lit, adding obscenity to his already evil grin. In this film lighting becomes more than just a means of correct exposure, it supports the characterisation as well.

– NG

The light source

The source of light is often deemed important, as an audience may ask where the light is coming from and why. But is this always important?

Lighting is a vitally important aspect of Andrew Birkin's *The Cement Garden*. There are a number of scenes where the light source takes on an almost ambiguous quality. One of these is when the boy, played by Andrew Robertson, runs out of his claustrophobic home naked. He dances around in the darkness and holds his arms open as if to embrace an invisible source of light. The source of light could be the moon or even a street lamp which is outside the frame, but it could also be symbolic: with the boy embracing the light of freedom or knowledge. The light could also be a metaphor, depicting the fact that he has finally seen the light and has freed himself of all the trouble and pain which has surrounded him up to now.

> Another example can be found in Frank Darabont's *The Shawshank Redemption.* When the main character (Tim Robbins) escapes from jail, he emerges from the filth – literally and metaphorically – and is engulfed by a bright source of light. It could be the moon peering out from behind storm clouds, or it could be lightning, but in the context of the story the source of light can also be seen as symbolic. The character could be basking in the light of his new-found freedom.
>
> – TLdR

The relationship between light and shadow

Examine the relationship between light and shadow. Why is half a face hidden in darkness as in *The Godfather?* And why are shadows so predominant in the room?

In the powerful opening scene of *The Godfather,* the image fades from black to reveal a close-up view of a face in a darkened room. Darkness envelops the character, who is in conversation with Don Corleone (Marlon Brando) and we know that a shady deal or an evil deed is being planned.

The only source of light in the room that we see at that moment is an electric light which reflects from the character's forehead. (Other sources of light such as light through blinds or table lamps are only revealed later.) The visitor is asking the Godfather for a favour, but as the man feels inferior to the Don, and guilty that he approaches him only now that he needs him, the lighting creates an almost comical effect. The man looks frightened, cautious and embarrassed. He is in an inferior position to the Godfather.

As the camera pulls back towards Corleone's point of view, darkness still surrounds the visitor, obviously reflecting his frightened state of mind and the atmosphere in a room where the discussion revolves around murder and death. Only later do other shadowy, dark figures in black suits appear from the darkness. They literally look like black ravens coming to life from within the shadows where they were "hiding" from our view.

Corleone is out of focus in the first shot and we see only the shape of his head and his hand which characteristically moves from his face towards the guest in an understated gesture. This intense darkness, with only smatterings of light on the character's forehead, his face and his white shirt which protrude from a black suit, set the mood for the entire dark, ominous, dramatic film about the inner workings of the Mafia.

We have literally entered the dark heart of the Mafia, where objects are viewed in black and white – right and wrong. There is no place for natural light in such a claustrophobic, menacing place where dishonesty, murder and deception are commonplace.

In David Lynch's *Lost Highway,* the character played by Bill Pullman is literally swallowed by darkness before his wife's gruesome murder. Some shots are in complete darkness and one is actually startled when

32. Darkness surrounds the hapless Fred Madison (Bill Pullman) who is doomed to be imprisoned for a vicious murder in David Lynch's *Lost Highway*. (Courtesy of Ciby 2000)

Pullman slowly appears from the pitch blackness. This reflects his nightmarish state of mind and the fact that his soul and his entire being have been swallowed by an evil darkness which could be inside him.

Reflecting intensity and texture

The lighting usually reflects the intensity and texture of nature and the surroundings. For instance, in *Lawrence of Arabia* certain scenes are harshly lit to reflect the cruel heat of an inhospitable place. In *Cry, the Beloved Country,* some scenes have a warm feeling about them, indicating the wonderful, friendly heat of the African sun.

In his narration, the character played by James Earl Jones says: "The hills are lovely beyond any singing of it." This is reflected in the rich, warm photography. Even some of the scenes in his office (as the young girl approaches him with a letter) have a warm, glowing feeling as his face is basked in light.

The hills indeed have a luscious, green colour as described in the narration. Even the Johannesburg skyline seen through the train window has a golden glow around it because it is "the city of gold". Only when the old man gets off the train and is robbed does the city take on a more sinister, darker look. But then again, when he sits around the table with his friends from the church, a warm glow comes from the lamp on the table. There is some warmth amid all the darkness, because of friendship and spiritual fulfilment. (Colour photo F, page xii)

Some directors glamorise the African sunsets, as in *The Ghost and the Darkness* or *Out of Africa*. The director controls the way we see the scene through his deliberate use of lighting which may not always reflect reality.

In most James Ivory films, on the other hand, a more subdued form of lighting also plays an important role. In contrast to the harshness of the African landscape, the England of *Howards End* and *The Remains of the Day* is not nearly as bright as a scene which takes place in, say, Italy during *Enchanted April*. Ivory's scenes have a subdued light, even if the scene takes place outside. The English weather is usually overcast and does not allow the same amount of sunlight in as, for instance, a film taking place in California.

Low-key lighting

A director uses low-key lighting if he wants shadows to dominate the screen. This technique is usually used to create suspense, sensuality, or both – as in *Body Heat* by Lawrence Kasdan. It is often used in horror films like Ridley Scott's *Alien,* to hide a menacing presence from the eager eye of the camera and to terrorise an audience. In the first shots of the Nostromo spaceship approaching the hostile planet, the ship itself looks like a monster through the clever use of low-key lighting. There is even something prehistoric about its shape, which is emphasised by the lighting.

Compare this shot with the romantic view Stanley Kubrick has of man's new toys (spaceships) in *2001: A Space Odyssey,* or Steven Spielberg has of a flying saucer in *E.T.: The Extra-Terrestrial.*

In *Alien,* as the three astronauts venture into the stranded alien spaceship, low-key lighting gives them a spooky, unearthly look. This effect is emphasised by the searchlights mounted on top of their helmets and the flashlights in their hands. These lights form a sharp contrast with the overwhelming darkness of deep space surrounding them. The faint streaks of light appear to be hopelessly inadequate, stressing the fact that the astronauts are up against a dark, unseen, treacherous force which is far larger and more dangerous than they expect. Their weapons (in this case symbolised by the searchlights) are powerless against this overwhelming, unknown menace.

The entire first half of *Lost Highway* by David Lynch is characterised by extreme low-key lighting. Note the dark bedroom where the characters played by Bill Pullman and Patricia Arquette sleep. Even the party they attend is dimly lit. It does not seem as if they have one bright light in their entire home, which of course reflects the fact that danger and death are lurking in the underlit rooms.

High-key lighting

A director uses high-key lighting when light plays a dominating role in a scene. He does not work with as much contrast as a director who, for instance, makes a *film noir* (black film). High-key lighting is usually used in situation comedies, soap operas, comedies and children's stories.

Most Hollywood (slapstick) comedies are lit in high key. Since the comic impact of the film lies in physical comedy, there are few shadows. This allows the audience to fully appreciate the physical stunts and gags which the actors employ to get their laughs. All the Jim Carrey films are lit in high key (with the notable exception of The *Cable Guy*). Films like *Ace Ventura, Pet Detective* and *The Nutty Professor* have lighting designs which aim to keep the entire frame well lit, so that none of the actor's actions goes unnoticed.

– NG

Different characters are often lit in different ways

Note the effective use of lighting in *Seven* in a scene in which the two investigators search for clues at the scene of a gruesome murder. The older cop, played by Morgan Freeman, is evenly though dimly lit, while the younger, less experienced cop (Brad Pitt) seems to be surrounded by darkness, with the light from his torch flooding the centre of the frame. This gives him an almost angelic, pure look on the one side, with an impenetrable darkness which threatens to swallow him on the other.

An ominous character is frequently lit from below to suggest a menacing, almost ghost-like presence. A hero or a main character usually has favourable lighting, often high key, to draw agreeable attention to him. A character of less importance is usually not favoured by the cameraman, to avoid distracting attention unnecessarily from the focal point.

33. Spooky low-key lighting gives the two cops in *Seven* (played by Morgan Freeman and Brad Pitt) an eerie, menacing appearance. Note how threatened especially Brad Pitt looks with the darkness which appears to engulf him, while the glaring light of the torch almost seems to burn him. (New Line)

Another way of suggesting a sinister presence is for a director to use back lighting and to cast the character in silhouette. In a murder mystery this technique can be used either to hide a character's identity, or to make him appear threatening or ghostly.

Flooding the scene with light

A director can also flood his scene with light, overexposing the frame, which often happens when somebody uses a searchlight or when a car approaches the camera. For a moment the viewer is blinded and thus disorientated, creating a sense of confusion. The searchlights in *Alien* have this effect as light suddenly and unexpectedly blinds the audience.

In *Lost Highway,* David Lynch floods an exterior love scene in the headlights of a car. The light seems to incinerate the characters and consume their souls. This excessive use of light is in line with the entire film's use of bizarre techniques to reflect man's subconscious. This flooding of light also gives birth to the final resolution in the shape of Bill Pullman. By using this technique, Lynch removes all traces of romanticism and literally turns the two lovers and their actions into a scorching, unromantic coupling from hell.

COLOUR

Bright colours

By using bright colours, a director attracts the viewer's attention to a character or a situation like a children's party or a field full of flowers, as Franco Zeffirelli does in *Brother Sun, Sister Moon* when a young soldier discovers the joys and beauty of nature. Unfortunately Zeffirelli overemphasises the use of colour, giving a false, plastic look to a scene which is supposed to be warm and beautiful, and so alienates his audience from the desired effect.

A director like David Lynch deliberately uses bright, kitsch colours in the opening sequences of *Blue Velvet* to comment on the working class's idealistic, television-inspired, rosy dreamworld hiding in the characters' subconscious.

A director often works with a high colour contrast to attract attention. This technique can be used in a symbolic way: for instance, a woman with loose morals may wear a tight-fitting red outfit, a nerd often dresses in dull greys, while a thug or a Mafia boss will dress in a dark suit.

The brash use of colour also has a role in comic strip cinema, such as *Dick Tracy* or *Edward Scissorhands,* where the director deliberately tries to imitate a fantasy world in which bright colours reign supreme. In *The Flintstones* and *Richie Rich,* the colours are also brighter than usual to imitate the dazzling colours used in the original strips.

Colour as a motif or symbol

Nicolas Roeg uses the colour red as a central motif throughout *Don't Look Now* because a young girl was wearing a red raincoat when she drowned. This colour dominates the entire film as everything red reminds the parents of that tragic incident, no matter where they go. Red in this case also has a symbolic meaning: it spells danger, is related to blood and violence, and eventually leads to another death.

> Krzysztof Kieślowski is a master when it comes to the symbolic use of colour – his *Three Colours* trilogy bears testimony. In each chapter, he makes deliberate use of one dominant colour in order to convey the desired message and emotions.
>
> In *Three Colours: Blue*, he uses blue symbolically to convey the wide range of feelings which the characters experience. Very little dialogue is required, because most of the vital information is conveyed through the use of this colour. In many of the scenes, particularly in the hospital, the blue shows us that the main character, portrayed by Juliette Binoche, has become cold and distant. The death of her family has made her oblivious to the world around her. She has become enclosed in her own little cocoon. All the warmth and love she once possessed has seemingly leaked from her body, leaving her cold and alone.
>
> –TLdR

Cool colours tend so suggest tranquillity, aloofness and serenity. Cool colours also have a tendency to recede in an image. Warm colours (red, yellow and orange) suggest aggressiveness, violence and stimulation. They tend to come forward in most images (Giannetti 1993: 20, 21).

> In Luc Besson's *The Big Blue*, colour enables us to accurately experience what the characters in the film are experiencing. The deep contrasting shades of blue below the surface allow the viewer to feel the serenity that the characters enjoy during a dive. The colours are cool and neutral, and assume an almost surreal nature. They can be seen to be cleansing the soul of all the impurities which forcefully confront it on the surface.
>
> –TLdR

Black and white

When one sees a film like *Seven*, it becomes clear that David Fincher literally made a black and white film in colour. With his low-key lighting, his dark, stark sets and his subdued use of colour (there is barely a bright colour in sight), he creates a grey, nightmarish world. In this world normal colour is almost completely absent, except in the horrifying final scenes – some of the only scenes to take place in bright sunlight. In this way, *Seven* reflects a world in which it is eternally night, also on a symbolic level.

Black and white usually gives a film a very formal look. As in most *films noirs,* the director creates tension between light and darkness.

> In contrast to the familiar look of a conventional colour photograph, a black and white picture carries the viewer immediately into the realm of abstraction. Because it renders colours as light or dark shades of grey, giving its subject new visual identities, black and white film is at its best when used to interpret rather than merely record. It is superb at capturing patterns and contrasts, textures and forms, and all manner of tonal relationships, from the most powerful to the most subtle (Boggs, 1996: 207).

Woody Allen often shoots his comedies, like *Manhattan,* in black and white, because colour does not play that important a role in the cultures he is presenting. The use of black and white also refers to the importance of the spoken or written word in black and white, as if on paper. A director like David Lynch creates a nightmarish, claustrophobic, almost surreal quality through his stark black and white photography in *The Elephant Man.*

Steven Spielberg makes exceptional use of black and white in the excellent *Schindler's List.* At the beginning of the film, we see some colour, particularly in the flames of the candles. This symbolically depicts that Jewish culture is still alive and strong, and burning brightly.

When the candles are snuffed out, the colour fades and we are left with a stark black and white picture. This is also symbolic. It shows that the flames of the Jewish culture are being threatened, and that its people are about to enter a dark period from which colourful bright scenes will be absent. This is also evident in a particularly haunting scene in the film in which we see a little girl in a red dress running across the black and white landscape which Spielberg has created. This brief glimpse of colour accurately depicts the ever-diminishing amount of hope and innocence that exists around her.

The black and white nature of the film accurately portrays the good and evil surrounding each of the characters, as well as the despair that existed for a number of years.

–TLdR

COSTUMES

Costumes too play an important role in visual design. Always ask yourself whether the costumes are neutral or whether the characters' clothing contributes to your overall impression of the film and in what way.

A character's clothes must be functional and fit the period in which the film takes place. In period films like *Farinelli, How to make an American Quilt* or *Restoration,* one should ask whether the costume

34.
Note the flamboyant costume and headdress used by director Gerard Corbiau in *Farinelli,* starring Stéfano Dionisi, which serve as an extension of the character's nature. (Unifrance)

designs serve their purpose and are realistic and accurate. If the film is of a particular genre, such as a Western or *film noir (The Quick and the Dead, Body Heat),* do the costumes reflect the essence of that genre and time period?

Restoration is a perfect example, as even the smallest detail is true to the period and the fashions inspired by the flamboyant sun king. Every detail of a costume must be authentic, as in *Portrait of a Lady* by Jane Campion or Mel Gibson's period piece, *Braveheart.*

Costumes or clothing are frequently used to reflect character, personality, social status, breeding or the lack thereof. The clothes a woman wears can reflect her moral character. In David Lynch's *Lost Highway* Patricia Arquette wears skin-tight, sexy costumes to emphasise her seductive curves and beguiling fatal beauty. So too in *Body Heat,* Kathleen Turner's Matty Walker wears tight, body-hugging clothes which emphasise her long, beautiful legs and her ample breasts. Her clothes alone ooze sexual charm, seductiveness and promiscuity. The same applies to the flamboyant drag queens of *The Adventures of Priscilla, Queen of the Desert,* where the clothes are as over the top as the personalities who wear them. These characters are making a definite statement with the flashy outfits they wear: the clothes reflect the women they would like to be.

Costumes can serve as an extension of an actor's screen persona. Take note of Charlie Chaplin's little tramp outfit, or the elaborate outfits Jim Carrey wears in the two *Ace Ventura* films, or the nerdish clothes worn in *The Nutty Professor* which emphasise the main character's weight, as well as the over-the-top outfits he wears when he is thin to complement his "new" muscle-bound body. Macho characters like Rambo *(First Blood)* or the cop in the *Die Hard* series often wear only vests to display their bulging muscles.

The Mafia characters in *The Godfather* and other films about the Mafia usually dress immaculately in formal suits (also note the strict dress code of the policemen who take the law into their own hands in *Mulholland Falls* by Lee Tamahori), while the youngsters' outfits in *Kids* are deliberately antisocial – a kind of rebellious statement against any kind of formalism and authority.

Costumes can even reflect a contrast in experience, age and personality, as the different outfits the two cops, played by Brad Pitt and Morgan Freeman, do in *Seven.* Sometimes older women dress flamboyantly, as Shirley MacLaine does in *Evening Star* to show a stubborn woman who refuses to grow old. Her body may be ageing, but not her mind. This is reflected in the clothes she wears, which would actually suit a much younger woman, although she still looks stunning in them. In teenage dramas, girls and boys usually wear tight-fitting jeans and muscle hugging T-shirts (cf. *Risky Business)* to reflect their youthful arrogance and body-conscious culture.

Directors often attract attention to a character and his frame of mind through the colour of the clothing he wears: villains are usually clad in black (note the Mafia in *The Godfather* and the dark, unflattering costumes most of the characters wear in David Lynch's nightmarish *Lost Highway*), while heroes wear white or light colours. See, for example, the clothes Tom Cruise wears in *Jerry Maguire,* while evil characters like Damien in *The Omen* are often clad in dark colours to reflect their diabolical nature. The girls in *Picnic at Hanging Rock* are dressed in pure white, while the repressed school principal, Rachel Roberts, is dressed in black. Promiscuous women are often clad in red as Jennifer Tilly is in

Liar Liar. Streetwise kids in clashing, slapdash colours indicate that they are rebelling against authority, as in *Carpool.* Colour can also be used in an ironic way, such as when a villain is wearing white (as Christopher Walken does in *The Comfort of Strangers*) to give him a cold, clinical, almost sterile look.

Costumer Tom Wolfe said: "Clothing is a wonderful doorway that most easily leads you to the heart of the individual. It's how characters reveal themselves" (Giannetti, 1993: 299).

If a director mixes clothing styles, as Baz Luhrmann does in the postmodern *William Shakespeare's Romeo and Juliet* or even in the flamboyantly stylish *Strictly Ballroom,* what is he trying to say? In the former the use of modern streetwear reflects the streetwise attitude of the characters. It also helps the younger audience, at whom the film is aimed, to identify more easily with the characters and their emotions. In *Strictly Ballroom* the excessive clothes and the kitsch hairstyles reflect the souls of the characters. For them it is all about appearance. Under the costumes are mostly empty souls. It is only when Scott brings about a revolution by exposing the organisers' and judges' greed, that some characters change.

Musicals like *Bugsy Malone, The Rocky Horror Picture Show* and *Hello, Dolly!* lend themselves to a wonderful array of colourful and striking costumes, while fantasy films like *Legend, 101 Dalmatians* and *Dragonheart* resort to fairy-tale costumes.

Even postmodern high-tech films like *Hackers* feature an almost surreal, styleless dress code to reflect characters who live in another world and who have very little in common with the "real" world. The same applies to the outrageous, but highly fashionable clothes the kids wear in *Clueless,* and Jean-Paul Gaultier's evocative combination of punk, primitive and classic in Luc Besson's *The Fifth Element. Waterworld's* shabby, torn, rough costumes help depict a world in which there is no remaining sense of realism and people simply wear the costumes to cover themselves or protect themselves from the elements.

In comic strip cinema, costumes can be deliberately overstated. Notice the Joker's costumes in *Batman,* the outfits the "cool" kids wear in *William Shakespeare's Romeo and Juliet,* as well as the elaborate, almost grotesquely overdone costumes of the drag queens in *The Adventures of Priscilla, Queen of the Desert* and actor John Goodman's designer tatters in *The Flintstones* which also reflect a feeling of the Stone Age.

Costumes can also reflect sexual and spiritual repression, as in *Portrait of a Lady* by Jane Campion, *Picnic at Hanging Rock* or *Witness* by Peter Weir or Martin Scorsese's *The Age of Innocence.* On the other hand, clothing also reflects sexual flamboyance, as in *Don Juan DeMarco* or Mira Nair's *Kama Sutra.* In other films such as *Prêt-à-Porter* by Robert Altman, people hide behind their costumes, thus turning the clothing into a main theme of the film.

Fabric also plays an important part in establishing a character. Compare the character of a woman who wears suede or some other expensive material (as the character played by Lauren Bacall does in *The Mirror has Two Faces* to remind her of her glorious glamour days) to a character clad in khaki (like Meryl Streep in *Out of Africa* or Val Kilmer in *The Ghost and the Darkness*) or in simple clothes like Streep in *The Bridges of Madison County.* The last example reflects a woman who is not interested in appearance but finds greater pleasure in other things such as her family and caring for her children.

35. Note the informal, tacky clothes worn by the streetwise oil rigger (Lionel Newton) in *Jump the Gun.* The character's free spirit, simple background and defiant nature are reflected in his choice of clothing. (Courtesy of Film Four International)

36.
The Joker (Jack Nicholson), made up to look like a demented clown, holds his own parade to celebate Gotham City's 200th anniversary in Tim Burton's *Batman.* (Warner Bros.)

37.
Lukas Haas as Donner wears simple clothes which on the one hand complement his well-defined body, while the loose shirt reflects his personality and advertises his youth and availability to prospective clients. It also shows a rebellious, convention-defying attitude. Scott Silver directed *johns*. (Courtesy of Overseas Film Group)

MAKE-UP

Another important element of visual design is make-up. With the vast number of fantasy films flooding the market, special visual and make-up effects artists are now becoming cinema's latest superstars. Ever since *An American Werewolf in London* won an Oscar for special make-up effects, make-up wizards have competed on the level of gory effects. (Ironically enough, the team responsible for the remarkable *The Elephant Man* make-up did not win an Oscar in the previous year.)

In horror movies, make-up artists have literally tried to out-do one another as far as gory detail is concerned (cf. films like *Friday the 13th, The Evil Dead* and *The Frighteners).*This has led to the effects becoming so excessive that they fail to convince or scare any more. In fact, they have the opposite effect: people often start laughing, as happened with *From Dusk till Dawn*.

There are a few exceptions, though, where make-up literally tells its own story and is so well designed that it contributes to a particular film's success.

In horror films like David Cronenberg's modern version of *The Fly* and Bernard Rose's *Candyman,* the effects are so perfectly integrated with the story that they are convincing on both a horror and realistic level. The same applies to Sam Raimi's *Darkman,* where a man's face is disfigured – yet beneath all the layers of make-up he still manages to convince us of his human qualities.

In *Eraserhead* and later *The Elephant Man,* David Lynch makes use of extensive and highly realistic make-up effects which also take on a symbolic quality. John Merrick's (John Hurt) grotesque make-up becomes symbolic of the huge emotional burden the character carries, because he is seen to be a freak and an outcast. Eventually Lynch succeeds in making us look past the make-up to discover the lonely, frightened, exploited and really beautiful human being.

The make-up for *Planet of the Apes,* a film about a community of ape-like people, and even that of the predecessors of man in *2001: A Space Odyssey* is so convincing that one is scarcely aware of the effects. This counts in the film's favour. The same happens to the dream-like creatures in Ridley Scott's *Legend* and the gorillas in *Greystoke: The Legend of Tarzan, Lord of the Apes* by Hugh Hudson. In the latter film Rick Baker and Paul Engelen were responsible for the amazingly realistic make-up effects which enable humans to portray apes and gorillas very realistically.

Make-up is not used only in science fiction films like the *Star Wars* trilogy or horror films like *A Nightmare on Elm Street.* It is often used to age a character, as is done with Billy Crystal in *Mr. Saturday Night,* when the actor aged fifty years in the film.

Make-up is also used to portray a character's horribly burnt or disfigured face as in *The English Patient* or the fat, bulging face of *The Nutty Professor*. (In the latter film Eddie Murphy's make-up took eight hours a day to apply.)

38. Through superb make-up, Billy Crystal as the stand-up comic Buddy Young Jr, ages fifty years in *Mr. Saturday Night*. (Courtesy of Castle Rock; Photographer: Bruce McBroom)

39. Eddie Murphy spent eight hours a day in the make-up chair to achieve the desired look of an obese clown in *The Nutty Professor*. (Copyright © 1996 by Universal Studios, Inc. Courtesy of MCA Publishing Rights, a division of Universal Studios, Inc. All rights reserved.)

40. Oliver Stone emphasises youthful patriotism and idealism in *Born on the Fourth of July* with Tom Cruise. (Copyright © by Universal Studios, Inc. Courtesy of MCA Publishing Rights, a division of Universal Studios, Inc. All rights reserved.)

Unfortunately, the make-up used in Mark Rydell's *For The Boys* and in another Bette Midler film, *Hocus Pocus* by Kenny Ortega, was so unrealistic that one was constantly aware of its shortcomings. The unconvincing make-up effects thus detracted from the story.

The reverse is also true: a good make-up artist can take years off a character, as happened to Tom Cruise in *Born on the Fourth of July,* when we see scenes of the young Ron Kovic as an idealistic school-boy, even though the actor was in his late twenties at the time. In *Once Were Warriors* the excessive tattoos of the Maori characters indicate their cultural standing, their masculine bonding and traditional roots.

41. Gangsters with traditional tattoos in *Once were Warriors,* directed by Lee Tamahori. (Courtesy of New Zealand Film Commision)

Make-up can also be used to transform a character completely in order to expose a side of him which he tries to hide from other people. An example is the (often unconvincing) transformation John Malkovich undergoes in the Jekyll and Hyde modernisation: *Mary Reilly.*

Another example of where make-up is literally used as a "character" in a film is in *How to Get Ahead in Advertising,* starring Richard E. Grant. A hideous boil on the character's neck starts to talk and turns into a monster-like alter ego which haunts and eventually almost destroys the character's life.

In *Dangerous Liaisons,* Glenn Close plays the part of an evil, conniving woman. After her peers hiss at her in a theatre (she was responsible for a tragic death when her sex games went awry), Close sits in front of a mirror and removes her elaborate make-up and beauty spots. We literally see a new character, the *real* woman, emerging from under the make-up. We discover a scared, tortured, haunted human being who only now realises what she has done, but it is too late for repentance. In *Strictly Ballroom* the selfish mother Shirley, brilliantly played by Pat Thompson, tries to hide her age and wrinkles behind excessive make-up. She literally "puts on her happy face". Unflattering close-ups expose the ageing and frustrated ex-ballroom champion and the wrinkles brought about by discontent.

Federico Fellini often uses elaborate make-up in his films to stress the artificiality and absurdity of a film and his larger-than-life characters. Many of them are usually circus people for whom grotesque make-up is normal, or prostitutes whose plump features are exaggerated through excessive make-up, as in *Amarcord.*

Make-up can also deliberately imitate comic book stereotypes like *Dick Tracy* and his friends and enemies, or sexual stereotypes in *The Rocky Horror Picture Show,* in which Frank N. Furter's almost grotesque red lips are emphasised by the make-up artist to suggest decadence, sexual ambiguity and promiscuity. The rest of his make-up gives him his alien look.

In *Philadelphia,* the make-up is extremely convincing, from the spots which start to appear on actor Tom Hanks's face and body, to his eventual "death mask" while he lies dying on his bed, a mere shadow of his former self. Robert De Niro's face achieves a puffy look in *Raging Bull* as his character is transformed from a lean fighting machine into a lazy, fat slob. De Niro gained a great deal of weight for the part, but make-up effects on his face also helped.

In Neil Jordan's *Interview with the Vampire: The Vampire Chronicles,* actors Tom Cruise and Brad Pitt have white faces which transform them into the living dead who never see the sun. Vincent Perez's pale make-up in Tim Pope's *The Crow II: City of Angels* gives him the appearance of a walking corpse obsessed with his own failures and melancholy nature.

The drag queens in *To Wong Foo, Thanks for Everything, Julie Newmar* also rely heavily on convincing make-up (under which the man is still

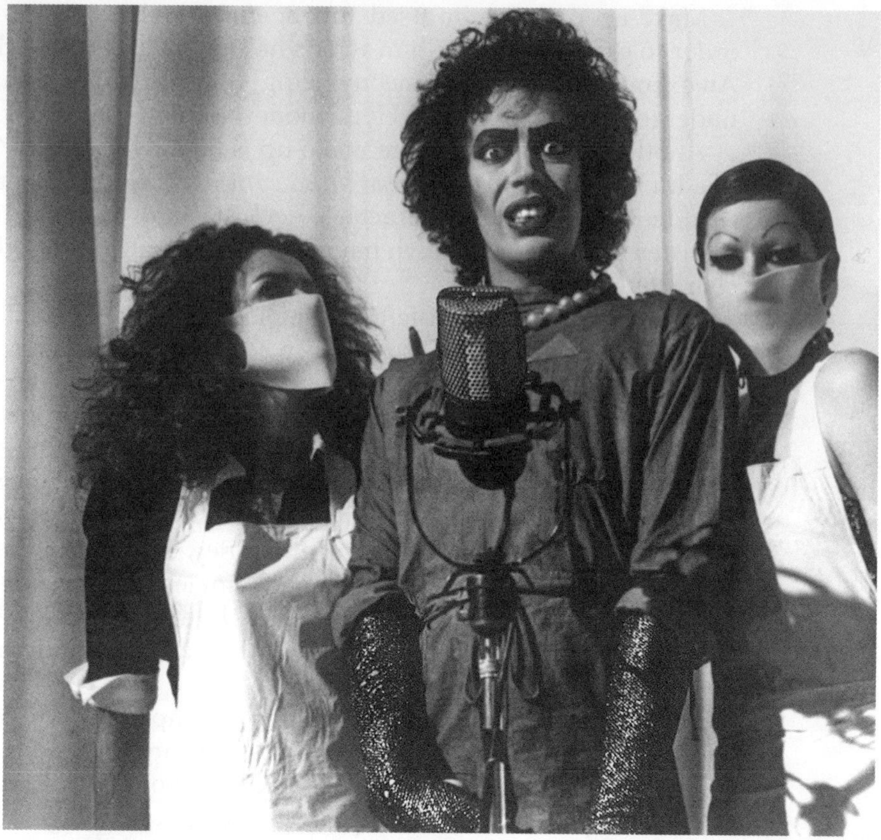

42.
Tim Curry's decadent make-up is a study in ambiguous and promiscuous sexual deviation and liberation in *The Rocky Horror Picture Show*. (20th Century Fox)

43.
Kirsten Dunst as Claudia and Tom Cruise as the sensual vampire Lestat in *Interview with the Vampire*. Note his death-like appearance through the clever use of pale make-up. (Warner Bros.)

44. Vincent Perez's death mask symbolises his character's dark, tormented nature in Tim Pope's *The Crow II: City of Angels*. (Miramax)

present) to be convincing as three "women" taking over a hostile, homophobic town.

The point is that make-up should enhance characterisation, not detract from the overall effect. This is why David Cronenberg, who is obsessed with physical disintegration, uses it so convincingly in *Crash*, where two characters (played by Rosanna Arquette and Elias Koteas) have convincing wounds which are also supposed to be sexually attractive in that particular context. (Colour photos I and J, page xiii)

EXERCISES

1. The art director is one of the most important contributors to the atmosphere a director is trying to create. Explain this comment with reference to suitable examples.
2. Through his use of lighting, a director often tells a particular story. Discuss this statement with relation to the four *Batman* films.
3. In *The Godfather* and *GoodFellas* there is a striking difference between the use of light and shadow. Discuss this tension.
4. Explain the difference between low-key lighting and high-key lighting. Illustrate with examples.
5. A director often works with a high contrast in a colour film to attract attention. Discuss and illustrate with examples.
6. Examine *William Shakespeare's Romeo and Juliet*, *Hamlet* and *Looking for Richard* as far as their costumes are concerned. How do these films differ from one another in this respect, and how do the directors make different statements through the different use of costumes?

5

Dialogue and sound

INTRODUCTION

The director of classic films like *Ran* and *The Seven Samurai,* Akira Kurosawa claimed: "Cinematic sound is that which does not simply add to, but multiplies, two or three times, the effect of the image" (Giannetti, 1993: 185). *The Jazz Singer* (1927) was the first film to use the spoken word and it introduced a whole new era to cinema. One can scarcely imagine a film without some form of sound nowadays. Even silent movies were accompanied by a live piano, an organ or even a full orchestra.

When a director uses sound he must decide which sounds are important and which are not. In this way, he imitates the functions of the human ear which also selects and even separates certain sounds. He should be careful not to allow a cacophony of sound to dominate or detract from the main action. If an intimate conversation takes place in a crowded restaurant, the audience should be able to hear the general background noises to set the scene, but the noise should not interfere with the conversation. One must still be able to hear each line clearly (depending, of course, on the speech patterns and style of conversation).

In Larry Clark's *Kids,* not every line of dialogue is clear in the scenes in public places because not all the dialogue is important, and Clark tries to create a sense of extreme realism. He also implies that much of the characters' dialogue revolves around one or two subjects only. So it does not matter if we do not catch every word – we have already heard the same information in other scenes. The same applies to Quentin Tarantino's naturalistic dialogue in *Reservoir Dogs,* where people talk about ordinary things like tipping while simultaneously planning a bank robbery.

The combination of foreground and background sound in *Kids* is justified because the background against which the scene takes place often has a direct influence on or relation to what is being said. In the case of *Kids,* the whole skateboard culture and the empty, drug-infested lives of the kids in the background reflects the very culture Clark is trying to expose in the conversation. The two themes therefore feed off each other and have a direct relationship.

However, in a comedy scene where every line is important, one is not interested in what the background people are saying. We may see their lips move and may hear a general hum in the background, but we do not necessarily hear what these people are saying. We focus only on the important conversation in the foreground.

One of the most remarkable instances of the use of sound is the opening scene of *Contact* by Robert Zemeckis. In this film a scientist, played by Jodie Foster, believes that there is intelligent life in outer space. She manages to make contact with what she perceives to be a superior race from another planet.

As the earth recedes into the distance during the film's impressive opening sequence, the audience takes part in a bizarre sound journey through the universe which has been bombarded by noise. One actually relives the entire history of sound, but at the same time one is escaping from it, until there is nothing left but utter silence. This silence, after all the jumbled noise, emphasises man's insignificance as he barely registers in the infinite pureness of the universe.

Also significant are the strange sounds with which the so-called alien race communicates. There is something dramatic and melodic, but at the same time eerie and even threatening in the pulsating sounds, which initially mean nothing until they are identified and analysed.

Zemeckis's film therefore displays not only considerable visual skills, but also striking sound effects, contrasted with the effective use of dead silences.

DIALOGUE

Through dialogue, a director, scriptwriter or character conveys the most important and obvious information to the audience. Several elements are important when judging the efficiency of dialogue and its effectiveness in a scene, as discussed below.

Economy Film dialogue must be used as economically as possible, and should differ from stage or radio dialogue in so far as the camera also serves as a narrator – therefore film dialogue should not overstate the obvious. It should not tell us what we are already seeing. If a character walks into shot wearing a red dress, a beehive hairstyle and a depressed look, the camera conveys all this information. In radio, another character may comment: "I suppose the red dress and beehive hairstyle have something to do with your depressed state of mind", because we cannot see the character. On film, all these elements are obvious and therefore it is not always necessary to convey this information in the dialogue, unless it is done for comic purposes. For instance a character could say: "You look great – pity the hairstyle went out with the sixties."

Dialogue should be used sparsely and should sound like the real dialogue of flesh-and-blood characters in a realistic situation. It should not be forced, stagy or superficial. Here is an example of effective film dialogue from *Body Heat,* screenplay by Lawrence Kasdan. In this scene, a down-and-out lawyer, Ned Racine, tries to pick up a stunning blonde, Matty Walker, as she walks past him. Eventually she will seduce him into murdering her husband:

RACINE: You can stand here with me if you want, but you'll have to agree not to talk about the heat.

WALKER: I'm a married woman.

RACINE: Meaning what?

WALKER: Meaning I'm not looking for company.

RACINE: Then you should have said I'm a *happily* married woman.

WALKER: That's my business.

RACINE: What?

WALKER: How happy I am.

RACINE: And how happy is that?

WALKER: You're not too smart, are you? I like that in a man.

RACINE: What else do you like? Lazy? Ugly? Horny? I got 'em all.

WALKER: You don't look *lazy*.

RACINE: Oh.

WALKER: Tell me, does chat like this work with most women?

RACINE: Some, if they haven't been around much.

WALKER: I wondered. Thought maybe I was out of touch.

RACINE: Can I buy you a drink?

WALKER: I told you, I've got a husband.

RACINE: I'll buy him one too.

WALKER: He's out of town.

RACINE: My favourite kind. We'll drink to him.

WALKER: He only comes up on weekends.

RACINE: Hahaha. I'm liking him better all the time …

(*Empire Magazine*, 1996: 146)

Each line is vitally important to the above scene and there are just the right number of words to get the message across. There is no need for additional dialogue, because the director's message has already been conveyed. Too many unnecessary words would result in a loss of effect. Good dialogue allows us to read a lot more into the scene than simply the words that are being spoken. By listening to the dialogue itself, the viewer is capable of discovering much more about the characters and their relationship with each other. This is known as "subtext", and is extremely important to good dialogue. The actual words become symbolic of a completely different train of thought.

The most important thing is that the dialogue in this scene is natural. The viewer gets the feeling from the very beginning that this conversation can actually take place. It is believable and not staged or forced.

–TLdR

Comedy In his comedies, Woody Allen often uses techniques such as unfinished sentences (usually reflecting the instability, insecurity or neurosis of a character) or overlapping dialogue (to indicate the nervous, often frenetic energy of the protagonist), or he portrays people frequently searching for words as indeed happens in real life. Count how often people use the words "you know" in Allen's comedies.

Think how often we look for the right word to describe a situation, or how frequently we interrupt other people or even ourselves and our own thought patterns or say "eh …" during a sentence while we are thinking or searching for a word. By imitating this style, Allen gives the impression that he is eavesdropping on a real-life situation which is actually happening at that very moment. Thus he creates a sense of spontaneity, even improvisation. Although Allen has certain gags built into his scenarios, the build-up to the gag follows a natural, unconventional, unforced pattern, making us believe completely in the character, the situation and what he is saying. The dialogue does not sound contrived.

The same applies to the carefully constructed dialogue used in *A Fish Called Wanda,* where the audience is constantly surprised by the originality and "blandness" (in other words straight-faced quality) of the gags, making them even funnier, because the writer does not place little markers around his dialogue, prompting us to laugh. The humour flows naturally from the situation.

In slapstick comedies like those of the Marx Brothers, Laurel and Hardy, and some films of Jerry Lewis, John Cleese, Barbra Streisand, Eddie Murphy and especially Jim Carrey's *Liar Liar,* the dialogue often functions like a machine-gun which is opened on an audience. It is a non-stop flow of one-liners and gags, some of which are quite vulgar. However, a good director will know when to stop. In *Ace Ventura, Pet*

Detective and *The Mask,* the scriptwriter and Carrey take their slapstick satire to the edge, but stop just short of overkill.

The same, unfortunately, cannot be said of Eddie Murphy's *The Nutty Professor,* directed by Tom Shadyac. In the scene where Murphy's character, now slim, stands on his knees in front of his girlfriend at a club and bellows out lame excuses, the dialogue carries on for too long. This tests the tolerance and endurance of the viewer to the limit. The result is that the dialogue starts losing its comic impact.

Drama Dramatic tension is usually built up through the careful, discerning use of the spoken word. Every word counts and contributes to the overall effect. In a good scene, one should not be able to change or remove one sentence without altering the natural rhythmic flow of meaning or effect of the situation.

Adapting a stage play for the screen therefore usually proves to be more difficult than writing an original script for a film, because the writer has to condense or adapt the dialogue for the benefit of the camera without losing its original meaning. For instance, a character may describe how beautiful Prague is on stage, but when the city is presented on screen, the viewer can see this for himself, therefore the dialogue has to be carefully adapted. Examples of great screen adaptations from plays include *Amadeus,* scripted by Peter Shaffer and based on his play; Edward Albee's *Who's Afraid of Virginia Woolf;* Julian Mitchell's *Another Country* and Neil Simon's comedies.

People often hide behind words or do not say exactly what they mean, as in *All About Eve, A River Runs Through it* and *Ordinary People.* They pretend to be talking about a certain thing on the surface, while they actually mean something completely different. This is referred to as "subtext" – that which lies below the surface.

A good example of subtext occurs in the final scene of Stanley Kubrick's *A Clockwork Orange*. Alex is recovering in hospital after an attempted suicide brought on by the government-sponsored treatment which was inflicted upon him. While in hospital, the minister of the interior comes to visit him. The minister expresses his regret at Alex's condition, and tries to shift the blame from himself and his government to a small group of radicals. Beneath this dialogue, however, lies the minister's true message. He wants to ensure that Alex does not tell the press of his terrible experiences at the hands of the justice system. The minister even goes as far as to offer him a bribe in the form of a job and a salary, although the word "bribe" is never mentioned.

Alex understands what the minister is really saying and, in his characteristically sarcastic manner, he agrees. We, however, are aware of Alex's true motives: he is willing to play along with the politicians, but will exact revenge in his own way – by reverting to his aggressive and sadistic

nature. In this example of subtext both characters are communicating on a level which is hidden under a mask of pleasantries and goodwill.
– NG

Dialogue should never be overtly self-conscious, except in cases such as the send-up of a genre, where the deliberate overstated use of corny, kitsch dialogue is meant as a direct comment on, or a send-up of an unreal, superficial situation. This happens in Tim Burton's darkly comical parody of the 1950s science fiction genre in *Mars Attacks!* The same can be said of the acid dark humour injected into the black comedies *The Addams Family* and *Addams Family Values* by Barry Sonnenfeld, as well as *The Pallbearer* by Matt Reeves, in which a funeral turns into a farce as characters attend the service of a man they pretend to know. When one of them has to make a speech about the unknown man, the irony of his words has his friends falling about laughing in church!

As far as natural dialogue is concerned, less is often more, as is proved in the *Three Colours* trilogy and Robert Redford's *A River Runs Through It.* The point in the latter film is that the strict father (Tom Skerritt) never really communicates with his sons on an emotional level. He says much without actually using words, which is not necessarily a good thing. His younger son, played by Brad Pitt, needs guidance, understanding and love, and never really receives enough of it. This feeling is conveyed by the sparse use of actual dialogue, although much of the subtext is explained in the voice-over narration. It is what is not said which carries as much weight as what is said.

45.
In *Before Sunrise* Ethan Hawke uses natural, unpretentious language as he sorts out his relationship with a French student (Julie Delpy) on a train journey. (Courtesy of Castle Rock; Photographer: Gabriela Brandenstein)

46. Craig Sheffer and Brad Pitt as two brothers who long for love, while Tom Skerritt stars as their religious father who is unable to express the deep emotion he feels towards his sons in Robert Redford's *A River Runs Through It*. (Buena Vista International)

Dialogue is often unnecessary. A look or a gesture may say more in certain situations than an entire page of dialogue. Another example of this from *A River Runs Through It* is where the father and his elder son (Craig Sheffer) look at the Brad Pitt character as he is catching trout. The father touches his son's knee and gives a faint smile. As the father has never touched his sons or displayed any physical affection before, this uncharacteristic gesture says more than a whole confession of fatherly love in dialogue.

Voice-over narration

Voice-over narration (i.e. narration which is not accompanied by a picture of the speaker) is often used when a book is adapted into a screenplay, or when we need access to the inner thoughts of a character.

In a book such as *The Prince of Tides*, written in the first person, the narrator's very personal and often flamboyant, even poetic way of describing a situation cannot always be conveyed in dialogue, therefore a voice-over is needed. Furthermore, the character is an English teacher who is in love with the power of the written word. The beauty of this character's written confession can only be conveyed in voice-over narration.

Another example of sparse, but very necessary voice-over narration by the older Christian Slater character occurs in *The Name of the Rose*.

The character philosophises about his master's immense wisdom and how it has influenced him. Each narration increasingly clarifies how much he respects his mentor and how much he learns from him.

In *The Shawshank Redemption,* the wise narrator (Morgan Freeman) gives us his impressions of the newly arrived inmate (Tim Robbins). From Freeman's tone we realise that Robbins is an extraordinary man who is able to beat the corrupt prison system in his own unique way. He is almost elevated to an icon through the narration.

> Voice-over narration works perfectly in *The Prince of Tides,* because it enables the viewer to see the story through the eyes of the main character. Whenever he finds himself in a difficult situation, we can associate with it completely, because he is able to explain to us how he got to that point. The film would have been tedious if each of these experiences had been depicted visually.
>
> Another outstanding example of effective voice-over narration occurs in the French film, *The Coming of Age.* The main character is a budding writer who writes about his life, his loves and the world around him. He communicates his abstract thoughts to the viewer via the voice-overs. Furthermore, the technique works in this film because the main character is often alone. Voice-over is very successful in this instance, as it allows the viewer to listen to the character's thoughts, which would otherwise have been almost impossible to convey.
>
> – TLdR

You should always ask yourself whether the narration is really necessary, or whether it detracts from the overall effect the director is trying to achieve. In *A River Runs Through It* the sad, nostalgic and poignant tone of the writer is extremely prominent in the book and Robert Redford's images succeed in conveying that atmosphere. The narration, however, often gently underlines the subtext and is therefore essential to the overall statement of the film. It enhances the atmosphere in a gentle, unobtrusive manner.

A narrator can set a certain mood, as in *To Kill A Mockingbird,* or can comment on the social and economic standing of a community, as in Martin Scorsese's *The Age of Innocence,* television's brilliant *Brideshead Revisited* and the Oscar-winning Dutch film *Antonia's Line* by Marleen Gorris, or even *Forrest Gump* by Robert Zemeckis.

The sober, down-to-earth Dutch narration in *Antonia's Line* serves to illustrate the immense wisdom gained by the narrator, Antonia's granddaughter, through her experiences. It sparkles with a subtle, unobtrusive humour which creates a feeling of well-being, humour and sadness at the same time. This is what the film is all about: man's humanity towards his fellowman, and the ability of the human spirit to overcome almost any obstacle, depending on how one looks at it.

47. Willeke van Ammelrooy, Marina de Graaf and Els Dottermans in *Antonia's Line*. (Courtesy of The Sales Group)

A voice-over narration can also tell us much more about a character than actual dialogue ever can. Notice Linda Manz's simple choice of innocent words in describing the situation she and her family find themselves in in *Days of Heaven* (she even stumbles over her words), or Woody Allen's paranoic, incomplete, nervous narration during *Manhattan*. Here is an extract:

ISAAC: "Chapter One: He adored New York City. He idolised it all out of proportion." Uh, no, make that, "He, he romanticised it all out of proportion." Better. "To him, no matter what the season was, this was still a town that existed in black and white and pulsated to the great tunes of George Gershwin." Er, no, let me start this over …

"Chapter One: He was too romantic about Manhattan, as he was about everything else …"

(*Empire Edition*, 1994: 114)

Sometimes a character needs to address the camera directly, one on one, to involve the audience in a more direct way, as Al Pacino does in his analysis of adapting Shakespeare for a modern audience in *Looking For Richard*. He asks us to participate and reminds us that we are watching a very personal film which we must analyse and to which we must respond as we go along.

The same happens at the end of *Bogus* by Norman Jewison, when a young boy's guardian angel, which he himself has created, addresses the audience directly to let them in on a secret: he does actually exist, and his job is to help lonely little kids find their place in the world.

CHAPTER

5

Dialogue and sound

48. Al Pacino analyses Richard III in a provocative contemporary reading of Shakespeare's play in *Looking for Richard*. (20th Century Fox)

The use of voice-over narration in Francis Ford Coppola's *Apocalypse Now* can be justified in that it provides information which may be difficult for an audience to see, such as Kurtz's personal records and files. The film is also in a sense a confession on the part of Captain Willard (Martin Sheen), and therefore he addresses the audience directly. Another advantage of the narration is that the audience gets a glimpse of the internal conflicts raging within Willard.

However, at times the narration becomes tedious and creates a feeling of overkill. This is especially apparent in the final part of the film where the visual horror of the jungle and the war is powerful enough without the irritating interruption of a narration which sounds overdramatic. This detracts from the authentic and convincing atmosphere of the rest of the film.

– NG

SOUND EFFECTS, VISIBLE AND INVISIBLE

Sound effects create a specific atmosphere or ambience. We often cannot see the source of the effects, which can heighten the tension or create a rich romantic atmosphere. For example, the chirping of crickets and other night sounds of the bush or country are often used to enrich the atmosphere and enhance a romantic scene which takes place against this exotic background.

The gentle sounds of the (visible) chimes in *Body Heat* not only create a feeling of sexual tension, cynicism and eeriness, but also become a kind of leitmotif for sex in the film – the sound frequently recurs whenever sex takes place.

Invisible sounds often have a much more devastating impact on the audience than anything visible. In Wolfgang Petersen's *Das Boot/The Boat,* most of the action takes place beneath the sea. As the men in their compact, claustrophobic submarine sink lower into the sea (this is also symbolic of their overall mental state) we hear the faint hum of the ship's engines; there are creaking sounds, as if the immense quantity of water pressing in on the ship is crushing it. Frequent sounds of steam hissing in the engine room and even water bubbling outside the ship create an atmosphere of great claustrophobic tension. We do not see the source of the sound, but the effect is devastating.

In Jean-Jacques Annaud's *The Name of the Rose,* the events centre around a dark, ominous medieval monastery where a murderer kills off innocent monks because he feels threatened by the knowledge they may acquire from a book by Aristotle. There is an eerie silence in some scenes. People often speak in hushed, subdued tones, so that an ordinary voice sounds like an explosion amid this deafening silence, underscored by dark, brooding music.

Perhaps the best use of sound and sound effects can be found in Brian De Palma's *Blow Out* where a sound-effects operator (John Travolta) records innocent sounds near a river as a general background for a film track. Inadvertently he records a car accident, which could also be a murder. However, before we hear the car, the night sounds he is recording all take on a sinister, often menacing tone. We cannot see what is creating these sounds and we know they are not threatening, but somehow they are elevated to greater importance by their closeness to the microphone and the emphasis De Palma places on them. Even the innocent conversation between two lovers assumes a sinister meaning.

Another good example of the use of sound or, in this case, a combination of sound effects comes from Martin Scorsese's *Raging Bull.* He uses a combination of sounds to give a more realistic, devastating impact to the heavy punches delivered by the boxer Jake LaMotta. When he receives the same punches, there is a heavy thud which literally reverberates across the cinema – it is as if we, the audience, are being hit, and we hear the distorted sound echo in our heads. Compare this almost surrealistic use of sound (often with the scene in slow motion) in *Raging Bull* with the more realistic, sharp sounds of the punches in John G. Avildsen's *Rocky* or the overstated, unrealistic punches in action films like *Metro.*

In *Midnight Express,* the sound of approaching footsteps could indicate imminent torture, even though we do not see the vicious prison guard approaching until later. We are also frequently aware of a wailing voice crying out over the stillness of Istanbul, or we hear the death-like scream of a peacock (signifying doom and loss of freedom) without actually seeing the source of the sound, which makes it even more terrifying.

In several of his films, notably *Eraserhead, The Elephant Man* and especially *Lost Highway,* David Lynch uses an unidentifiable low humming sound which accompanies most of his scenes. This disorientates us and warns us of dangers that lurk outside the frame. It also warns us that we are now dabbling in the world of nightmares, strange sounds and surrealism.

The volume of the sound effects (often accompanied by a music score) usually increases as a scene nears its climax, which heightens the dramatic effect. This technique is also used in chase or action sequences like in *Speed* or *Twister* by Jan De Bont and especially in *Metro,* although in this film the director often deliberately misleads us by having the music swell to a crescendo without anything significant happening. For instance, in the bathroom scene the character Ronnie Tate (Carmen Ejogo) closes the bathroom mirror more than once and we expect to see the bad guy standing behind her.

In *Alien,* by the time the John Hurt character discovers the eggs, we are used to the low humming sounds, the astronaut's breathing or the wind howling. Even Jerry Goldsmith's score is subdued and barely noticeable. But when the character peers into the open egg, the "face-hugger" suddenly jumps onto his helmet with a sharp, screeching, high-pitched sound. This very loud sound resembles a lightning bolt compared to the dark, ominous, subdued sounds we have been subjected to until then.

THE MUSICAL SCORE

Music in films has made possible an artistic blending of sight and sound, a fusion of music and movement so effective that the composer Dmitri Tiomkin was moved to remark that a good film is "really just ballet with dialogue" (Boggs, 1996: 238). Music underlines or highlights the atmosphere a director is trying to create. It should never hijack or dominate a film, unless the story is about the music, as in *Amadeus* or *Immortal Beloved.*

A great deal of irony is evident in the music from the final scene of Miloš Forman's *Amadeus*. Salieri is speaking to a priest about the greatness of Mozart and the mediocrity of all others. He tells how he has spent his whole life trying to outdo Mozart, and in the end how he has just had to accept his own mediocrity. A composition by Mozart plays in the background as he speaks, making it all the more ironic. We even hear Mozart's annoying little laugh behind the music, a laugh that symbolically tortures Salieri. The extreme irony is that although Salieri outlives

Mozart, he has to live with the knowledge that he will eventually fade from the pages of history. Wolfgang Amadeus Mozart, on the other hand, will live on in the hearts and minds of music lovers for all eternity – irony indeed!

– TLdR

Howard Shore's score for *The Silence of the Lambs* is also very effective. One hardly notices the music, but subconsciously one is very aware of it as it creates an uneasy, uncanny feeling and speaks a visual language which resembles an ominous whisper. In *Das Boot/The Boat,* Klaus Doldinger's magnificent score imitates the dark, mechanical sounds of the U-boat's engines and often hums like a bad headache in the back of the audience's mind.

Music speaks its own language, and one can scarcely imagine films like *The Third Man, Picnic at Hanging Rock, Under Fire* or *Blade Runner* without it. But why do directors use music rather than other natural sounds?

Music enhances the atmosphere

Music often comments directly on a specific scene or arouses certain emotions. Think of the manipulating music during the death scenes in Franco Zeffirelli's *Romeo and Juliet* or in the final sequences in *Ghost* and *Pretty Woman,* where swelling, melodramatic music tells us exactly how we should react to the images.

Music often warns of approaching terrors in the dark (compare *Halloween, Seven, The Frighteners*), or it scares us witless as a hand suddenly falls out of a closet right in front of the camera and a loud crescendo of music prompts us to jump out of our seats. In *The Shining,* Stanley Kubrick often uses horrifying, mechanical, thumping sounds to accompany the young boy's visions which climax in the apparition of twins in the corridor or a frightening ghost image. He literally terrorises us with his music. Also compare the music in the scene in which Jack Torrance (Jack Nicholson) breaks down a door with an axe to kill his family.

Conversely, music can set a cheerful, happy-go-lucky atmosphere as in the *Mother* credit sequence, directed by Albert Brooks. It can enhance a romantic atmosphere or prompt us to cry when a main character dies, as in *Evening Star* or *Shadowlands.*

Music can inspire us. Take the "Captain, my Captain" scene in *Dead Poets Society,* where the boys heroically stand on their desks to show their support for Mr Keating. It also stresses their rebellion against the archaic school system as the music swells into a triumphant ode to the power of knowledge.

On the other hand, the gentle, soothing musical motifs used during the rain sequence in *Diva* perfectly imitate the sensitive sound of raindrops and give the scene an almost melancholy, saintly, romantic atmosphere as the postboy finds himself in the same company as his beloved

CHAPTER
5
Dialogue and sound

49. Patrick Swayze and Demi Moore get their hands all messy in an erotic scene from *Ghost* by Jerry Zucker. (Courtesy of Paramount)

diva. To him it is a timeless, religious experience. He is in the presence of a genius.

Music is used ironically in *The English Patient:* while the English officers and adventurers and some of their wives are celebrating Christmas in Cairo, Count Laszlo de Almasy and Katherine are making love in a room adjacent to the courtyard. While "Silent Night" is being sung, Gabriel Yared's stirring music often intrudes to accompany the lovers, then mixes with the (then crude sounding) Christmas song, before the music swells to prominence again. Harsh reality therefore often intrudes during their love-making, but when their passion becomes overpowering, the lovers do not hear the Christmas carol – which may also serve as their conscience, as Katherine's husband is present at the singing. This is an example of brilliant juxtaposing of music.

The sentimental opening song creates the perfect atmosphere for the fairy-tale romantic comedy *My Best Friend's Wedding*, starring Julia Roberts and directed by P.J. Hogan.

Initially, the film seems to be saying that marriage is a woman's ultimate goal. This is why the song, lip-synched to Ani DiFranco's "Wishin' and Hopin'" seduces us into believing that if a girl prays, hopes and cheats hard enough, she will meet her prince on the white horse because that is her right. In reality the film's message is a thinly disguised and highly entertaining critique on America's sentimental and selfish obsession with marriage. A bewildered audience find themselves disliking the heroine, played by Julia Roberts, for her selfish and self-destructive behaviour.

This adult fairy tale gets a further twist when the heroine does not get her man. There is no traditional happy ending populated by stock characters who glamourise the concept of marriage. Who wants to be as "happily married" as Dermot Mulroney and Cameron Diaz if you can have unselfish friendship the way Roberts and her gay friend, played by Rupert Everett, enjoy!

A great example of the effective use of music to enhance the atmosphere can be found in *Kolya* when the young boy's recollections of his stay with his adopted father in Czechoslovakia is summed up in his singing of "The Lord is my Shepherd" during the final scenes. The words, carefully sung in his young and innocent voice, get an even more significant meaning because the whole film has been composed like a hymn to humanity and each familiar line takes on a new, divine meaning. Love was the greatest gift anybody could have given him. The pureness of his voice and the innocence with which he sings the words turns this scene into perhaps one of the most touching, honest and beautifully crafted ones of the nineties.

Music creates rhythm

This technique is often used in musicals or animation fantasies where singing creatures or actors bellow out a song to the specific rhythm of an orchestra. The images are often choreographed to the music. Think of "Under the Sea" from *The Little Mermaid* or, on a more realistic level, Bob Fosse's inspiring "On Broadway" sequence from *All That Jazz*, or Alan Parker's darkly cynical comment on the British school system in the "Another Brick in the Wall" sequence from *Pink Floyd: The Wall*. In *Strictly Ballroom* the entire film has been constructed like an elaborate dance. Some scenes literally follow the rhythm of the music.

In the title sequence from Jonathan Demme's *Philadelphia*, we go on a melancholy journey through the last year in the life of a lawyer who is dying of Aids. The montage consists of images taken from a moving vehicle/plane. At first it has the appearance of a rhythmic travelogue on Philadelphia. But Bruce Springsteen's Oscar-winning "Streets of Philadelphia" (and often slow motion photography) make us aware that we are experiencing the city through the eyes of a man on a final journey. He is bidding everything he took for granted a touching farewell.

Music suggests underlying tension

We may not always be aware of the sinister motives of a character or the ironic tone of a scene. By using the right music, a director often draws our attention to such facts or creates a new vision. Think of Jerry Goldsmith's eerie score for *Alien*. The uncanny, unearthly sounds gently tease our nerves as the astronauts scrutinise the egg chamber in the derelict spaceship. The music does not pinpoint the danger directly, but merely suggests that something is amiss. It almost becomes a lullaby of terror.

Music sums up the entire film in one theme

In *Gone with the Wind* the great, swelling sounds of Max Steiner's score perfectly embody the style, atmosphere and temperament of the entire production with its melodramatic flair, tragic romances and fierce emotional and physical battles.

The soundtrack in *Jaws* by John Williams has a mindless, mechanical and ominous tone which is always used when the shark is approaching or threatening a victim. It suggests mystery, death and fear, and is as fearsome as the white shark itself. Simply listening to the sound already tells us everything we need to know about the monster and the tone of the film. Other similar examples include the music of *Star Wars*, the *James Bond* films, *Superman, The Mission, The Omen* and *The Dollar* trilogy.

One of the best and most hauntingly effective scores is that of Hans Zimmer in John Schlesinger's *Pacific Heights*. Each movement of this symphonic suite has been written to underscore a particular scene. In the beginning, when the couple move into their dream house and discover the ambience of the place, Zimmer uses melancholy, romantic music. This melody changes abruptly to take on a menacing tone once the psychopath, played by Michael Keaton, makes his appearance. It later changes to a chaotic dissonance as their lives fall apart. It even assumes an Oriental sound when a Chinese couple move in.

Unfortunately, dominating music can also detract or simply serve as a decoration or a means of covering the weak spots in a film. Examples are Randy Newman's pretty, but overdone score for *Come see the Paradise* by Alan Parker and the melodramatic music for *Legends of the Fall* which rises and falls at the slightest provocation. The music must be integrated with the scenes and images; it must not dominate or detract.

Music recreates an era

Music from a certain era is often used to evoke a feeling of nostalgia. In *That Thing You Do,* Tom Hanks's songs were especially composed to recreate the sound of the sixties when the Beatles and Rolling Stones reigned supreme. Therefore some of the songs have a distinct Beatles flavour. Woody Allen often uses nostalgic music in his films, like *Radio*

50. Brad Pitt in pensive mood as a reporter bent on revenge after having been abused as a boy in a reformatory in *Sleepers*. (Courtesy of PolyGram)

Days which celebrates the golden era of radio when the songs were at the height of their popularity. The same applies to the films *Forrest Gump* and *The Big Chill.*

Music can be used as an ironic comment

Directors can often use songs or music as an ironic comment on situations. In *The English Patient* we hear "I'm in Heaven" while Katherine's husband, Geoffrey Clifton, sits in a car drinking in front of the building in which his wife is making love to one of his friends (De Almasy). These words are extremely ironic if his situation is taken into account, but of course perfectly reflects the state of mind of the lovers.

The use of the happy-go-lucky song "Singin' in the Rain" while a thug (Malcolm McDowell) viciously beats up and kills a helpless woman in *A Clockwork Orange* is unexpected, yet effective. It creates an ironic contrast with the visuals, making them more shocking, while showing how carefree and happy Alex feels when he is doing what he does best – inflicting pain upon others.

The use of "We'll meet again" in the final sequences of *Dr Strangelove* is a further example. This optimistic song is accompanied by shots of nuclear weapons exploding. The words of the song become extremely ironic because mankind has been destroyed by its own creations and no-one will ever meet anyone else again.

Other films which employ this technique include the use of "What a wonderful world" in *Good Morning, Vietnam* by Barry Levinson, accompanied by shots of villages being bombed with napalm; and the childlike innocence and fragility of the "Étude" by Chopin in *The Killing Fields* by Roland Joffe which is juxtaposed with similar images of death, destruction and violence. It is taken to kitsch extremes in John Woo's *Face/Off*, though, when a boy listens to "Somewhere Over the Rainbow" during a massacre.

In the final sequence of *Shallow Grave* by Danny Boyle the upbeat "Happy Heart" is accompanied by slow motion shots of the three characters laughing and joking. Since we have witnessed the acts of betrayal and violence the three have directed at one another, the music in fact becomes ironic. It helps to support the idea that innocent exteriors can mask evil.

– NG

In *Chariots of Fire*, the character Harold Abrahams is shown training for his next race and the song, "He is an Englishman", ironically enough sung by him, accompanies the training montage. Because he is a Jew and therefore something of an outsider, the speech he later makes about his patriotism as an Englishman gives a new and special meaning to this song. Also note the formal, melodious way in which the song is sung, reflecting a proud and formal attitude with just a hint of irony.

In *One Flew Over The Cuckoo's Nest* the repressed patients who are subject to the iron will of Nurse Ratched are forced to listen to "soothing" music which is supposed to calm their "aggression". In reality though, the music antagonises them, because it is too loud. The smooth sounds of the song "Charmaine" also serve as an ironic comment on the patients because, while this music is bellowing over the loudspeakers, McMurphy (Jack Nicholson) confuses their carefully monitored emotions by upsetting Nurse Ratched's iron routine.

Music is used to reflect the inner thoughts of a character

By using the right, often understated music, a director can reflect the inner thoughts or turmoil of a character which cannot necessarily be put into dialogue or reflected through acting.

In *Shine* by Scott Hicks, the pianist (David Helfgott) suffers a nervous breakdown while playing Rachmaninoff's Third. During the sequence there is a shot of his fingers hammering at the keys. We do not hear the music, only the mechanical sounds of his fingers upon the keys, emphasising that his mind is going, that he is not hearing what he is playing any more, and that the whole exercise has become mechanical. We literally go into his mind as the world stops around him and he is aware only of his fingers moving mechanically.

> In *Three Colours: Blue*, Krzysztof Kieślowski effectively uses music to reflect the inner thoughts of the character. This is particularly evident at the end of the film where he tilts into a shot of the Juliette Binoche character crying. There is no real acting and no dialogue. All he uses is soft understated music to convey what she is thinking. This is all that is needed for the viewer to realise that, although the character's family is dead, she will need to discover and experience love once again in order to carry on living.
>
> –TLdR

Music is used as leitmotif

A certain musical motif is often repeated to evoke a conditioned response. When we hear the lonely harmonica, we recall the avenging Charles Bronson character in *Once Upon a Time in the West*. When we hear the ominous deep-sea sound from *Jaws* we remember the great white shark which immediately evokes terror because we associate it with a certain image. The five-note motive the aliens use to communicate with humans in *Close Encounters of the Third Kind* turns into a language of its own and is frequently repeated during the film.

Travelling music is used to accompany montages

By using an entire song or a certain theme to accompany a series of images which tell a complete story, a director comments on what is happening on screen or suggests the passing of time. There are many examples, such as the Maurice Jarre building-the-barn music from *Witness*, the training montage music by Bill Conti from *Rocky*, the bridge-building theme by Jerry Goldsmith from *The Ghost and the Darkness* or the exploration of the desert during the early scenes of *The English Patient's* music by Gabriel Yared.

Music is used to accompany opening and closing credits

The music which accompanies the credits sets the tone for the rest of the film, and the credits often blend in with the score. Vangelis's rousing, heroic music sets the tone perfectly for the opening credits of *Chariots of Fire*. Graceful movement accompanied by sacred-sounding music underline the main theme very effectively.

> One of the most powerful credit sequences in cinema is from David Fincher's *Seven.* Both the score and the actual style of the credits set the tone for the rest of the film in no uncertain terms. We feel that we are entering a world of murder, madness and confusion and fear for our own lives. Even the unsteadiness of the titles seems to depict that all is not right, and that something evil is about to confront us.
>
> – TLdR

Music is used to create comic tension

Music used in comedies is usually referred to as "mickeymousing". Dissonant, unharmonious and false sounds, sometimes used in fast motion, can create a playful, comical, farcical atmosphere. The music used for these sequences can often exist only if accompanied by images, otherwise they are merely sounds or discordant melodies which do not make much sense, as in *George of the Jungle.*

> In *The Mask* by Charles Russell, many of Jim Carrey's antics are accompanied by zany or weird sound effects. They stem from traditional, animated family-orientated films. This "mickeymousing" heightens the cartoon feel of the film, as well as suggesting the spontaneous nature of Carrey's character.
>
> – NG

Music can reflect a certain atmosphere

In the late nineties, alternative music, including grunge and heavy metal music, is very fashionable, which is why so many "cool" films incorporate this kind of music. This is done not only to reflect a culture, but also to make the film accessible to an audience which otherwise may not have bothered to see it. Baz Luhrmann deliberately uses alternative music in *William Shakespeare's Romeo and Juliet* to capture a modern teenage audience which identifies with the music. The same applies to *Trainspotting*.

The soundtrack used by Danny Boyle in *Trainspotting* is very popular. The music is effective in showing the progression of youth culture from what it was in the past to the rave culture of today. Although the songs are very popular and well known, the music never dominates the film because Boyle succeeds in blending the visuals with the music. The result is that the music has more of a subconscious effect on the audience.

Another example of where music is used to reflect a certain culture is in *The Crow*. The Gothic and industrial-style music adds to the film's dark, mysterious and brutal atmosphere. Again the soundtrack never dominates, even though the songs are well known outside the context of the film.

– NG

One of the finest examples of the harmonious interplay between the music of two vastly different cultures can be found in *Deliverance* by John Boorman. A group of yuppie city dwellers decide to experience the freedom of unspoilt nature before a dam is built in a certain place. Along the way at a petrol station they meet a backward family. The son with his banjo looks like a moron. One of the city men, played by Ronny Cox, plucks at the strings of his guitar. Suddenly the boy with his banjo responds. There is a remarkable rapport between "the civilised" and "the primitive". For one brief moment there is harmony because the characters are "speaking" the same language in a combination of the smooth, more sophisticated sound of the guitar and the less melodious, more earthly sound of the banjo. Each reflects a different culture which blend for a timeless moment. Unfortunately the urban dwellers' arrogance in the following scenes quickly ends this moment of cultural harmony.

SILENCE AS A PLOT DEVICE

Silence can often be even more devastating than any sound effect. Because silence can make us uneasy or create expectations, it stimulates our imagination. We wonder what secrets are hidden in the silence. It is as if our hearts stop beating as we await the next sound. This does not mean that the entire scene takes place in silence. Occasional sounds like the creaking of a floorboard or a whisper can interrupt the silence, drawing our attention to the immense stillness surrounding or threatening the characters.

Silence is used very effectively in Stanley Kubrick's *2001: A Space Odyssey*. At one point in the film, the Gary Lockwood character exits the spaceship to repair a fault. The computer, Hal, cuts off his support and he floats helplessly away into the darkness. Kubrick cuts out all the sound, thus depicting the nothingness and the horror of being completely alone in an unknown universe.

– TLdR

In *Three Colours: Blue,* Julie dives into the swimming pool as if she is diving into her own subconscious. As she disappears beneath the water, not a sound disturbs the tranquillity. She stays underwater for quite some time, creating a sense of unease. (Is she drowning? Has something happened to her? Does she want to commit suicide?) When she finally surfaces, the silence is broken by her gasping and the sound of water splashing. This contrast shocks us (and her) back to reality.

When the small boy races his tricycle through the empty, haunted corridors of the Overlook Hotel in *The Shining* by Stanley Kubrick, the sound of the wheels on the floor suddenly disappears when he hits the carpets on the floor. This break in a monotonous sound suggests that we may anticipate another, even more horrible sound or occurrence. In this way, Kubrick draws our attention to the spooky, eerie silence in the hallways.

In *The English Patient,* Katherine admires the beauty and almost unearthly stillness of the desert at night. This scene is violently interrupted by an approaching sandstorm. One moment there is perfect stillness in the desert, and in the next an explosion of ferocious winds bursts onto the soundtrack like a detonating bomb. This contrast suggests that their relationship is going to be thrown into immense turmoil very soon. It also refers to the unpredictable moods of nature, which echo the uncertainty of their relationship. Their love is also threatened by the violence of war which, like the storm, is raging on the horizon.

SOUND AS A TRANSITIONAL DEVICE

Before a new scene starts, the director prepares us for what is going to follow with the relevant sound effects while the present scene is still incomplete. Thus he not only achieves a smooth transition, but also points to the relationship between the two scenes. For instance, in *Apocalypse Now* we already hear the sound of helicopter blades as the Martin Sheen character watches the arms of a fan. This conjures up images of a helicopter in his mind. A little later a helicopter flies over the room where he is staying.

The same applies to *The Chamber* by James Foley, in which a young, inexperienced lawyer (Chris O'Donnell) tries to save his racist grandfather from the gas chamber. The sound of a cell door closing before we actually cut to a scene in the jail emphasises the hopelessness of the characters' situations as the grandfather's death is inevitable. This happens in other scenes too where, for instance, we hear an angry mob chanting before we see them, thus heightening the dramatic impact of

51.
Chris O'Donnell as an idealistic young lawyer searches for the truth in a case against his racist grandfather's conviction for the murder of innocent people in *The Chamber*. (Copyright © 1996 by Universal Studios, Inc. Courtesy of MCA Publishing Rights, a division of Universal Studios, Inc. All rights reserved.)

the situation and carrying our emotions from one scene to the next without breaking the tension or flow.

SOUND TO LINK TWO OPPOSING IMAGES

The unexpected linking of two contrasting sounds can often be used to shock or surprise, thereby heightening the dramatic effect of the second sound.

One sound can also change into another similar sound, although the sounds may have vastly different origins. For instance, a woman is murdered on a train. She gives a loud, high-pitched scream which carries over into the next scene and is taken over by the same high-pitched sound of a train's whistle. In this way, the tension and horror are carried over into the next scene, and an innocent, everyday sound takes on a different, more ominous meaning.

SLOW MOTION SOUND

This technique is usually used when an image changes from ordinary speed into slow motion, emphasising its distorted, unsettling or irritating qualities.

In *Mother*, the Albert Brooks character is annoyed by his mother (Debbie Reynolds) who constantly gossips about his problems to complete strangers. As he nears breaking point we realise that another comment about his private life may lead to a confrontation with her. This is indeed what happens as they are doing their shopping and she discusses his problems with a shop assistant. Suddenly her speech slows down as she talks in slow motion. There is a close-up of her mouth, emphasising that the son is extremely annoyed by what she is saying.

One of the most famous examples of slow motion sound comes from *2001: A Space Odyssey* where Hal, the computer, slowly "dies" as David Bowman (Keir Dullea) disconnects his cables, nuts and bolts. His "speech" starts to slur and as the bolts are loosened we can literally hear his thought processes reversing to the time when his brain was being assembled. Hal, the computer, "talks" more and more slowly until he sings "Daisy", the song he learnt when he was still a "young" computer. The disintegration of the machine and its thought processes are brilliantly conveyed through this slow regression of sound until it stops completely, like a record player with a flat battery. The very mechanical sound reminds us that Hal is an imperfect creation of man which has ceased to function. The irony is that Hal is the most human "character" of all in *2001: A Space Odyssey.*

In the infamous massacre from *The Wild Bunch,* Sam Peckinpah sometimes uses slow motion sound, but often increases the volume to the level of distortion, creating a scene of havoc and chaos in which too many men die senseless deaths. The pace and volume of the sound stress the terror of their death and draws our attention to the intense horror of the moment.

EXERCISES

1. Should every line of dialogue always be clear? Discuss the importance of dialogue and its clarity in relation to films like *Kids, The Saint, Hamlet, Bullets over Broadway* and *Pulp Fiction.*
2. Discuss the different elements which are important when judging the efficiency of dialogue. Give examples.
3. An invisible sound source is sometimes more effective than a visible one. Discuss with examples.
4. How important is the music score to a film? Name the various contributions the music score makes to a film.
5. Discuss silence as a plot device, with examples.

6

Editing

Editing literally means joining one shot or strip of film to another in the most effective way. Film-makers have often stated that the most important contribution cinema has made to the twentieth century is the art of editing. Vsevolod Pudovkin, one of the great Russian directors of the silent era noted that the selection, timing and arrangement of shots into a film continuity serve as the crucial creative act in the production of film: "If a film narrative was to be kept continually effective, each shot must make a new and specific point" (Reisz & Millar, 1984: 15, 30).

In this chapter the term "editor" will be used, but of course, the director plays an equally important part in the selection or sequence of shots. He compiles a storyboard and shoots his film in a particular order. Consider the famous Hitchcock plane attack in *North by Northwest* or the Odessa steps sequence in *The Battleship Potemkin* as scenes which an editor has assembled. The thought process and construction, and often the very act of editing, are done by the director in collaboration with his editor. Editing enables the director to create a sense of depth and places him in a commanding position to guide the audience's reactions, because he is able to choose what the viewer sees at a particular moment.

Consider the following imaginary scene. A man is wrongfully accused of a brutal murder. He is hunted down by a police officer and finally caught. Once apprehended the suspect is taken to an interrogation room where the officer questions him. During the shoot the director has instructed the crew to film the following shots:

- A flashback shot of the place where the murder took place, complete with chalk outline and police barriers.
- A flashback close-up shot of a gun firing.
- A wide shot showing both the suspect and the officer in the interrogation room.
- An over-the-shoulder shot of the officer from the suspect's point-of-view.
- An over-the-shoulder shot of the suspect from the officer's point-of-view.
- A close-up of the suspect.
- A close-up of the officer.
- A high-angle shot of the suspect sitting alone in the room.
- A low-angle shot of the officer leaving the room.

The director's budget allowed him the freedom to film the entire scene from each of the above-mentioned angles, and therefore the editor has many options to consider when editing the scene together.

Edit 1.

In the first version of the edit the editor/director has decided to focus on the suspect by utilising the relevant close-up and over-the-shoulder shots. Since the editor and director have in this case decided to concentrate on the innocent man the audience develops sympathy for the man in this version of the edit. This version ends with a high-angle shot of the suspect sitting alone in the room.

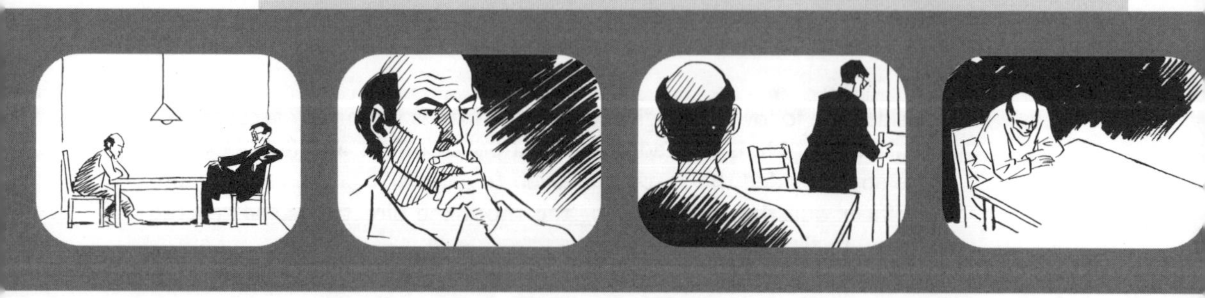

Edit 2.

In the second version of the edit however the emphasis is placed on the officer. Here the editor has manipulated the point-of-view of the audience so that they will see the situation through the officer's eyes. By forcing the audience to look at close-ups of the interrogator the director may succeed in creating doubt in the minds of the viewers as to whether or not the suspect is truly innocent. This version ends with an intimidating low-angle of the officer leaving the room.

Of course these are only two options available to the editor, but there are a multitude of approaches the editor may consider. The editor may decide to shift the focus during the scene back-and-forth between the officer and the suspect as the balance of power between the two characters shifts. This flexibility is what gives the editor an enormous amount of power over how the film will look, and is also why the director will often work in close association with the editor.

– NG

Sergei Eisenstein developed the art of montage, by which he juxtaposed shots for symbolic rather than narrative reasons. He was one of the great Russian directors, screenwriters and theorists, whose first film, *Strike,* features a scene of police killing striking workers. He suddenly cuts to a shot of cattle being slaughtered in an abattoir, which, technically speaking, has nothing to do with events on the screen. However, in a metaphorical sense, it is a direct comment on the previous sequence. In this way Eisenstein directly links the two images and comments upon the ruthless and barbaric slaughtering of innocents.

THE SEQUENCE

When a director uses more than one location, allows time to lapse and shows several points of view to portray a certain event, that part of the film is referred to as a "sequence". The different shots woven together in one sequence (or montage) form a unified whole.

In almost all the sequences in Oliver Stone's *Natural Born Killers*, every manipulated image is meant to shock, distract or disconcert the viewer. It is as if we, the viewers, are switching between television channels or have gained entrance into the media-polluted minds of the protagonists, played by Woody Harrelson and Juliette Lewis. Stone deliberately disrupts the "orderly" flow of images and turns it into chaos, manipulating our vision of reality and rhythm to create a sense of extreme aggression. He intentionally calls attention to his editing to make this point.

> The machine-gun style of editing which Stone applies to *Natural Born Killers* is done for a specific reason. Today's youth has an attention span of five seconds – the length of the average shot in a music video. Therefore the editing style, as well as the visual style of *Natural Born Killers* is identical to techniques used in music videos. Stone illustrates how we have become anaesthetised to violence, and that he needs to employ these flashy techniques just to keep our attention. This is ironic, since we would like to believe that a realistic depiction of violence would hold our attention anyway. Stone also demonstrates how the media is responsible for popularising violence for profit and higher ratings.
>
> The shortcoming of Stone's technique is that for the duration of the film he never slows down. This results in the film becoming monotonous, despite all the "bells and whistles".
>
> – NG

Editing has been described as a jigsaw puzzle, often consisting of anything from twenty hours of raw footage to even a hundred or more which has to be assembled and ordered to convey a story in a certain way. The editor chooses the most effective shots to convey the message, and places them next to other similar or contrasting scenes. He organises images in a specific time frame.

This is called the "language of cinema", by which a story is built up from several different components without interrupting its natural flow, unless the director's style and message require the editor to do so. It is as if we, the viewers, are moving our lines of vision from one perspective to the next, in order to take in the entire scene and focus on its most important aspects.

When selecting certain shots and deciding upon the length of these shots, editors must keep the following aspects in mind.

THE PACE OR TEMPO OF THE FILM OR SCENE

A shot lasts for a certain time. You must question the reason for the length of the shot and why the director, in collaboration with the editor, decides on this length.

In the first *Alien,* Ridley Scott seldom affords us the opportunity to study the alien and we are only allowed quick glimpses of it. However, in Jean-Pierre Jeunet's *Alien Resurrection* we get longer glimpses of the monsters, because by this time we are familiar with their horrifying details and are no longer shocked by them. The camera often lingers on the monsters, especially the queen who gives birth to a creature which adopts Ripley (Sigourney Weaver) as its reluctant mother.

Modern action films like *Air Force One, Double Team* and *Men in Black* often have such a frantic pace that the viewer is left breathless. The audience is never allowed to recover from the exaggerated thrills, which turn these films into little more than special-effects vehicles with a slim storyline.

The style of these films often resembles that of music videos, in that very few scenes last more than a few seconds and the viewers are therefore unable to take them in (is it because the director is too scared that they will lose interest?). The film rushes from one often meaningless scene to the next, without exploring the current scene's possibilities.

In *Secrets and Lies,* Mike Leigh's camera stays on the two women for minutes on end after they have discussed the fact that they are mother and daughter. It is an unflinchingly frank portrayal of two people who have had to be completely honest with and about themselves. They are only now discovering each other and having to come to terms with the fact that they are related. The situation is further complicated by the fact that the daughter (Marianne Jean-Baptiste) is black and her mother (Brenda Blethyn) is white. They come from vastly different backgrounds which on the surface seem to be irreconcilable.

By keeping the camera on them for a long time, any protective cutaways, special lighting or flattering camera angles are removed: the two women are completely exposed emotionally – even "naked". They have to confront and solve their problems without any flashy, artificial cinematic techniques, which makes their situation even more realistic. While these characters are thus exposed, we have free access to their full range of emotions in an unflinching, unmanipulative way. This brilliantly explores both the tragic and comic subtext of the scene. A whole life is reviewed in one single shot and two people come to terms with a lifetime of problems. They sit next to each other, almost as if they are trying to bridge the huge gap between them in a physical way. This unedited shot has another function: it stresses the irony of their spiritual predicament as opposed to the physical situation.

In Wolfgang Petersen's film *Das Boot/The Boat,* a new lieutenant is introduced to the interior of a German U-boat. In one long, uninterrupted scene which lasts seventy seconds, the character is taken through several "rooms" or parts of the cramped submarine in hand-held shots until he ends up in the machine room. By not editing, Petersen perfectly conveys an atmosphere of claustrophobia and realism. We are imprisoned with the characters in the small, confined space from which there is no escape.

We are aware of the crowded atmosphere, the smells of the men, the heat as well as the clustered quarters in which several men are cramped together. They are very aware of the danger of tons of water surrounding the submarine which could crush them should they venture too deep into the unknown. Petersen seems to be saying: you are in a real submarine where there is scarcely room to move and you can suffocate at any moment. Even the movements of the cameraman are stifled and confined to hand-held shots.

In *The Godfather's* opening shot, the camera slowly pulls back from a face in close-up until it finishes just behind the Don Corleone character who is listening to a man's plea for a demented kind of "justice". This long scene allows us to orientate ourselves to a world which is forever in darkness and where fraud, evil and murder reign supreme. Quick edits between Corleone and his visitor would have destroyed this uneasy, formal and intimidating atmosphere.

In *Cinema Paradiso,* Giuseppe Tornatore starts his film with a ninety-second lyrical sequence in which the camera focuses on a tranquil sea seen through a curtained window. A mother is phoning abroad from Sicily in an attempt to locate her son. The camera slowly pans back to give the impression of tranquillity, loneliness and natural beauty, as if we are watching a painting slowly coming to life. Had the director edited this sequence (e.g. if he had cut to the mother and the person she is phoning during the credits) the atmosphere would have been very different.

Quick, aggressive editing on the other hand can indicate restlessness, anger, confusion, fear and excitement, as in the sequence in which the volcano erupts in *Dante's Peak* and the famous bus sequences in *Speed* by Jan De Bont. Also note the dramatic monster scenes in *Jurassic Park* and *The Lost World: Jurassic Park,* as well as *Men in Black.*

In one of the typical scenes in *Speed,* De Bont frequently cuts between the Sandra Bullock character at the steering wheel (usually in shuddering, unstable camera movements) and Keanu Reeves as the cop barking out instructions (often seen from the back in equally unsteady movements, imitating the unstable bus). There are several overhead shots of the bus travelling at high speed and point-of-view shots of the bus

52. Volcanologist Harry Dalton (Pierce Brosnan) and town mayor Rachel Wando (Linda Hamilton) flee an active volcano as *Dante's Peak* unleashes a stream of lava. (Copyright © 1997 by Universal Studios, Inc. Courtesy of MCA Publishing Rights, a division of Universal Studios, Inc. All rights reserved.)

53. Jeff Goldblum, Julianne Moore, Richard Schiff and Vince Vaughn explore reports that "something has survived" in the dinosaur roller-coaster ride, *The Lost World: Jurassic Park* by Steven Spielberg. (Copyright © 1997 by Universal Studios, Inc. Courtesy of MCA Publishing Rights, a division of Universal Studios, Inc. All rights reserved.)

swerving between cars and careering into the face of oncoming traffic, traffic arrows and signs, police cars pursuing the bus, the bus's speedometer and the reaction of the frightened passengers. With his quick, aggressive cutting, De Bont creates a feeling of unbearable tension, uncertainty and desperation. He also stresses the hopelessness of the situation and the bravery of the two main characters who are trying to prevent the bus from reverting to a slower speed, upon which a bomb will explode.

Similar techniques were used in the famous car chases in William Friedkin's *To Live and Die in L.A.* and *The French Connection,* as well as in the cable car chase in Thomas Carter's otherwise inferior *Metro* and the brilliantly done bus and train crash in *The Fugitive.*

The same applies to Danny Boyle's *Trainspotting.* Through his quick, hostile cutting and his frequent use of freeze-frames, we feel as if we have been injected into the bloodstream of a junkie and are experiencing an all-time high, to be followed by hallucinations and a very depressing low.

Slow, leisurely editing is usually used in tranquil love stories such as *The Bridges of Madison County* by Clint Eastwood or the romantic scenes in *Diva* by Jean-Jacques Beineix. Also note the leisurely, formal style of editing used in *Chariots of Fire* where the runners may be fast, but the world and society around them linger over every decision.

Joel and Ethan Coen's editing in *Fargo* is also a case in point. To match the leisurely, rural "nothing-ever-happens-in-a-sleepy-town" theme of the film, the Coens stress the slow pace of the town shaken out of its slumber by a kidnapping which turns into a murder. The Coens seem to be saying that the murder may have woken some of the residents for a short while, but afterwards they will revert to hibernation and their small town slumber. Even the investigating officer (Oscar winner Frances McDormand) takes the murder in her stride. She seems to be more interested in her household problems or in an old flame, who threatens her cosy existence, than in the seriousness of the crime. These impressions are gained mainly from the editing.

JUXTAPOSITION

Juxtaposition means placing two elements or shots next to each other usually for a contrasting or shocking effect. Juxtaposing enables the editor to guide our emotions from one image to the next so that we understand their relationship and meaning. Thus he can build suspense, shock us or even move us to tears.

A classic example of juxtaposition occurs in Steven Spielberg's *Schindler's List.* At one point in the movie, Amon Goeth, portrayed by Ralph Fiennes, is abusing his domestic help, played by Embeth Davidtz. At the same time in a different area, Schindler (Liam Neeson) is attending a Jewish wedding ceremony, where a number of people are kissing. The juxtaposition of evil with the few glimpses of happiness successfully creates intense shock.

–TLdR

In *Strictly Ballroom,* the grandparents of the girl who wants to dance with Scott teach them the sounds of the street which should reverberate in their hearts as they dance. This lesson and their tense, though excited, faces are juxtaposed with the agile feet of the older man stamping out an infectious rhythm. Two styles of dancing meet in this sequence as the unexciting movement of Scott's feet is suddenly ignited by the passion he discovers in the old man's style. Also note the juxtaposing in the same film as the president of the dance federation tries to obstruct Scott's path to participation. During these scenes, Baz Luhrmann intercuts to Scott gliding smoothly on his knees to centre stage. No obstruction can prevent him now.

In *The English Patient,* Kip, Hana's lover, is trying to defuse a bomb near a bridge. American soldiers celebrating victory approach the bridge – the trembling caused by their vehicles could cause the bomb to explode. Hana, afraid that she will once again lose a friend or loved one because she sees herself as "bad luck", is cycling towards her lover. These three scenes are intercut and juxtaposed to create agonising tension. Will the bomb explode? Will the Americans understand that they are inadvertently endangering somebody's life? And will Hana arrive in time to see her lover being blown up?

Of course, the scene turns out completely opposite from what we expect, but by juxtaposing those scenes, Anthony Minghella makes us realise once again how many innocent casualties formed a part of this senseless war, and how vulnerable human beings are in a war situation. This complements one of the film's themes: the scarred survivors of the war who are trying to heal themselves and the horror of the casualties inflicted upon them and their loved ones. The theme of loyalty (Hana cycling to her lover) is also stressed in this scene.

CONTINUITY OR LOGIC

The editor or director, or both, are responsible for allowing the action to flow in a continuous, coherent way from one shot to the next, so that one scene logically follows the next. For instance, a character approaches a house. We cut to

- an outside view of the house,
- the man approaching the front door,
- his opening of the door,
- his entry as seen from inside,
- a close-up of him looking at a vase of flowers on the table,

- him putting down his brief case on top of a letter meant for him,
- his closing of the door,
- his sniffing the flowers and
- exiting the lounge.

There are exceptions, where editing follows an illogical pattern to create a surrealistic feel. Consider the opening sequence in *Blue Velvet*, where we see shots of the townsfolk going about their everyday business juxtaposed with a man watering a garden and his discovery of a severed ear.

Another example occurs in Peter Jackson's *Heavenly Creatures*, where the editing disorientates the viewer by cutting from a seemingly normal scene to an "illogical one". Two girls who are attracted to each other are to be separated forever. Before their parents force them to split, Pauline and Juliet are allowed to move in together. They are ecstatic. The director, Peter Jackson, uses an unstable camera, as well as lots of zoom-ins and dolly shots to recreate their excitement. Quick edits dominate the sequence. As they start dancing, the scene changes to an imaginary Alice-in-Wonderland-like moment. The girls joyfully dance with moving statues, declaring themselves to be mad and therefore mercifully different from the world which suppresses them.

This scene is intercut with two quick shots of a guillotine's blade, suggesting that they may later find themselves at the mercy of a court after a vicious murder. Suddenly Jackson cuts to a scene from *The Third Man* in which the character Harry Lime runs from the authorities through the sewerage system. This jolts us from one dark fantasy to the next, and also implies madness because, like the girls, we are frequently surprised by unexpected images. The images unsettle and shock us, reflecting the girls' emotional turmoil and their descent into obsession and madness.

TRANSITIONS

The film-maker often wants to jump from one sequence or scene to another without forming a bridge. For instance, a man with a gun has to walk across a street and into a building to find his wife in the arms of another man in a hotel room. We are not interested in his entire journey across the street, through the lobby and up the stairs, as this has no relevance for that particular scene. Therefore the editor cuts out the unnecessary journey. We just see him closing the door of his car, looking up at the silhouettes against the curtain, and in the next shot he appears in the corridor and approaches the door of the bedroom. If a director does not want to do a cut as suggested above, he can use several other techniques, as discussed below.

To reflect Scott's turmoil in *Strictly Ballroom*, the camera circles him as he practises for the championships – a determined expression on his face. During this movement the director, Baz Luhrmann, cuts to him in exactly the same position, the camera still on his face, but as it pulls back, Scott has perfected the movement he was practising – now he is wearing different clothes and is dancing at the Pan-Pacific championships. This smooth transition also signifies that he has decided to stick to the rules ... for the moment.

The dissolve technique

One shot merges or blends with another by means of superimposition. This often happens when a character thinks back to his past.

In *The English Patient*, the past and present are often linked by a very slow, lyrical fade as Count de Almasy (Ralph Fiennes) thinks back to the beauty of the desert or his discovery of the greatest love of his life. The slowness is in perfect sync with the leisurely, poetic style of director

Anthony Minghella and the fact that the hero's mind slowly wanders off to the past which, compared to the hell in which he now finds himself, is paradise. It is almost as if he loses himself in the past.

The same applies to the lyrical style in which Carroll Ballard shot *Fly Away Home*. Amy, the thirteen-year-old girl played by Anna Paquin, remembers her dead mother when she stays on the farm with her eccentric father (Jeff Daniels). The poetic quality of the story and the lingering shots of the exquisite beauty of the unspoilt area in which Amy discovers sixteen unhatched eggs, cause Ballard frequently to use slow dissolves. This technique suggests the immense sadness and fond memories with which the girl remembers the past. It also paints a sensitive, slow-moving montage of the hatching of the eggs and the development of the chicks into adult geese. It could be argued that these scenes are far too slow and conscious of their own beauty, but they still manage to convey the desired atmosphere.

The wipe technique

With a wipe a scene is pushed off the screen by using a line. The line can have any shape and may move in any direction. The wipe is often specifically used to evoke a period feel. The next scene follows the line. In *101 Dalmatians,* a wipe is used once to suggest a time lapse, but in *Ed Wood,* Tim Burton frequently reverts to this technique to create a feeling of time and place, and also to imitate the kind of technique frequently used by directors in B-grade science fiction movies.

54. In *The Spitfire Grill*, director Lee David Zlotoff's style is slow and relaxed to reflect the time warp in which a one-horse town finds itself. The pace changes dramatically when Percy Talbott (Alison Elliot) arrives. (Courtesy of Castle Rock; Photographer: Aaron Rapoport)

George Lucas makes use of this technique in the *Star Wars* trilogy to signify a major change in distance from the previous shot. The wipe also creates the feeling of literally watching a sweeping epic of immense proportion.
– NG

The jump-cut technique

With this technique the artist cuts from a character in one scene to the same character doing something different, usually in the same scene or location. A jump cut implies an abrupt transition which often disorientates the viewer or takes him by complete surprise.

One of the best examples of this occurs in *Basquiat,* a film about the life and early death of the famous graffiti artist, played by Jeffrey Wright. To comment on his strange frame of mind (he frequently used drugs and had very little in common with normality), the director (Julian Schnabel) shows him painting graffiti on a wall in New York. He then jump cuts to the finished graffiti painting or sentence. We therefore see Jean Michel Basquiat writing two words, then suddenly seven, and then the sentence is complete.

The same technique is applied in the more obscure *The Passion of Darkly Noon,* where the life of a religious and misguided fanatic (played by Brendan Fraser) jumps from one eccentric moment to the next in quick, rapid movements. It is as if he moves to a different position and to a different time-frame every time we blink our eyes. During these movements we also become aware that his mind is disintegrating into psychotic madness.

55. Director Serguei Bodrov uses a naturalistic, simple editing technique in *Prisoner of the Mountains*, starring Serguei Bodrov Jr. (Courtesy of Fortissimo Films)

The same technique is used for the sex orgy in *A Clockwork Orange* as discussed previously in the section on fast motions in Chapter 3. In *Citizen Ruth* the Laura Dern character, usually high on glue, lies in the bath blinking her eye. Her vision jumps from left to right as she looks at her feet and the taps in the wall. The director (Alexander Payne) uses jump cuts between the two perspectives because we see everything through her eyes.

A classic jump cut can be found in James L. Brooks' *I'll Do Anything*. The lead character (portrayed by Nick Nolte) is about to audition for a role in a film and is rehearsing a few lines in the make-up room. The director focuses on his face in the mirror, using jump cuts very effectively to portray all the emotions going through his head at that moment.

Trainspotting also uses jump cuts. At one point Spud is applying for a job. He appears before a selection panel, but is too high on drugs to concentrate. The director uses jump cuts to portray the character's hyperactivity and anxiety.

– TLdR

Match-on-action cut In Stanley Kubrick's match-on-action cut in *2001: A Space Odyssey*, a prehistoric ape tosses a bone into the air and it changes into a spaceship. Several million years pass in a fraction of a second. In this way Kubrick comments upon man's use of tools and how these tools have changed during millions of years of evolution. Man still uses tools, but now they are a thousand times more advanced. It was the dawn of knowledge when primitive man discovered that he could use objects around him as weapons or tools to his advantage. This saved him from extinction. The question, however, is whether man has really changed spiritually over all these millions of years.

A flip-frame This technique can be compared to turning a page, where one scene flips into another just as we turn from one page of a book to another.

Fade in and fade out One shot fades from black into a recognisable image, or it fades from an image to black. This technique is used to suggest a big jump in time, or when a character loses consciousness, as happens to Billy Hayes in *Midnight Express.* In *Three Colours: Blue,* Krzysztof Kieślowski uses four fade outs as he returns to the same point in time, indicating that time stands still and means nothing to the main character, Julie.

Parallel cutting With this technique an editor or director may jump between two scenes which seem to be disjointed and occur at the same time.

One of the best examples of parallel cutting is the baptism and massacre sequence towards the end of *The Godfather.* As Michael's godchild is baptised, rival Mafia bosses are murdered on his instructions, lending an ironic flavour to the baptismal ritual. On the one hand we see life and salvation bestowed upon a child with the godfather present; on the other we witness the consequences of the new godfather going to war and killing his rivals. It is salvation versus destruction and punishment. The contrast is heightened further when Michael, played by Al Pacino, also has his godchild's father killed after the baptism. He is almost himself turned into a kind of "god" who gives the last rites. Through the juxtaposition of the christening and the murders, Coppola makes the ultimate ironic comment. This sequence is also called a "montage".

Parallel cutting also occurs in *The Cement Garden* by Andrew Birkin. A boy masturbates; the director intercuts this action to his father who is covering the garden with cement and dying of a heart attack. The significance here is that while life is being "created" on the one side, life is ebbing away on the other. Both characters are subjected to shuddering movements, although the dying father is experiencing anguish while the boy is experiencing a new-found pleasure associated with youth as he discovers himself. As life "enters" in one scene, life exits in another.

In *The Name of the Rose,* an innocent hunchback is burnt at the stake by the hypocritical religious order under the Spanish inquisition. At the same time, an intelligent philosopher and monk (Sean Connery) accompanied by his novice (Christian Slater) discover the cause of all the deaths: a poisoned book, written by Aristotle about the basis of laughter as medicine to the human mind. The murderer abhors this discovery, because this knowledge, according to him, could mean man losing his fear and therefore his respect for God. This indirectly implies that the monks would lose their power, which "comes from God".

Flash backs and flash forwards

This technique links with the dissolve technique to reflect jumps in time. The best known example of a flash forward exists in *Don't Look Now* by Nicolas Roeg. A couple (Donald Sutherland and Julie Christie) have recently lost their daughter in a drowning incident for which they hold themselves responsible. They are unable to have intercourse for a while. In the love scene in Venice (the city of love), Roeg jumps forward in time. In one scene we see their two naked bodies making love, while in the following scene they are putting their clothes back on, before Roeg cuts back to their sensual love-making, showing that this action is not about sex, but about love. In this way he stresses the fact that this is a fleeting, almost unreal event in their tortured lives, a small moment of bliss away from the torture of guilt. By means of this technique, Roeg also de-eroticises the sequence (someone once called it the exact opposite of a strip-tease), thus contradicting critics who called it soft porn.

By flashing forward Roeg states that they are, and will always be, two people even when united during love-making. The tragic event has split and separated them forever, even in their most intimate moments. He also stresses that after the sexual act their greatest fulfilment is in the happy afterglow of having been together, of loving, of finding comfort and consolation with each other. Their being together almost becomes a memory as it is happening.

Some people would argue that the entire *Jacob's Ladder* by Adrian Lyne is a flash forward in which a wounded, dying Vietnam soldier (Tim Robbins) is given the opportunity to see what his life would have been like if he had decided to live. In the end, instead of living to witness his destruction by a hostile country which abandoned him, he chooses death. Thus he is saved from the grim reality which would have awaited him, and which was shown to him in forward flashes, had he chosen to live.

On the other hand, by flashing back a director places greater significance on the scenes in the present, because suddenly they acquire an ironic, multilayered meaning they would not have had otherwise. Another good example is *Citizen Kane,* where the whole film is told in flashback as we try to solve the mystery of Rosebud along with the characters. So too in Joseph Losey's *The Go-Between,* we see a mysterious man arriving at an equally mysterious house in the rain. Only later do we realise that it is Leo, the main character in the flashbacks, who as a young man witnessed a tragedy at this house which froze him sexually. He has come "home" one last time to put the demons to rest, to make peace, and the film is his recollections of what happened.

In *Another Country,* a journalist questions a spy, Guy Bennett, who defected to Russia (played by Rupert Everett) about his reasons for leaving England and "betraying his country". In the flashbacks, Guy strongly attacks the repressive English public school system. In *Sophie's Choice,* the main character (played by Meryl Streep) explains to Stingo, her obsessed writer friend, what drove her to self-destruction as she relives (in a flashback) her horrific moment of choice before being sent to a concentration camp during World War II.

A freeze-frame

A director sometimes freezes a character in mid-action – often to immortalise him, as in *Butch Cassidy and the Sundance Kid,* when George Roy Hill freezes the image of the two outlaws who are surrounded by the law and apparently meet their death when they storm into the line of fire in the end. By freeze framing this action, the director etches this picture into our minds. The characters therefore do not really "die", but live on in our minds forever. The same applies to Ridley Scott's freeze-frame in *Thelma and Louise* as the two women unite in death and to Danny Boyle's *Trainspotting* (see the section on freeze-frames in Chapter 3).

In *Chariots of Fire* Ben Cross as Harold Abrahams makes a triumphant leap. Hugh Hudson freezes on this action and the picture turns into black and white. As the camera pulls back, the image becomes a newspaper story. In this way Hudson creates expectation and tension for Abrahams's race against Liddell and also immortalises one of the great runners of that time.

The ripple technique

In *Strictly Ballroom* a freeze-frame ripples to life, as if somebody has disturbed the tranquillity of the surface. These ripples change into the parents, Doug and Shirley, who had supposedly been photographed doing their most triumphant dance.

Photographs or stills

A director sometimes uses a series of photographs to compress time or to tell a visual story through static pictures. When Billy Hayes (Brad Davis) arrives back in America after his terrifying treatment at the hands of the Turkish prison authorities in *Midnight Express,* we see him reunited with his parents and girlfriend in a series of photographs, as if from a newspaper. By avoiding a melodramatic reunion in the final moment of the film, Alan Parker sustains the tension in the viewer who has sat through this harrowing two-hour ordeal. He carries the freeze-frame of the climax of the film over into the still photographs.

In the previous scene Hayes, dressed as a prison warder, escapes from jail and does his triumphant little jump into the air on which Parker freeze-frames. Here too it is as if we are looking at newspaper photographs which emphasise the fact that this is a true story and that history has been made.

In *The Fugitive,* Andrew Davis uses black and white images which appear to be photographs which come to life as the wife of Dr Richard Kimble (Harrison Ford) is viciously murdered. By using this technique, Davis suggests that Kimble is reliving something that has been described to him in court and by the police – he has not seen most of it himself, and therefore imagines what it could have looked like. The images are also fragmented, as he cannot quite remember everything which happened after he was confronted with the killer. The pain and shock blur or "freeze-frame" his memory.

By using extreme distortion of sound in these sequences (almost as if photographs are being taken and the flashbulb is exploding in the microphone), Andrew Davis places us inside the mind of Dr Kimble. This extremely violent editing technique shocks us, stressing the senselessness of the action, and also creates the impression that these scenes are nightmares which frequently recur in Kimble's mind the moment he dozes off or his mind starts to wander.

The spinning technique

Here an image revolves at great speed in a circular movement, usually starting as a newspaper headline which revolves until the headline fills the screen. This technique is used in *Citizen Kane* to propel the scene from one headline-making event to the next, especially since this story is made up of headlines and revolves around the newspaper world.

In *Strictly Ballroom* a mock newspaper headline, "New Steps Rumoured", spins while the president of the dance federation denies that there will be new steps. The same technique is applied to stress his rules. The use of newspaper headlines emphasises the fact that these people take their craft extremely seriously.

56.
Mark Herman's easy-going, leisurely editing is often interrupted by closely cut scenes as the brass band starts to fight for its survival and tempers flare. Ewan McGregor and Tara Fitzgerald star in *Brassed Off*. (Courtesy of Film Four International)

Compression of time

A whole lifetime can flash by in seconds if a director or editor uses several carefully chosen quick shots in rapid succession. During the bridge-building scene in *The Ghost and the Darkness,* Stephen Hopkins deals with the main construction of the bridge in a few seconds as we see the workers constructing it. In reality it took months. But when presented to us by Hopkins, the bridge develops significantly but continuously in each shot. Also note the many training montages in *Chariots of Fire.*

The same applies to the passage of months during which the Alec Baldwin character in *Ghosts From the Past* continues with his life while he gathers evidence to bring a racist murderer back to trial. In a short montage the film skips over his marriage and ensuing period in a few seconds to avoid detracting from the real issue at hand: his fight for justice.

In *Midnight Express,* Billy Hayes lands in an asylum. To avoid going through the months of emotional torture the character endures, Alan Parker chooses a few shots of him either wandering around or sitting staring blankly into space. In other shots, he walks around in a circle with the other prisoners, until he finally regains the moral and physical strength to walk against the circle's prescribed movement.

The montage technique

The montage is related to the compression of time, and is a term derived from the French word "monter", which means to assemble. It was originally used as a general term for editing, but is now used to mean those forms of cutting that deliberately draw attention to the juxtaposition of a series of images. This makes one aware of the editing technique. The montage is a series of shots and sounds which do not seem to have a logical pattern, but form a kind of a miniature short story, as in *The Godfather's* christening montage.

> In creating a montage, the editor uses visual and aural images as impressionistic shorthand to create a mood, an atmosphere, the transition in time and place, or a physical or emotional impact (Boggs, 1996: 165).

In the shower scene from *Psycho*, Hitchcock exploits two of the biggest drawcards in cinema: nudity and violence. By placing the character in the shower, he not only succeeds in portraying her as being "vulnerable" (and therefore completely defenceless), but also suggests to the audience that they are seeing a naked Janet Leigh. The entire scene is an assault on the senses. As the attack takes place, Hitchcock changes our perspective several times, and to several extremes. The result is a disturbing and harrowing scene as the perspective rapidly switches between neutral observers, assailant and victim. Another result of this rapid cutting is that the attack seems to take longer than it actually does, adding to the shock experienced by the viewer.

– NG

An example of a montage can be found in George Roy Hill's *Butch Cassidy and the Sundance Kid*. The Paul Newman character takes Katharine Ross for a ride on his bicycle. In the background the famous melody "Raindrops keep fallin' on my head" is playing. We see various shots without dialogue portraying the developing affection between the two characters. This montage seems out of place in the film, yet is very effective in visually conveying what is happening between them.

– TLdR

One of the most touching and brilliant montages of all time is the final sequence in Krzysztof Kieślowski's *Three Colours: Blue*. As Julie finally finds spiritual freedom and sheds the baggage which has stifled her emotions since the death of her family, she puts down the phone and pulls the page with notes written on it towards her. It is now obvious that she may have written some of her husband's music herself, or improved on his score. The words from 1 Corinthians 13 in the Bible about the importance and power of unselfish love serve as the binding motive here.

Kieślowski literally blends a whole series of images in this montage which sums up Julie's emotions, her life and her attitude towards her own existence now that she has been liberated. He shows Julie making love and enjoying the passion that goes with it, as well as expressing her emotions for the first time. He now connects other static characters who, until now, have played a rather passionate part in her life – like the boy who witnessed the accident, and her mother who could not communicate with her at all. Both these characters stir in her imagination and move into her real life through the liberating experience of finally releasing the notes from paper and turning them into music – a metaphor which also applies to her spiritually being freed from constraints.

There is a touching scene in which the entire frame is filled with Julie's eye. It fades into black and the camera moves to Julie who now finds the strength to actually cry for the first time. It is a liberating experience – away from her self-banishment and away from her tangled emotions. A woman who up to this point had focused only on herself, now moves outside this mindset to a new found freedom through music. Kiešlowski himself has said of this sequence: "To love is a beautiful emotion, but in loving you immediately make yourself dependent on the person you love" (Stok, 1995: 215).

EXERCISES

1. Editing is the most important contribution cinema has brought to the twentieth century art world. Do you agree?
2. When selecting certain shots, editors have to keep several factors in mind. What are they?
3. What does juxtaposition mean? Explain with examples.
4. Name the different ways in which a director can achieve a transition in time.
5. The montage can be seen as a "poem in miniature" or "visual shorthand". True or false? Write an appreciation.

7

Setting

> Settings are not merely backdrops for the action, but symbolic extensions of the theme and characterisation. Settings can convey an immense amount of information or location (Giannetti, 1993: 281).

Cinema-goers can read several motives into a director's choice of setting, as discussed below.

SETTING AS AN EXTENSION OF A CHARACTER'S FRAME OF MIND

One of the earliest examples of a setting reflecting a character's frame of mind can be found in *The Cabinet of Dr Caligari* made in 1919 by Robert Wiene. A hypnotist turns a somnambulist into a murderer, but the question arises whether the whole film is not perhaps a figment of a deranged mind. This idea is reflected in the lopsided, twisted, abstract and skew sets which seem to be out of proportion and which have been used deliberately to reveal the hallucinatory state of mind of the main character. He is telling the story and we see the action through his perspective.

The dark rooms in which the serial killer in *Seven* executes his vile murders are also a reflection of his bizarre, distorted frame of mind. Everything is dark, clustered, smelly and is viewed in low-key lighting.

Roads filled with carnage, parking garages with cars huddled close together and motor wrecks at the side of a road reflect the twisted sexuality of the protagonists in David Cronenberg's *Crash*. The wrecks can be seen as an extension of their own twisted souls or sexuality and the coldness they feel towards each other. The sex is also usually mechanical, another theme reflected by the use of cars.

In *101 Dalmatians*, Cruella de Vil, played by Glenn Close, has designed an office for herself which resembles a spider's web. Stark lines and an open office cluttered with new age furniture and people-unfriendly shapes and lines indicate that she is a troubled, dark, selfish character who traps people (and animals) in her web.

SETTING AS A DIRECT INFLUENCE ON SOCIAL BEHAVIOUR

Lee Tamahori's *Once Were Warriors* starts with the perfect picture postcard version of what New Zealand is supposed to look like. As the camera pulls back, we see the grim reality: an industrialised city dominated by cars and open pipes which pollute the clean air the country is supposed to have. The camera then cranes down and follows a woman (Rena Owen) who has just done her shopping and is on her way to her house. We see what she sees – but for us it is a new experience, an introduction to an (alien?) setting which is familiar to her. But by looking at the people around her, we can understand that this setting has created or directly influenced the people who make up her life.

There is, for instance, a boy who lives in an abandoned car wreck under a congested highway. By looking at the graffiti on the wreck and the run-down interior, we understand why the children behave the way they do, as this is what they see and experience every day. The setting reflects their inner lives and states of mind. It is no wonder they are so aggressive, demotivated and depressed. Upon entering their houses, we discover that they come from cramped, dirty dwellings with small backyards filled with washing. The air is polluted, and their friends huddle in cluttered bars full of aggressive drinkers. Other characters, like the son's highly tattooed friends, sweat aggressively in graffiti-smeared gymnasiums surrounded by barbed wire.

In this regard also note the influence the decaying, soiled and cramped Turkish jail has on its characters in *Midnight Express*, the reformatory on the boys in *Sleepers*, or the jail on the inmates of the Shawshank prison in *The Shawshank Redemption*.

In *Paljas* by Katinka Heyns the dry, desolate landscape has a direct influence on the characters' state of mind, reflecting their isolation and loneliness. When the circus train arrives, it serves as a striking anachronism which brings about an unexpected and colourful change in the characters' existence. Also note that Heyns never overindulges in the raw beauty of the landscape – she only hints at the beauty behind the barren horizon.

57.
A scene from *Paljas*, directed by Katinka Heyns. (Courtesy of Sonneblom Films)

SETTING AS A REFLECTION OF A CHARACTER

A character *is* often his house. He builds a place or surrounds himself with objects which reflect his personality.

In *Citizen Kane,* Xanadu is a palace built by a powerful man. It represents the corruption of innocence and idealism by material goods. Xanadu is filled with priceless art works, most of them in storage where no-one will see or appreciate them. It represents Kane's devolution from a man who only sought the truth, to someone who believes that greatness comes from collecting massive amounts of objects and artefacts. His biggest mistake is to think that he can also collect people in the way he does furniture or statues.

In the end, Kane does not have a single friend, but only a house filled with treasures that are cold and hostile. Even though the house is full of priceless riches, in reality it is as empty as its owner's soul. The character and the house are so closely interlinked that when Kane starts dying, his mansion also starts slipping away in decay and ruin.

–NG

SETTING AS AN IMITATION OF REALITY

A director may create an "unreal" world in such a realistic way that he convinces us that it actually exists.

In the science fiction trilogy *Star Wars, The Empire Strikes Back* and *The Return of the Jedi,* the directors, among them the creator of the series and the director of the original, George Lucas, create fantasy worlds that are completely plausible. The planet on which Luke Skywalker grows up is reminiscent of a rural community on earth and exudes a people-friendly ambience, yet at the same time has a specific and alien look. The same applies to the interior of the spaceships, the famous bar scene where different interplanetary creatures intermingle over a drink, and the galaxy which forms their playground.

Ridley Scott also gives his own realistic impression of what Los Angeles could look like in the year 2020 in *Blade Runner,* when the Japanese are supposed to have taken over the city drenched by an eternal acid-polluted rain.

Other films which recreate fantasy (or real worlds which may exist, but still have to be discovered) are *2001: A Space Odyssey* by Stanley Kubrick, *Batman* and its sequels, David Lynch's *Dune* with its huge sandworms, the hereafter in *Contact*, the town in *Dante's Peak* which is dominated by the threatening yet beautiful mountain, *Jurassic Park, Volcano* as well as *The Poseidon Adventure's* upside-down ship. Of course, perhaps the most realistic space set ever built is the Nostromo along with its lifeboat, the Narcissus, in Ridley Scott's *Alien,* the egg chamber and the derelict spaceship with its dead space jockey, as well as the surface of the alien planet, all designed by H.R. Giger.

Although these locations do not exist and were recreated on sound stages, they are so realistic that we accept them without question. (Compare them to the slapdash, kitsch space settings of *Dark Star* and Ed Wood's *Plan 9 from Outer Space,* where the spaceships are literally pot lids covered with foil and hang from the roof on visible lines.)

A director often reinterprets a "real" location, which may give it a superficial look, but still is convincing in that particular genre. Think of the flamboyant sets for *Cleopatra* in the 1963 version by Joseph L. Mankiewicz, or the recreation of 5th Avenue in *Hello, Dolly!,* or the arena where *Ben-Hur's* famous chariot race takes place. Perhaps one of the best and most realistic time period sets ever was that built for *Restoration,* as it perfectly reflected the flamboyance and vanity associated with England's sun king, or the construction of the Titanic in James Cameron's film, *Titanic.*

SETTING AS A DECORATION

A setting can often form a breathtaking and striking background to an intimate story (as in Sydney Pollack's *Out of Africa*), and it can complement the action or the film's overall theme.

In John Ford's westerns, such as *The Searchers* and *Stagecoach,* the desolate and majestic Monument Valley serves as a kind of natural monument, as does the Grand Canyon in Lawrence Kasdan's film of the same name. Monument Valley is literally a testimonial to the majestic grandeur of God's creation – a vast, largely uninhabited country, strikingly beautiful. Man looks small and insignificant against the vastness –

even if he is as macho and strong as John Wayne. The stunning background also serves as a "character" in these films, as other parts of the West do in Clint Eastwood's *Unforgiven,* Walter Hill's *Geronimo: An American Legend* and Kevin Costner's *Dances with Wolves*. It has a direct influence on the story, as characters often battle the elements. The directors, however, always stay with their stories and never allow the setting to dominate the dramatic narrative.

It is interesting to note that Eastwood exposes the West's romantic, picture-friendly image in *Unforgiven's* hostile, windswept plains. The strange, desolate "beauty" is motivated and integrated into the story. Note the simple yet strong house which the character played by Clint Eastwood built for his family. There is nothing picturesque or glamorous about the house whatsoever. It is functional, stark and strong, yet gives a melancholy and desolate impression. It has been designed for survival and lacks the touch and care of a woman. The house is therefore almost symbolic of the main character, who had stopped living after his wife died and had built a cold exterior around himself to keep the hostile world out.

One of the most striking uses of setting is found in *The Devil's Advocate* by Taylor Hackford, in the scene where the devil (Al Pacino) shows his novice, Kevin Lomax (Keanu Reeves), that the new city of New York could be his if he is sly enough.

There are no railings on top of his sky-scraper, while exquisite waterfalls tumble into the granite abyss, changing the face of the city completely. These waterfalls soften the stark lines of the other buildings and force us to look at this familiar city through new eyes. The reflection of the buildings in the artificial pools gives it the appearance of a granite fairy land which we too would like to own.

This sequence is a parody of the scene in the Bible where the devil tries to tempt Christ in the desert. The fact that Pacino stands right on the edge with his back to the void suggests that he fears nothing. He is the prince of darkness and the king of the city. He can change the appearance of his property as it suits him to impress his viewer.

The interior of the new luxury apartment of the Lomaxes seems cold and hostile, compared to their warm, more homely surroundings in the South. When Mary Ann Lomax (Charlize Theron) can not decide on the right colour scheme, we realise that she is going to settle for the wrong one, which will alienate her even more from her new home and eventually from her husband.

In a film like Franco Zeffirelli's *Brother Sun, Sister Moon,* the director unfortunately falls in love with the beauty of the Assisi countryside. His camera literally gets lost in the beauty and brightly coloured flowers which somehow look artificial and unreal. The setting becomes kitsch, contrived and ineffective as the background to a touching story about a young man who discovers spirituality, nature and himself.

Many critics have noted that the abundance of wild life on the train journey in *The Ghost and the Darkness* is exaggerated. In contrast there is a noticeable absence of the very game the Val Kilmer character admires on his train journey when they reach their destination where the bridge is being built.

SETTING THAT TAKES ON A SYMBOLIC MEANING

A setting may represent an idea or a theme. The huge, desolate, eerie hotel in *The Shining* has, on the one hand, been created by Stanley Kubrick to terrorise viewers. Upon closer examination though, it also has a symbolic meaning.

This empty hotel with its massive halls and the endless empty corridors symbolises Jack Torrance's (Jack Nicholson) frame of mind and the embodied evil. Later it becomes clear that Torrance may (or may not) be a reincarnation of an evil, possessed caretaker of the hotel who decades before had slaughtered his wife and twin daughters. The hotel is literally an incarnation of that evil, madness and confusion as it spews forth blood from an elevator, has doors opening by themselves and attracts strange and evil spirits. The huge maze also can be seen as a metaphorical extension of Torrance's state of mind which itself is like a maze from which there is no escape, except into madness (represented by the dead-end corners).

In *The Name of the Rose* the monastery, and especially the maze leading to the library, can also be seen as symbolic. The sets of the library and monastery reflect the narrow-minded suppression of knowledge and banning or smothering of emotions. Since most characters are eagerly searching and thirsting for knowledge and enlightenment which are withheld from them, the library – the source of knowledge – is situated at the end of a maze. It is almost impossible to find. The dark and eerie house and motel in *Psycho* also symbolise repression and unadulterated evil.

SETTING AS A MICROCOSM

The word "microcosm" means a miniature representation of something, or "little world". For instance, a group of people who find themselves on an island, ship or plane symbolise a certain part of the community as each one represents a certain culture, way of thinking, mentality or social standing. The place where they find themselves almost becomes the planet itself, summed up in a single location, like in *Robinson Crusoe*.

In Miloš Forman's brilliant *One Flew Over the Cuckoo's Nest*, the asylum in which a sane man, played by Jack Nicholson, is locked up is a microcosm of repressive society. The film is about a rigid system, represented by Nurse Ratched, which punishes those who dare to step out of line, which destroys individuality and kills people emotionally when they try to rebel. As Pauline Kael (1975–80: 84) puts it, it is like being buried alive:

58. Danny Boyle's realistic setting for *Trainspotting* perfectly echoes the culture of drug pushers and addicts, played by Ewan Bremner (Spud), Ewan McGregor (Renton), Robert Carlyle (Begbie) and Jonny Lee Miller (Sick Boy). (Courtesy of Film Four International)

> Nurse Ratched runs the place for the Combine, the secret power centre that controls society. The Combine sends society's non-conformists to the hospital, and Big Nurse forces them into submission – if necessary, by turning them into vegetables. Chief Broom's view is a psychotic metaphor for a society awaiting revelation, and the revelation comes in the person of ... McMurphy (Jack Nicholson).

The best example of setting as a microcosm is *The Lord of the Flies* (especially the earlier Peter Brook version which is better than the 1989 Harry Hook version). A group of schoolboys are stranded on an island and revert to uncivilised, instinctive, often primitive behaviour when they are forced to survive without the help of adults and there is no civilisation to guide or influence them. Their primal natures emerge and take over. Each of these boys represents a certain kind of person (a leader, a nerd, the voice of reason, the bully, his victim, the adventurer, etc.). The island is symbolic of our civilisation or the world we inhabit, which is filled with these different kinds of people.

Some may argue that the dining room in *The Last Supper* serves as a microcosm too. It is almost like a court and an execution room, as several of the self-righteous characters represent a radical, leftist section of civilisation. The guests who pay them a visit and are poisoned, represent an extreme rightist vision which includes homophobes, racists, and other conservatives.

SETTING AS A REFLECTION OF PERIOD

One would expect the set in period pieces like *Barry Lyndon, The Age of Innocence, Dangerous Liaisons* and *Little Women* to be accurate representations of that time. Even the young Ron Kovic's house in *Born on the Fourth of July* or the movie set of *Ed Wood* should accurately reflect the economic and social standing of that society.

If a drama takes place during, for example, the French Revolution, one expects the sets to be true to the style of that period to the last detail. This is usually the case, as in *The Madness of King George* by Nicholas Hytner, where the rich, lavish and elaborate sets are true to the court of King George III in the late eighteenth century. Also note the quaint gardens and delicate furniture which adorn the rooms in Ang Lee's *Sense and Sensibility*.

In Martin Scorsese's *The Age of Innocence* the narrator frequently draws our attention to the hypocritical splendour of the upper classes' houses. The sets are reflected in the dialogue: "The Beaufort house had been boldly planned. Instead of squeezing through a narrow passage to get to the ballroom, one marched solemnly down a vista of drawing rooms." As the narrator describes the house, we see the bold red curtains, the huge arrays of flowers, the flamboyant dresses, the decorative paintings (among them a scandalous nude!) and other decorations. The narrator makes us aware of the falseness of this display of splendour, because the Beauforts decorated the house according to the expectations of society, not necessarily as they may have wished to. This reflects their hypocritical nature.

On the other hand, when we cut to the luxurious interior of Mrs Mingott's house, we find warmth and friendliness in the pink colours, the excessively dramatic pictures of French fiction, and the many paintings of dogs. She resembles a contented, friendly, plump Christmas pudding, surrounded by her equally overfed dogs, and this is reflected in the furniture and colours she has chosen.

A FINAL LOOK AT SETTING

Settings can also be exceptionally realistic if a director decides to shoot on the actual location, as in documentaries like *Hoop Dreams* or dramatised documentaries with their hyper-realistic style, like *The Battle of Algiers*. In this film the scenes are extremely realistic and were filmed at the actual places where the incidents took place.

In *Edward Scissorhands*, director Tim Burton creates contrasting sets which accurately convey the personalities of the different characters. Edward, played by Johnny Depp, stays on a large mountain which overlooks the small suburban town in which the film is set. The castle in which he lives is dark and old, creating a shroud of mystery which suggests that he has been living in his own little world, oblivious of everything around him. The town, on the other hand, has an almost plastic quality. It is brightly lit and everything looks the same, suggesting the blandness of the people's conventional lives.

The contrasting sets assist in accurately portraying the differences between the eccentric and all-too-human Edward and the shallow townsfolk. They stress that Edward is an outsider and that even though he can use his extraordinary talents to make the people accept him, he will always be different.

–TLdR

In musicals, the sets are often artificial, cardboard kitsch which is convincing in a "story book", unrealistic sort of way. Examples are the sets for *Seven Brides for Seven Brothers* and *Singin' in the Rain,* where the sets are obviously studio-built and the lighting artificial. However, a director like Alan Parker prefers a more realistic look to his musicals, as *Fame, The Commitments* and *Evita* prove.

EXERCISES

1. Settings are not merely backdrops for the action, but symbolic extensions of the theme and characterisation. Settings can convey an immense amount of information. Discuss.
2. How can a setting reflect character? Discuss and give examples.
3. Setting can take on a symbolic meaning. Discuss *The Shining, Underground* and *Once were Warriors* in this regard.
4. Setting often imitates reality. Describe the success or failure of this so-called "reality" with regard to *Titanic*, the *Star Wars* trilogy, *Blade Runner, Alien 1, Jurassic Park* and its sequel.

8

Acting

INTRODUCTION

An actor is like a living recording device. He is the spokesperson responsible for conveying a large part of a film's message. He also brings the characters in a film to life. Through his expressions, body language, appearance, dress and use of voice, he helps to communicate what the writer or director is trying to say. He is the most obvious tool a director can use to make a point. However, this is exactly the problem: he should not merely be a tool, but should operate and function as a believable, clearly defined and convincing human being.

SINCERE AND CONVINCING PERFORMANCES

An actor's performance should be entirely convincing, unaffected and frank. Of significance is the honesty of the character and the accurate portrayal of the emotions he or she conveys. If a particular character has inconsistencies or eccentricities, these must be portrayed as totally believable and be communicated in as natural a way as possible. Inconsistencies can be found in characters like "Superman" or "The Shadow", where the person involved is both a nerd and a hero, or both evil and honourable.

In *Fargo,* the character portrayed by Frances McDormand does a fine balancing act between her middle-class way of life in a small town and the investigation of a murder. It is this duality which she handles so amicably that results in the comic and dramatic tension in the film.

The actor must make the character as true to life as possible, as

Robert De Niro does in his portrayal of the outsider anti-heroes in *Raging Bull* and *Taxi Driver,* both for Martin Scorsese.

Al Pacino is one of the few actors of his generation with the ability to captivate an audience totally, allowing them to lose themselves in the characters he portrays. Credibility is the primary reason for his outstanding performance. He draws us into the heart of a character, leaving us either uplifted or repulsed. Occasionally, as in *Scent of a Woman,* he manages to achieve both. In this film, he portrays Lt. Col. Frank Slade, a man trapped by blindness and alcoholism. The character has two sides: one is that of a heavy drinker, full of self-pity and anger and the other is a man with a gentle nature and a sense of style and humour, a man he had long since forgotten existed.

Pacino's performance is completely credible: we never doubt that everything could have happened to one man. He takes us on a roller-coaster ride, allowing us to experience every emotion that the character experiences. We slowly learn to understand him and have compassion for his situation. We see that he is really a romantic at heart, for example, when he explains the scent of a woman to the Chris O'Donnell character in a plane on the way to New York.

–TLdR

59. Martin Brest's *Scent of a Woman* revolves around the friendship between a blind ex-serviceman, played by Al Pacino, and his high school companion Chris O'Donnell.

60.
In all his films, Clint Eastwood usually portrays the same kind of character with slight variations. Even as a selfish burglar who witnesses a murder in *Absolute Power* (which he also directed), the audience remains on his side because of the Eastwood charm and persona. (Courtesy of Castle Rock; Photographer: Graham Kuhn)

THE ACTOR AS PART OF A TEAM

Although the actor's role is often crucial to the success of a film, he is still part of a team (scriptwriter, director, editor, cinematographer, etc.) and should never dominate a film completely. This often happens in action thrillers where the names of stars like Jean-Claude van Damme or Bruce Willis are larger and deemed to be more important than the film. Unfortunately the same seems to be happening to an excellent actor like Nicolas Cage, who has now turned into an action hero after films like *The Rock, Con Air* and *Face/Off*, where he is required only to look worried or macho. What a waste of talent!

In a masterpiece like *The Silence of the Lambs*, the acting is of an exceptionally high standard, but so are the script, the music, photography and directing. None of these elements draws particular attention to itself. They are all perfectly integrated, which is why this film is regarded as one of the greatest films in modern cinema. From their first meeting there is a spark, a strange kind of respect between Hannibal Lecter and Clarice Starling – a theme which runs through the entire film. However, although these characters dominate the film, the interaction of minor characters like Clarice's superior, played by Scott Glenn, is just as strong.

CHAPTER

8

Acting

61. Anthony Hopkins, Jodie Foster and Scott Glenn in *The Silence of the Lambs.* (Orion Pictures)

MANNERISMS

Actors should avoid mannerisms which could detract from their performance. Some actresses pull their hair back and lock it behind their ears, only to repeat this meaningless gesture when their hair falls forward again. This does not contribute to their characterisation in any way, but rather detracts from it and exposes their inability to find a meaningful way of portraying their characters. Note how often actresses like Cameron Diaz and Jennifer Aniston repeat these gestures, especially in films like *She's the One.*

THE STANISLAVSKY METHOD OF ACTING

Great actors such as Dustin Hoffman, Marlon Brando, Robert de Niro and Jennifer Jason Leigh often use the Stanislavsky method of acting in which they literally "become" the character they are portraying. They live the part every moment they are playing it, even off set.

If a character is required to put on weight, as happened to Robert De Niro in *Raging Bull* or Toni Collette in *Muriel's Wedding,* such an actor will physically add several kilograms to his or her weight to achieve the desired effect, while other actors like Eddie Murphy in *The Nutty Professor* simply rely on the convenience of costumes and make-up. (Of course, one could not expect Murphy to go to such an extreme.)

Daniel Day-Lewis literally helped to construct the pioneer village in which his character stayed in *The Crucible* and lived in the same circumstances as his character would have done. When playing a cripple in *My Left Foot,* Day-Lewis asked to be treated as a cripple and to be carried on and off the set because the character could not walk. Actors sometimes also ask to be addressed by their characters' names.

62.
Daniel Day-Lewis as Christy Brown, a handicapped Irish writer-artist who suffered from cerebral palsy and Brenda Fricker as his mother in *My Left Foot*, directed by Jim Sheridan. (Miramax)

The question now arises whether a performance is inferior if an actor does not go to these extraordinary lengths. (Nicolas Cage had his front teeth pulled for *Birdy* and Tom Cruise wanted a drug injected into his legs to paralyse his lower body for a few hours in *Born on the Fourth of July*.) Of course not. Not all actors approach a role with such conviction or dedication, nor is it always necessary. Actors such as Shirley MacLaine, Emma Thompson, Ralph Fiennes or Robin Williams study the script and the words and give the required performance when the camera is rolling, but slip out of character once the performance is over.

This technique does not influence their acting in the least, nor make it inferior to other performances. These actors have mastered the technique of good screen acting and can give a professional performance when required. It is up to the actor to decide how to prepare for the part and how much research to put into the preparation.

FILM ACTING AS OPPOSED TO STAGE ACTING

Film acting generally portrays great intimacy, which separates it from stage acting. As the camera is able to capture an extreme close-up, a blatant display of emotion can result in overkill, as often happens in Eddie Murphy comedies, especially *The Nutty Professor.* This merely irritates and distracts the viewer. Several scenes in this film are so over the top that Murphy alienates his character from the audience, rather than endearing him to them.

Even though an actor like Jim Carrey goes way over the top with his facial gymnastics in all his films, he still manages to endear himself to his audience, because he makes it clear, especially in *Liar, Liar* and the *Ace Ventura* series, that there is often a lonely human being hiding behind all the contortions, who may be too scared to reveal his inmost feelings. His antics may be a desperate desire for acceptance. Carrey came closest to expressing these hidden anxieties in his finest portrayal to date, namely in *The Cable Guy*. He even managed to project deranged paranoia in the criminally ingenious Riddler in *Batman Forever*.

63. Jim Carrey's grin and strangely transfixed stare hint at his character's mischievous and extravagant mood swings (often resulting in manic yet motivated overacting) in *Liar Liar*. (Copyright © 1997 by Universal Studios, Inc. Courtesy of MCA Publishing Rights, a division of Universal Studios, Inc. All rights reserved.)

On stage, an actor may have to overact or exaggerate for the benefit of the audience in the back rows, while in cinema even the smallest gesture can be brought within touching distance of the audience in an extreme close-up. In cinema, therefore, actions or emotions are rather suggested in a subtle, unobtrusive way. Consider the subtlety of the Edward Norton character in *Primal Fear,* and note how he underplays each emotion, even during his outbursts or most gruelling moments.

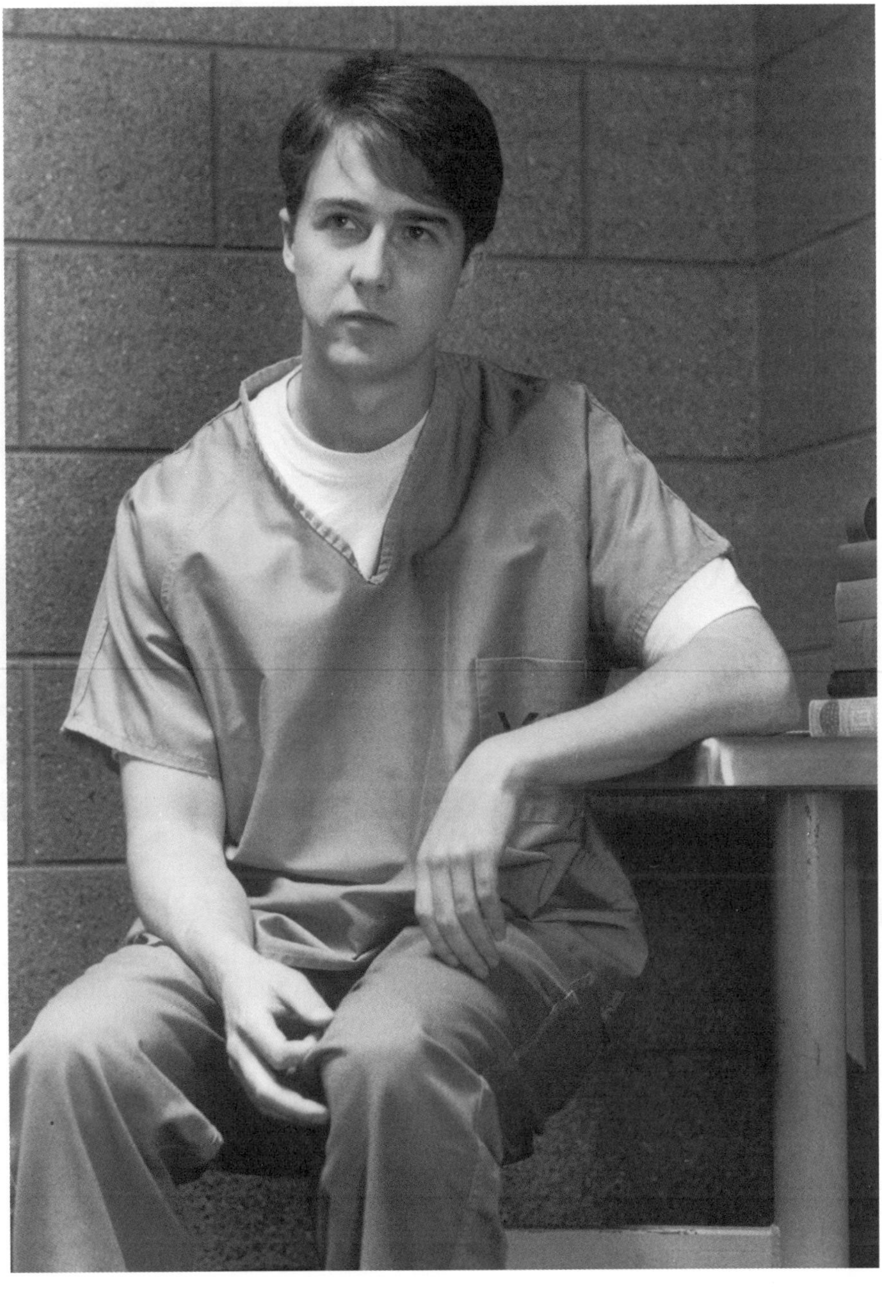

64. Edward Norton won a Golden Globe for his portrayal of a psychopath who deceives psychiatrists, the church and the law with his dual personalities in *Primal Fear*. (Courtesy of Paramount)

CHAPTER

8

Acting

65. Nicole Kidman in *Portrait of a Lady*, directed by Jane Campion. (Courtesy of PolyGram)

A MECHANICAL PERFORMANCE

Actors may sometimes give too little of themselves with the result that the performance is not convincing. Much of the "action" may be taking place inside their minds, but they may be unable to convey it, as happened to Nicole Kidman in *Portrait of a Lady* where her performance was artificial and often lifeless. Her calculated movements and expressions were prescribed by a director, and are not born from within as Barbra Hershey's are in the same film.

Compare Kidman's introverted performance with Juliette Binoche's courageous characterisation in *Three Colours: Blue*. Most of the action takes place in Julie's subconscious or in her mind. Binoche manages to convey each nuance by skilfully underplaying her emotions, but still allowing them to register for the camera. One can actually read her mind without the help of a voice-over or any other effects.

OVER-THE-TOP PERFORMANCES

On the other hand, an over-the-top performance, like Shirley MacLaine's in both *Terms of Endearment* and *Evening Star,* can be so artistically controlled and brilliantly executed that it does not jump out of the frame. MacLaine's flamboyancy is cinematically justified and never reads as excessive or false. She knows just how big to play for the intimate eye of the camera. The same applies to Glenn Close's "controlled" over-the-top performance in *101 Dalmatians,* where she imitates the comic book style of acting of the original cartoon character.

An actor who is in danger of turning into a parody of himself, and who frequently hijacks a film and runs away with it, is Jack Nicholson.

66. The deliciously over-the-top, fur-loving Cruella deVil (Glenn Close) in *101 Dalmations.* (Disney)

He is at his best when a director like Miloš Forman keeps a firm hand on him, as in his best performance in *One Flew Over the Cuckoo's Nest.* In this film, he skilfully underplays his devilish grin and his eyes have only a hint of madness which could also be taken for mischievousness. Pauline Kael (1975: 87) refers to his smile as a shark's grin. He is more like a naughty schoolboy enjoying his obnoxious tricks and daring authority to punish him.

In *The Shining*, unfortunately, his excessive madness and larger-than-life performance turn Torrance into a nightmare clown who is a terror machine, rather than a crazed, tormented human being. In films like *Hoffa* and *A Few Good Men*, though, his performance is controlled and totally convincing, and he does not over-indulge as he does in *Batman*.

Comedies often require overacting, as Jim Carrey proves in *Liar, Liar*. Compare an extravagant Eddie Murphy performance (in, for example, *The Nutty Professor*) to the performances of comedians like Charlie Chaplin or even John Cleese in *A Fish Called Wanda* and *Fierce Creatures.* The latter actors skilfully underplay the extravagance of their larger-than-life characters to such an extent that they are totally convincing as human beings, and do not appear to be clowns performing at a children's party. Also note John Cusack's understated performance in *Grosse Pointe Blank.*

67. One of the world's top comedians, John Cleese, in the black comedy *Fierce Creatures*. (Copyright © 1996 by Universal Studios, Inc. Courtesy of MCA Publishing Rights, a division of Universal Studios, Inc. All rights reserved.)

THE CHALLENGES OF MODERN FILM ACTING

In a cinema industry currently dominated by special effects and computer graphics, actors sometimes have to imagine the character or effect opposite them, as happens to Bob Hoskins in *Who Framed Roger Rabbit?*, Helen Hunt and Bill Paxton in *Twister*, Julianne Moore in *The Lost World: Jurassic Park*, as well as Michael Jordan in *Space Jam*.

These actors realise that their performances are now being challenged or even overshadowed by larger-than-life events, and must come across even more strongly than usual to make an impression against popular cartoon characters or forces of nature. Consider in this regard the spewing volcano in *Volcano*, or the raging torrent of water as happens to Christian Slater in *Hard Rain* (also called *Flood*), or the sinking of the Titanic in James Cameron's *Titanic*.

CONTINUITY IN ACTING

Since filming can take anything from one month to a period of years to complete, performances have to be perfectly timed and constructed to convey every nuance of a character's development. An actor should never anticipate emotions or events. Continuity in a performance, aided by the director of course, is extremely important in this instance.

If an actor does the final scene of a film at the beginning of the shooting schedule, he should combine all the emotions he has experienced up to that moment in that particular scene, even although he has not filmed any of the preceding scenes yet. This makes film acting an exceptionally difficult form of acting. Certain emotions may have influenced the character's final behaviour, or he may not have lost a loved one yet when a certain scene is filmed. He should keep all of these factors in mind when doing a sequence out of continuity.

CASTING

Casting plays a major part in the credibility and success of a performance. In some cases an actor's true character spills over into the roles he plays.

Robin Williams is a good example of character casting. He has always been cast as someone who is extremely eccentric for a single purpose: comedy. Any of his films immediately shows you that he is in his element; he always gives a fresh view of life and circumstances. Williams has a talent for seeing the lighter side of life. His performances are impressive because he knows exactly to what level of eccentricity he can take the characters. In *Dead Poets Society*, for example, he proves that he can grapple with serious emotional issues, while still retaining a hint of spontaneity and a sense of humour. His spot-on performance of a teacher who wishes to guide instead of dictate, stands out above his other roles. He proves in this role, as John Keating, that his real-life eccentricity can accommodate serious comment on human affairs.

Williams' performances are convincing because he plays his role true to himself. You never feel that he practises for hours to be a character he is not. The directors of his films should also be credited for casting him in roles which suit his personality. He is well known for his improvisation on set, and that keeps his performances fresh. He is never tied down by the script and enters the persona he is interpreting totally. He never loses sight of the film as a whole, however, and that is possibly why his performances never detract from the greater impact of the film.

By comparison, consider Ralph Fiennes's performance in *The English Patient.* Although the screenplay calls for an understated character, Fiennes appears to have taken this to the extreme. He remains relatively expressionless throughout the entire film (the scenes in which he is severely burnt add to this). It is all very well to play a character so coolly and calmly, but to take the underplay to such an extreme has only one result: the audience cannot relate. A character which is too understated distances the audience. The problem seems to be that Fiennes has got stuck in this emotionless method since his role in *Schindler's List.* Although his performance in that film was appropriate, it is not so in *The English Patient.* It is difficult for us to believe that a character who never shows his emotions (even when alone) has experienced love.

– NG

Nobody was convinced that the husky-voiced Demi Moore could portray the conservative Hester Prynne in *The Scarlet Letter* – the actress carries a history of promiscuous parts. (At the time, she had just finished *Disclosure* and never injected enough variation into her new performance to separate it from her previous ones.) Her previous characters interfere with the tortured and sexually tormented soul she is trying to portray. It is Demi Moore on screen, not the character. The situation is made worse by the modern style of director Roland Joffe (especially the sensual, soft-porn bath sequence), which further alienates the audience from both character and material.

Arnold Schwarzenegger and Sylvester Stallone have both tried to play weaklings *(Last Action Hero, Oscar),* but because audiences have preconceived ideas about them, and perhaps because of a lack of versatility, they are not at all convincing. They simply play variations of their own screen personae and do not register as real people, but rather as symbols or stars, as happened with actors like John Wayne and Humphrey Bogart in the past.

The opposite can be said of actors such as Brenda Blethyn and Marianne Jean-Baptiste in *Secrets and Lies,* and even David Thewlis in *Naked,* both films by Mike Leigh. Because they were unknown faces at the time, we associated those actors with the parts they played com-

68.
Demi Moore has attempted to portray diverse characters – unfortunately not always with equal success. Here she mourns her husband in *Ghost*, one of her more successful films. (Courtesy of Paramount)

pletely. If, for instance, Kim Basinger had portrayed either of the women in *Secrets and Lies*, or Tom Cruise the Thewlis part in *Naked*, the films would not have had the same impact. These actors would not have suited the roles, nor would they have been able to bring the same originality to the parts as the original cast. (Colour photo N, page xv)

Both Bette Davis and Katharine Hepburn refused to be typecast and were responsible for some of the most memorable, but varied acting performances in cinema history. This does not mean that new faces should always be employed to portray complex characters. A case in point is Leonardo DiCaprio's magnificent performances in *The Basketball Diaries*, *What's Eating Gilbert Grape* and *This Boy's Life*. Like famous character actors such as Robert De Niro, Dustin Hoffman, Gene Hackman, Vanessa Redgrave, Al Pacino and Jennifer Jason Leigh, DiCaprio is a chameleon who totally "inhabits" the body of the character he plays. He seems to be a completely different human being each time he appears on screen. His approach to each part, from Romeo in *William Shakespeare's Romeo and Juliet* to Rimbaud in *Love and Eternity* (also known as *Total Eclipse*), is fresh and original.

Two actors who have always given good performances, but have never had the chance to flex their true acting muscles, are Guy Pearce and Russell Crowe, who play two young cops caught in the middle of an inquiry into police corruption in *L.A. Confidential*, directed by Curtis Hanson. Crowe previously played characters from vastly different backgrounds in *The Sum of Us* and *Romper Stomper*, while Guy Pearce is known as the good-looking hero from television's *Neighbours* and the drag queen in *The Adventures of Priscilla, Queen of the Desert.*

In *L.A. Confidential* they prove that they are two of the best actors of their generation, as they ably display both the human side and the immense frustrations which form part of their daily lives. Pearce is tough yet also slightly vulnerable with a sensitive streak, underlined by his nerdish glasses. The determined lines around his mouth suggest that he is ambitious and will pursue truth and honour at all costs. Crowe's character is bombastic and often violent, a volcano waiting to erupt.

When these two men on the same side of the law, but with different agendas, confront each other towards the end of the film, we realise that two respectable cops are wasting precious time by fighting each other, therefore falling into the trap set by the real culprit. The true evil is still hiding inside the police force and still has to be confronted.

The real revelation, though, is Kim Basinger in the part of a hooker who is hired to blackmail powerful businessmen and cops. She has a melancholy, lonely but also extremely tough quality which Basinger brings out in what is certainly her best performance to date.

The same applies to Charlize Theron in *The Devil's Advocate.* Although not on the same level as Kim Basinger's performance, Theron proves that she can hold her own against two well-known actors such as Keanu Reeves and especially the powerful Al Pacino. She convinces as the glamorous and innocent girl from the deep South who becomes the suicidal, depressed victim of the devil's master plan to cause a rift between her and her husband.

TYPECASTING

Typecasting means that an actor repeatedly plays similar character roles in different films. Certain actors are often assigned the parts of villains, others those of heroes, and audiences expect to see them in the same roles in every film.

James Woods and Christopher Walken tend to fall into this trap, as most of the characters they portray are either psychopaths or dark, tortured souls. Note, for example, Woods's excellent performance in *Ghosts From the Past.* When on occasion such an actor tries to act against type, as Woods does in *Immediate Family,* the character fails to be convincing because his previous performances or screen personae are so etched into our memories that we cannot accept him in a different role. Woods did manage somehow to break out of this mould and portray a comic character *(The Hard Way)* or rogue *(Diggstown),* but he is seldom convincing in the part of a straightforward hero.

Anthony Hopkins, on the other hand, proves the opposite when he moves from being the psychopath in *The Silence of the Lambs* to gentler roles in *The Remains of the Day, Shadowlands* and *Howards End,* although he failed to be convincing in Alan Parker's over-the-top *The Road to Welville* or *Surviving Picasso* by James Ivory. Even a handsome actor like Val Kilmer refuses to be stereotyped. Think of the criminal character he

69. One of the best actors of his generation: Anthony Hopkins whose chameleonlike qualities allow him to portray any conceivable character with total conviction – from a cannibalistic murderer to the highly sensitive author/lecturer C.S Lewis. Here Hopkins poses with Debra Winger as an American writer, Joy Gresham, who falls in love with him in *Shadowlands.* (Spelling Films)

portrays in *Heat* as opposed to the charming and seductively intelligent hero in *The Saint*.

STEREOTYPING

Stereotyping literally means an idea (or performance) which has grown stale through fixed usage. Characters or actors represent a certain mindset or personality, and fit into our preconceived ideas of a certain kind of character.

Male hairdressers, for instance, are usually stereotyped as limp wristed and effeminate (although *Shampoo* with Warren Beatty temporarily put an end to that stereotype in the seventies!), while drug lords usually wear dark glasses and hats, have marks on their faces, often wear an eyepatch and only speak in monosyllabic tones, sometimes reverting to expletives.

Most villains in action films have scars, are dressed in black or are physically unattractive. However, directors often deliberately exaggerate their awkward, larger-than-life qualities to achieve a certain effect. Tim Burton intentionally overstates these elements with the Joker and the Penguin in *Batman* and *Batman Returns* because these are unrealistic, stylised comic strip characters who were never intended to be taken seriously. The same applies to the grotesque Agatha Trunchbull (Pam Ferris) in *Matilda* and Cruella deVil (Glenn Close) in *101 Dalmatians.* In children's films, the bad characters often have to be quite repulsive, because they fit into a fable or fairy tale mould. This is also true of horror series like *Halloween, Friday the 13th, A Nightmare on Elm Street* and *Scream.*

One cannot really describe Jean-Claude Van Damme as an actor. In reality he is a symbol, a stereotype hero who does not say much and reverts to violence to solve a problem. He is rather like John Wayne in those classic John Ford westerns. Van Damme repeats the same physically demanding performance in every role he takes and gives the audience exactly what they expect. He usually plays variations of the same character who, at a certain stage, gets rid of his shirt and flexes his muscles. This formula seems to work for certain audiences, as he repeats the same mannerisms in every part.

The same applies to performers like Steven Seagal, who have become stereotyped victims of their own image. Seagal does not even attempt to act and his performances barely register on screen. Sylvester Stallone, on the other hand, who has frequently been typecast as a fearless action hero in the *Rambo* and *Rocky* series, surprises audiences with his performance in *Cop Land,* in which he had to put on weight in order to sprout a middle-aged pot-belly. He plays against his heroic appearance and even manages not to slur his speech!

On the other hand, a radiant actor like Tim Robbins (who is never typecast) may stray into an inferior film like *Nothing to Lose* in an attempt to explore a thinly drawn character which fails to do his talent justice.

In films which pretend to reflect reality, grotesque villains actually become comical and fail to be convincing or to register as human beings. Think of the thugs in movies like *Dead Presidents, Judgment Night* or any Jean-Claude Van Damme film. One can identify the villain immediately, as he has "baddie" written all over his face and attitude.

However, not all crime bosses dress in black suits and have scars on their cheeks, and not all psychopaths are damaged individuals with mad, shimmering eyes and a vicious snarl. Compare the villain in *Metro* (played by Michael Wincott) to the much more believable psychopath in a film like *Citizen X*. Often great actors inject a kind of humanity into bad characters, making them more credible and humanly acceptable, which is why we fear them more than the stereotypes in other action films.

Jeremy Irons in *Die Hard with a Vengeance* is a much more interesting and multifaceted character than the Bruce Willis hero. The same applies to Gary Sinise as the demented kidnapper in *Ransom* and to Robert De Niro in *Heat, Angel Heart* and *The Fan*. Although they are suspect and evil killers, they are still convincing as (deranged) human beings – the kind of person we would pass in the street or scarcely notice in a crowded room, which is why they are even more frightening. Their appearance is normal and their behaviour unobtrusive until they are confronted with the wrong situation. Think of Sally Field's multifaceted performance in *Sybil* in this regard.

By comparison the Ray Liotta caricature in *Turbulence,* the villains in *Set it Off, The Crow II: City of Angels* (they even exceed comic strip standards for villains!) and *The Shadow Conspiracy* are often so unreal that we are not scared of or even repulsed by them. They may even become laughable.

REPEATING THE SAME PERFORMANCE

An actor's performance may also be judged according to his or her previous performance in a similar part. For example, John Malkovich does a brilliant characterisation of the sly, seductive and evil Valmont in *Dangerous Liaisons*. Unfortunately, he repeats the performance in *Portrait of a Lady* where his characterisation is not credible, and one questions the heroine's motives for falling in love with such an obviously evil, manipulative character. The audience can see right through Malkovich's ill-judged performance which is devoid of any of the "sensitive seductiveness" the character is supposed to have. His portrayal in *Mary Reilly* also repeats the techniques he uses in *Dangerous Liaisons,* although his performances in *Of Mice and Men* and as the villain in *In the Line of Fire* are his best to date. It is a pity he has spoiled these with his stereotype villain in *Con Air*.

The same applies to Hugh Grant who, since *Four Weddings and a Funeral,* has turned the stiff upper lip, stuttering and nervous British upper-class nerd into a caricature. He reverts to the same habits and

70, 71, 72. The three faces of John Malkovich as Dr Henry Jekyll in *Mary Reilly* (Columbia Tristar); as Lenny, a sweet but feeble-minded man whose powerful frame, uncontrolled by his childlike mind, causes trouble in *Of Mice and Men* (MGM); and as a gun-toting psychopathic criminal in *Con-Air* (Buena Vista International).

73.
Brad Pitt disregards his golden boy looks as he digs a grave as a psychotic killer who murders at random in *Kalifornia*, directed by Dominic Sena. (Courtesy of PolyGram)

affectations in films like *Nine Months, Sirens* and *The Englishman who went up a Hill, but came down a Mountain* and has become a prisoner of his own predictable techniques.

Brad Pitt, on the other hand, tries to act against his pretty-boy good looks and gives credible performances in films like *Twelve Monkeys, Seven* and *Kalifornia.* However, when he is cast as an Irish terrorist in *The Devil's Own,* his performance is superficial, as if he does not believe in his own character. One questions director Alan J. Pakula's motives for casting Hollywood's leading romantic man (currently voted the sexiest man alive by women) in such a devious, misguided part. From the onset, the audience is sympathetic towards him and perhaps even hopes he will get away because of his angelic good looks and soft eyes. However, if Edward Norton or James Woods had played that part, would we have felt the same about the character?

ENSEMBLE ACTING

Ensemble acting means individual actors interact to achieve a certain standard of acting in which all the performances are considered equal. There are no stars who dominate the film. All parts are usually similar in proportion and make an equal contribution to the overall effect.

Ensemble acting is usually found in Woody Allen films like *Everyone says I love you,* or films in which a group of characters get together (for instance over a weekend) to sort out certain problems, or to relive the past, as happened in *Love! Valour! Compassion!*

In this film the director Joe Mantello deliberately chose not to use any big names (with the exception of Jason Alexander of *Seinfeld*) to bring the eight gay men to life who get together over a series of weekends to discuss their relationships, friendships and life in general. The fact that the viewers are not familiar with most of the actors or have preconceived ideas of what they are going to do, further enhances their enjoyment of the picture, as the relatively unknown actors are completely convincing in their respective parts.

Not all ensemble casts benefit from using unknowns. *Little Women*, directed by Gillian Armstrong, features an illustrious and well-known cast consisting of Susan Sarandon, Eric Stolz, Christian Bale, Claire Danes, Kirsten Dunst, Trini Alvorado, Gabriel Byrne and Winona Ryder. These actors never act against each other or try to steal the limelight. The director also does not focus the audience's attention on a certain star or character. They are all equally important in bringing Louisa May Alcott's immortal story of love and family to the screen.

Peter's Friends, The Big Chill, Grand Canyon, The Last Supper, Jump the Gun, Singles, I Love You to Death and *Beautiful Girls* are examples. No actor steals (or tries to steal) the show; they all contribute in equal parts to the whole.

The performances of all the actors in *Jump the Gun* are a case in point. This is the story of a group of outcasts in South Africa who are trying to adapt to a new country with new challenges. They often have to revert to devious means to survive. The characters, portrayed by South African actors, are totally credible, especially because of their splendid interaction with one another, a possible result of improvisation. Their body language, vernacular and attitude reflect people who find themselves in hell, where they are making the best of their survival skills and are even enjoying the new face of their country.

GROWTH IN A CHARACTER OR PERFORMANCE

A character usually changes from the beginning of a film to the end. Depending on his experiences, the hero learns from his mistakes. He may start off as a two-dimensional character (in other words he is either good or bad), but may develop into a multifaceted human being who tries to change his ways, a certain situation or his own life. Some characters, on the other hand, are incapable of changing, and this should also be reflected in the actor's performance.

In *Seven* Brad Pitt's detective David Mills undergoes a radical change after his traumatic confrontation with the serial killer John Doe. Mill's nervous energy and bright eagerness are destroyed by evil, transforming him into a deranged shadow of the motivated fighter he used to be.

In Stanley Kubrick's *A Clockwork Orange,* Alex is a vicious murderer who has no respect for other people's lives or anything held sacred by

74.
Gugu (Baby Cele) and Minnie (Michelle Burgers) in Les Blair's comedy about contemporary life in Johannesburg, *Jump the Gun*. Life is hell and they're loving it! is what the film seems to be saying. (Courtesy of Film Four International)

society. During the film he is subjected to torture under the pretence that the government is "reforming" him. He pretends to change in order to get out of this situation (he learns how to use society and the government against themselves) and is artificially turned against violence. However, he quickly reverts to his old ways once the effect of the drugs and the conditioning are reversed. Therefore he changes for a short while, but only superficially. In the end, he is exactly the same person as the one we encounter in the bar during the first scenes. To make matters worse, he is let loose on the streets again to continue his abominable deeds. He may have changed on the surface as far as the public is concerned, but when he says: "I was cured all right" he is still as unscrupulous and wicked as in the beginning. Malcolm McDowell reflects this brilliantly in his portrayal.

The same can be said of characters like the autistic person in *Rain Man*, played by Dustin Hoffman. He is incapable of communicating or changing, and Hoffman expresses this in his performance, although a certain humanity and affection for his brother does shine through. (The unscrupulous, streetwise Ratso in *Midnight Cowboy* is perhaps one of his best-known performances as the character who learns some hard lessons and consequently changes his ways. Unfortunately the wisdom he acquires comes too late.)

The boxer Jake LaMotta in *Raging Bull* (portrayed by Robert De Niro) remains unaffected by what happens to him; he does not learn nor

CHAPTER

8

Acting

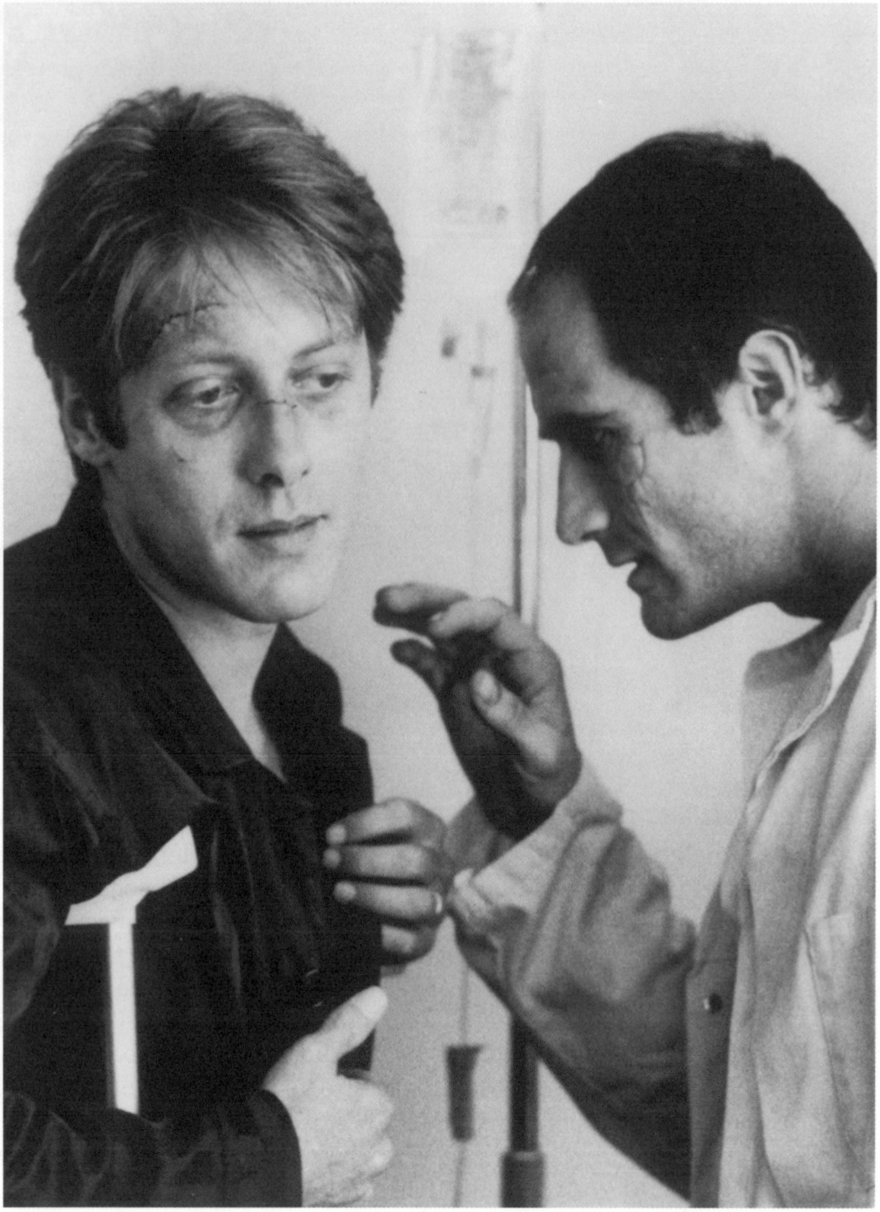

75. James Spader, here with Elias Koteas in a scene from *Crash*, is rarely typecast and is known for playing offbeat characters who provide him with a great challenge. (Courtesy of MDP)

wants to learn. In Mike Figgis's *Leaving Las Vegas* the alcoholic Ben (Nicolas Cage) fails to change even after meeting the prostitute, Sera (Elisabeth Shue). The film starts when he acquires his death wish, and this wish remains with him during the entire film. He also frequently asks Sera not to try and change him or to ask him to stop drinking.

In most films, however, the characters undergo immense changes, which are reflected in the actors' performances.

In *Marvin's Room*, an independent mother, Lee (Meryl Streep), has rejected her sister, Bessie (Diane Keaton) and neglected her son

(Leonardo DiCaprio). She has turned into a hard, relentless woman bent on self-destruction and annihilating her son. Through the interaction with her kind, loving sister who suffers from leukaemia, Lee begins to realise the importance of love, forgiveness, unselfish giving and family. In the end she not only accepts her son with all his shortcomings, but changes into a mother who sees the errors of her ways, rejects her stubborn selfishness and reaches out to the people around her. This change is revealed in Streep's touching and convincing performance.

In the beginning she speaks in hard, aggressive tones and is always on the defensive. She does not seem to care and frequently reprimands her son for small misdemeanours. However, as she gets to know him better, she gradually changes into a softer (though still tough) character who is able to communicate with her family and relate to them on a more human level. She realises how important her son is to her and how much she loves him. Unfortunately, overt sentimentality and clichés somehow spoil the film's overall effect.

The characters portrayed by Timothy Hutton in *Ordinary People,* Daniel Day-Lewis in *The Unbearable Lightness of Being,* almost all the boys in *Dead Poets Society,* the Morgan Freeman character in *Seven,* Rena Owen as Beth in *Once were Warriors,* the characters portrayed by Tim Robbins in *The Shawshank Redemption* and Tom Cruise as Jerry Maguire in the film of the same name all undergo similar transformations.

TECHNICAL, WINDOW-DRESSING PERFORMANCES

Some actors or actresses are incapable of, or are not required to, register fluctuating emotions and merely serve as decoration. This often happens in action films where the woman who accompanies the hero on his mission takes no real part in the action (in fact, she may even slow him down), but is always immaculately dressed and has make-up that can withstand the most severe circumstances.

These characters are often known as "stock characters" who could just as well have been part of the furniture. An example is the stunningly beautiful Carmen Ejogo (as Eddie Murphy's British girlfriend) in *Metro* who is pretty to look at, but is given no chance whatsoever to prove her abilities as an actress. Other examples are Kim Basinger in almost every part she has ever played, excluding *Fool For Love,* Mark Hamill in the *Star Wars* trilogy, Whitney Houston in *The Bodyguard, Waiting to Exhale* and *The Preacher's Wife,* Sofia Coppola in *The Godfather Part III* and even Tom Cruise in *Cocktail,* where nothing is required of him other than to look good.

Although the characters may influence the story's development, the actors are given no scope to develop the characters. (In Basinger's, Coppola's and Houston's cases, the actresses do not even seem to have the talent to inject new life into their characters, resulting in a stale, simply decorative performance.)

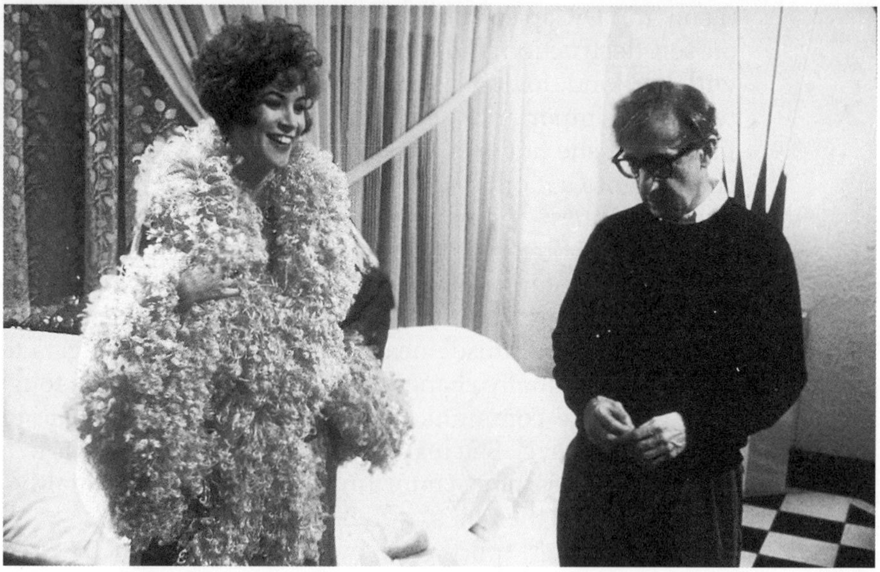

76.
A scene from Woody Allen's comedy *Bullets over Broadway* starring Jennifer Tilly. (Miramax)

IMPROVISATION

Improvisation means making up the performance as the actors go along. They may have a basic idea of where the scene is leading, but they have the freedom to make up their own dialogue and movements as the scene is being shot. It is often said that many scenes in Woody Allen movies, although they have a basic script, are influenced by improvisation, allowing the actors to develop the characters as they go along. The same applies to *Jump the Gun*. This technique is frequently used in documentaries or experimental film-making. Director Larry Clark has stated that *Kids* was carefully scripted, nevertheless one still gets the impression that many of the scenes were improvised as far as the dialogue is concerned.

CASTING INFLUENCED BY PHYSICAL ATTRIBUTES

In this case an actor or actress is used simply because he has big muscles or she has a large bosom. They are not really required to give outstanding performances, as their bodies do the "acting" for them. Pamela Anderson in *Barb Wire* and Arnold Schwarzenegger in the *Conan* films are examples. The same applies to the woman with the large breasts whom Jim Carrey meets in the elevator in *Liar, Liar.*

SMALLER PARTS AND CAMEOS

Great actors often make (uncredited) appearances in films in a small part which lasts for only a few minutes. Other actors may be required simply to stand in the background as part of a group or a crowd, or serve as a waitress or messenger. Even though their performances (if they can be described as such), may not really influence the eventual outcome of the film, it is still important that they are always convincing, even if only seen in the background. A bad performer or self-conscious extra can detract from the main actor's performance at a crucial moment.

EXERCISES

1. Al Pacino will always be Michael Corleone from the *Godfather* trilogy. Do you agree?
2. Madonna has been described as a singer who desperately wants to be a serious actress. Has she been successful up to now? Discuss by referring to her performances up to and including *Evita.*
3. Who do you regard as the best actors and actresses among the new generation and why?
4. Because the camera can enlarge an eye a hundredfold, film actors should not overact as they may do on stage. Is this true? Discuss by referring to the performances of Jim Carrey, Eddie Murphy, Anthony Hopkins and Juliette Binoche.
5. What is meant by typecasting and stereotyping? Discuss with examples.

9 The director

The director can be compared to a general in charge of a vast army of artists, ranging from the actors, the writer, the cinematographer, technicians and researchers to location scouts and even publicists. He is responsible for the end product which he has often conceived or nursed from its infancy.

He may have read a book in which he saw cinematic possibilities, as Stanley Kubrick did with Stephen King's *The Shining*. Once he has obtained financial backing, often from big studios, he sets about choosing a scriptwriter, who may also be himself. He also casts the film, usually with a casting director who suggests his clients or the right stars for certain parts, especially for supporting and smaller parts. The director then goes into pre-production, which means he starts to prepare for the actual shooting of a film. He chooses locations, collaborates with the costume designer, set designer and the rest of his team and finally starts rehearsing with the actors.

Each director works differently. For instance Mike Leigh, who made *Naked* and *Secrets and Lies*, works on an improvisational level with his actors. He gets them all together, talks to them, gets their ideas on their characters, helps them to develop their characters and often puts them in fictional situations, not necessarily in the script, which the actors then re-enact to get a more complete view of their characters.

Directors like Stanley Kubrick rehearse every scene, every movement and every nuance with meticulous precision. He had Shelley Duvall repeat her screaming scene (when the axe crashes through the door in *The Shining*) 128 times until she gave the exact tone required. He also made Tom Cruise and Nicole Kidman rehearse a scene in *Eyes Wide*

Shut, then sent them home, rewrote the scene and had them return for a new rehearsal. He also had Cruise repeat another scene 93 times for the same film.

A director like Woody Allen often does not give that much direction before shooting starts. He lets his actors act out a scene in front of the camera after plotting the movements. He frequently relies on their talents, abilities and innovation to produce new ideas, and thereafter he reacts to what has been done.

Directors often come from acting or technical backgrounds, so they know exactly what can be done in front of a camera. Some, like *Amadeus's* Miloš Forman, have been formally trained at film schools. (Forman studied under Milan Kundera in Prague.) The same applies to Martin Scorsese. Others, like Robert Redford or Clint Eastwood, are actors themselves – therefore their actors respect their direction because they speak from experience.

Stanley Kubrick, Lawrence Kasdan and Ridley Scott started as, respectively, a magazine photographer, a screenwriter and a maker of music videos and television commercials, therefore their demands on their technical crew are exact and based on experience. This also explains why Kubrick's films like *Barry Lyndon* are always visually overwhelming, as he works in close collaboration with his cameraman, but they are not always actor-friendly.

The director often has to play psychologist when working with a temperamental or inexperienced actor. He is responsible for coaxing the best possible performance from an actor, as Robert Altman did with his group of actors in *The Player* or Mike Leigh with his brilliant cast for *Naked.* William Wyler had to work with the temperamental Bette Davis on more than one occasion and eventually knew exactly how to handle her to get the required performance.

Directors hire assistant directors on second units to work with crowds and extras, or to shoot second-unit scenes. These may include shooting a vast landscape or the rising sun, which does not necessarily require the director's expertise, although he will give exact instructions regarding a certain scene if he cannot be present during the actual shoot. The director will, of course, interfere if a crowd scene, for example, does not have enough zest. While Madonna was singing from a balcony, Alan Parker often managed the crowds in *Evita* like an orchestra conductor although his assistant directors had got them together and rehearsed their reactions.

THE DIRECTOR'S STYLE

A director makes us see things the way he wants us to see them. He is usually regarded as the "narrator" of a film and influences the way we view a particular subject.

Style literally means a distinctive, characteristic manner of expression. Luis Bunuel's films, for instance, can never be confused with those

77.
Auteur director Robert Altman directing a scene from *Short Cuts*. (Spelling Films)

of any other director. He is a pioneer of surrealism whose films, according to *Brewer's cinema* (Brewer, 1995: 81), frequently attack organised religion and conventional morality. He has confessed that religious education and surrealism have marked him for life, as is evident from the famous eye-slicing scene in *Un Chien Andalou,* the parodying of the Last Supper in *Viridiana* and the exploration of frustrated lust in *That Obscure Object of Desire.*

Directors fall into two categories: The auteur director and the studio director. "Auteur" usually means an independent director who puts his personal stamp on every aspect of the film. He usually produces it and is often responsible for the script. In other words, he does almost everything himself. Directors who are regarded as auteurs include Federico Fellini, Alfred Hitchcock, Francis Ford Coppola, Bernardo Bertolucci, Robert Altman, Stanley Kubrick, Ingmar Bergman, Joel (and Ethan) Coen, Alan Parker, Woody Allen, Frank Capra, David Lynch, Mike Leigh, Akira Kurosawa, Louis Malle, Orson Welles, Oliver Stone, Francois Truffaut, Jean-Luc Godard and Martin Scorsese, to name but a few.

Auteurs' individual styles and narrative structures are evident and one cannot mistake their pictures for those of anybody else. Quite often certain motives, themes or techniques are repeated in their films. For instance, Woody Allen frequently uses long, unedited scenes in which the camera does not always favour the protagonist or person who is talking. Stanley Kubrick has a taste for deep-focus shots with the cam-

78.
Oliver Stone in a pensive mood on the set of *Natural Born Killers*. (Warner Bros.)

79.
The Coen brothers, Joel and Ethan, during the filming of *Raising Arizona*. (Courtesy of PolyGram)

era tracking in front of or behind people walking in a constricted space like a corridor, as seen in *The Shining* and *A Clockwork Orange.*

> Mike Leigh is an auteur in every sense of the word. With his provocative style, he attempts to oversee just about every aspect of his production. This authoritarian approach is evident in films like *Naked* and *Secrets and Lies*.
>
> In *Naked*, for example, his approach contributes stylistically to his message. The drained texture of the locations and the use of wide, distant deep-focus photography are all tools which he uses to convey the message of the film. Particularly in *Naked*, these techniques are used to depict the fact that he believes society has lapsed into a state of decay. By establishing his own creative style, Leigh, like all the great directors, places his personal stamp on this production, without which the film would be just another story, no different from the work of other directors.
>
> –TLdR

Other directors, sometimes nicknamed "studio directors", adhere to every whim of studio heads and have no control over the final product. They do not have "final cut" the way most auteur directors do. They simply bring a movie in on time and under budget and allow the producers to re-edit or re-shoot scenes after negative audience reactions. Their films all look the same and, apart from the director's name, are indistinguishable in style from the next film. Action directors often fall into this category or directors of average but unoriginal pictures like *Extreme Measures* (Michael Apted), *Volcano* (Mick Jackson), *No Way Out* (Roger Donaldson) or *Daylight* (Rob Cohen).

The work of studio directors contrasts sharply with that of auteur directors like John Ford (*The Searchers*), Peter Jackson *(Heavenly Creatures),* Alan Parker *(Mississippi Burning),* Mike Leigh *(Naked, Secrets and Lies)* and Peter Weir (*Dead Poets Society*), who put a very personal and provocative stamp on to every scene in their films.

Subjective style

A subjective style relates to a film-maker's emotions, prejudices, likes and dislikes. He presents his material from his own personal perspective, as Oliver Stone does in *JFK,* or Jim Sheridan in *In the Name of the Father* (a true story about four men wrongly convicted of an IRA bombing, starring Daniel Day-Lewis and Emma Thompson). Sheridan was accused of distorting the facts and manipulating the truth to suit his own dramatic needs.

Other directors who have a highly individualistic style include Danny Boyle (*Trainspotting* and *Shallow Grave),* Roman Polanski (*Tess* and *Chinatown),* John Singleton and Spike Lee, Baz Luhrmann (*Strictly Ballroom*), Richard Attenborough (*Gandhi*) and Neil Jordan (*Michael Collins*).

Objective style Objective film-making means functioning independently from general conceptions, not being influenced by current fashions or views, presenting facts in an undistorted way without allowing emotions or biases to influence the vision, and portraying an event or story as realistically as possible. For example, *Jump the Gun* presents the average South African in everyday situations without manipulating the audience's response in any way. It is an objective, unbiased portrayal of everyday life, although not all the critics agree.

80. Illeana Douglas as a woman who learns about life, love and music the hard way in *Grace of my Heart*. (Copyright © 1996 by Universal Studios, Inc. Courtesy of MCA Publishing Rights, a division of Universal Studios, Inc. All rights reserved.)

Further examples are Richard Linklater's youth comedy-drama *Dazed and Confused,* and some John Ford dramas like *The Searchers*. The audience has to make up their own minds. Allison Anders perhaps aspired to giving an objective view of a woman who is exploited and misused in the music industry in *Grace of my Heart,* but does not succeed because overt sentimentality often creeps in and spoils an otherwise good movie.

Several questions now arise which can lead to an interesting debate. Was Miloš Forman objective when he presented the editor of *Hustler* magazine as vile, selfish and obnoxious in *The People versus Larry Flynt*? Did Alexander Payne aspire to objectivity as far as the glue-sniffing Ruth is concerned in *Citizen Ruth*? A director's objective or subjective style is often influenced by the subject matter or his own background.

Subject matter

Some directors have been accused of making the "same" film and statement over and over again. It has been said that Spike Lee, excellent auteur that he is, is obsessed with racism in modern America, and that this message is repeated in every movie he has ever made, even *Girl Six.* He seems to be preoccupied with the same theme and style of film-making, which he repeats in every cinematic outing. Some of his best and

81. Controversial director Spike Lee.

most acclaimed works include *Malcolm X, Do The Right Thing, Get on the Bus* and *Jungle Fever,* while *Girl Six* and *Crooklyn* are described as having a flamboyant style which hides an empty core.

One can sometimes identify directors from the themes they choose. Hitchcock loved horror and a theme often found in his movies concerns a person wrongly accused of a crime, who then desperately tries to prove his innocence. *The Wrong Man* and *North by Northwest* are two examples. Mike Leigh shows a tendency towards depicting outsiders, discarded by society, who frequent the streets of London *(Naked)* or who are trying to survive dysfunctional lives *(Secrets and Lies)*. Ron Shelton, who is himself a sportsman, often chooses sport as an overriding theme in his films, as in *Tin Cup, White Men can't Jump* and *Bull Durham*. The

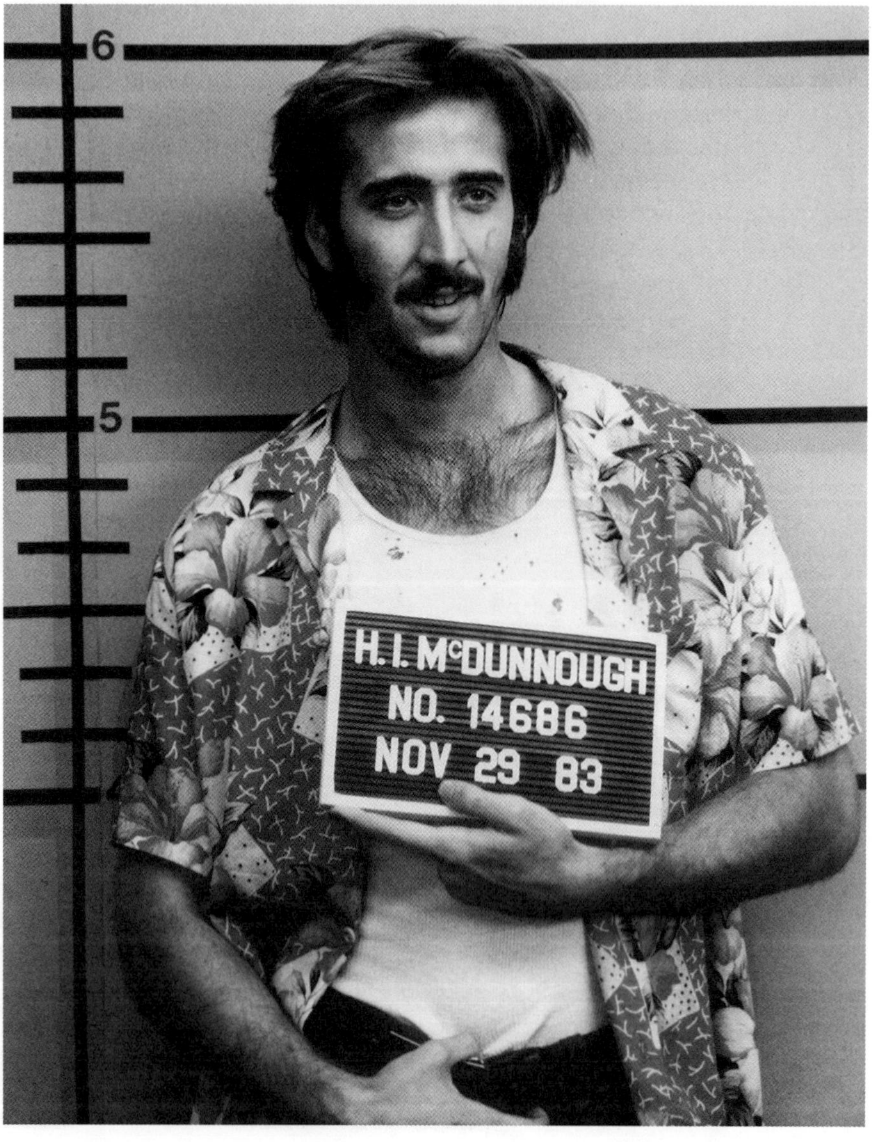

82. Oscar winner Nicolas Cage in one of his most engaging performances as the ex-convict who kidnaps a baby in the Coen Bros' *Raising Arizona.* (Courtesy of PolyGram)

sport mentality is often parodied or compared to behaviour in other levels of society.

On the other hand, many auteur directors cannot ever be categorised as far as their subject matter is concerned. Alan Parker (*Fame, Mississippi Burning* and *Shoot the Moon*), Stanley Kubrick (*Barry Lyndon* and *Eyes Wide Shut*), Robert Altman (*Three Women* and *Nashville*) and Martin Scorsese (*Taxi Driver, The Age of Innocence, After Hours*) are cases in point.

The director's background

Personal experiences may directly influence the subject matter the director chooses. For example, Spike Lee has a fiery temperament and an outspoken opinion of studios' treatment of African American artists. As mentioned earlier, Lee seems to be preoccupied by the theme of racism.

It is said that Hitchcock's father had him locked up in a jail cell as a young boy for five minutes when he committed a minor household misdemeanour – this may explain his preoccupation with characters accused of and punished for crimes they did not commit. (However, the story varies from biographer to biographer.)

Emir Kusturica frequently explores the cultural division in the former Yugoslavia in films like *Time of the Gypsies, When Father was away on Business* and especially *Underground*. Himself a victim of that civil war, all his films are about survival, presented with wry humour. Larry Clark, the director of *Kids*, was a photographer of teenage boys and in this way got to know street kids on home turf and the way they lived. His experiences with these children are responsible for his controversial *Kids*.

Directors who are willing to expose their souls on the screen are amongst the most highly regarded artists in the industry. An artist can only be honest about one thing – his or her personal perception or feeling towards a subject. This requires a fair amount of courage, because once your heart is shown to the world you open yourself to attacks from every flank.

A director whose honesty is apparent in his work is Krzysztof Kiešlowski. This Polish director draws from a personal source since his early documentary work (concerning the issues and problems of his country) to communicate a realistic and unglamorous setting populated with complicated characters. The film *Camera Buff* is said to hint at Kiešlowski's understanding of how the artist must be prepared to roll with the punches when he moves from obscurity into the social spotlight.

Kiešlowski remained true to his personal philosophy throughout his career. His medium became more than mere celluloid since he preferred to mould raw emotion the same way a sculptor manipulates clay. He paid the ultimate price for his honesty (he died shortly after completing the *Three Colours* trilogy), but he lives on through his work of art.

But a feature film should always stand on its own feet. It should not require a knowledge of the director's personal history in order to be appreciated. If this knowledge is essential to understanding a film, then the meaning of that film will become a mystery to a large segment of the audience. Alan Parker, for example, follows no specific formula in the selection of his subject matter or the style he employs. Compare *Pink Floyd: The Wall* and *Angel Heart*. The contents of these films are totally different. Accordingly, Parker's style of tackling the subject matter is also different. Since he prefers to adapt his style to a manner which best supports the content, the form of his films always matches the content, making him a great director. *Pink Floyd: The Wall* required a totally over-the-top music video-like style, while *Angel Heart* required a surreal, threatening, yet believable and realistic style.

On the other hand, all Oliver Stone's films in some way deal with the Vietnam conflict. It is obvious that he has never been able to justify the ordeal he had to undergo earlier in his life. It seems that in every film he is trying to find someone to blame for the horror of that war – from the press to president Nixon. In Stone's case, it is advantageous for the audience to know that the director was personally involved in the Vietnam conflict. Only then can his statements be fully appreciated.

– NG

THE DIRECTOR AS A "SUPERSTAR"

There are a few directors whose names alone attract their intended audience, which is why some of them always make the kind of films that are expected of them. Steven Spielberg is perhaps the most famous director in the world today next to Alfred Hitchcock, and people usually know what they are letting themselves in for when going to see a Spielberg film.

Spielberg usually concentrates on a magical incident which changes the world of ordinary people in small-town America *(Always, E.T.: The Extra-Terrestrial, Hook)*. His films normally centre around larger-than-life characters in larger-than-life situations (the *Indiana Jones* trilogy, *Jurassic Park* and its sequel). But Spielberg has also made a very personal and deeply disturbing film, *Schindler's List,* which reminds us never to forget what happened to the Jews during World War II. This film is vastly different in subject matter and tone from many of his other films.

The same applies to Woody Allen who tried to imitate Ingmar Bergman with *Interiors.* Other directors who have achieved "superstar" status and whose names are as well known as their films are John Ford, Oliver Stone, David Cronenberg (especially after *Crash* and *The Fly* in 1986), and to a lesser degree Francis Ford Coppola and Martin Scorsese.

When actors turn to directing, they are already well known and are also referred to as "superstar directors", like Warren Beatty *(Reds),*

83.
Director Robert Redford, here in a scene from Phil Alden Robinson's *Sneakers*. (Copyright © 1992 by Universal Studios, Inc. Courtesy of MCA Publishing Rights, a division of Universal Studios, Inc.

Robert Redford *(Ordinary People, A River Runs Through It)*, Clint Eastwood *(Unforgiven, Absolute Power)*, Mel Gibson *(Braveheart, The Man without a Face)* and Kevin Costner *(Dances with Wolves)*. It therefore takes a very brave and unselfish "superstar" director, like Spielberg, to break free from audience expectations and to deliver a truly original film which one would not normally expect in his body of work.

SOCIAL RESPONSIBILITY

A director often sees his task as a social responsibility to draw attention to a certain matter from which others may shy away. Jonathan Demme tackled discrimination against homosexuals head-on in *Philadelphia* in his unflinching and unbiased portrayal of this issue.

Oliver Stone also sees himself as a kind of "conscience of the American people" and touches on controversial issues or raw nerves in American society which are not necessarily government- or establishment-friendly. The same applies to a director like Lee Tamahori who in *Once were Warriors* exposes the shameless exploitation of women by heartless, selfish and abusive husbands who force them to survive in grim situations, and also the vast difference between whites and Aborigines in contemporary New Zealand.

The opposite is also, unfortunately, true. As brilliant a film-maker as Quentin Tarantino is (his *Pulp Fiction* and *Reservoir Dogs* have been immortalised as great works), he attempts to make violence "cool". His script for *From Dusk till Dawn* is an example of irresponsible and reckless film-making (the director is Robert Rodriguez). Some viewers feel that it is irresponsible to present violence as funny (as in the car scene in *Pulp Fiction,* where two thugs are more concerned with the dirty ceiling than with the fact that they have accidentally blown a man's brains out). Other directors who fall into this category include John Woo whose exploitation action thrillers like *Bullet in the Head, Face/Off* and *Broken Arrow* are nothing more than vehicles for special effects with gratuitous and often unmotivated explicit violence.

Many directors would argue that they do not see their role as a "responsible" one. Many merely want to entertain and feel they should be allowed to do so. However, those whose movies raise awareness, like Antonia Bird's *Priest* or Kenneth Loach's harrowing *Ladybird, Ladybird* about a single mother who tries to keep her children, or Gillo Pontecorvo of *The Battle of Algiers* fame, are often regarded as more important than their commercial colleagues.

CHOICE OF ACTORS

The director works on a very personal level with his actors. Directors often favour certain actors with whom they strike a rapport and who understand best what message they are trying to convey.

Possibly the best example of such a partnership is Robert De Niro and Martin Scorsese, who have worked together on a number of films such as *Mean Streets, Taxi Driver, Raging Bull, Cape Fear, Goodfellas, Casino* and *The King of Comedy*. Alfred Hitchcock had an affinity for blondes and most actresses in his movies are blondes. John Ford used John Wayne in many of his westerns, turning him into a kind of western icon. Sydney Pollack has made seven films with Robert Redford, among them *Out of Africa.* Ingmar Bergman, who also had a relationship with Liv Ullmann, cast her in most of his best-known films like *Cries and Whispers* and *Scenes from a Marriage,* often opposite Erland Josephson, while Spike Lee cast himself in many of his own films, and Nicolas Roeg favoured his wife Theresa Russell.

The merits of this practice are, however, debatable: a director may extract the same performance from the actor every time or, as in De

Niro's case, may stretch the actor's talents to the ultimate and be responsible for some of the greatest performances of all time. One somehow feels that Sydney Pollack got the same range of emotions from Redford every time, while Alan J. Pakula elicited a completely different performance from Redford in *All the President's Men.*

NARRATIVE STRUCTURE

The narrative structure means the way in which the director constructs his material or tells his story. He may choose a tight, formal structure in which the film never ventures into an experimental phase, like Martin Scorsese's *The Age of Innocence,* David Lean's *A Passage to India* or Ken Russell's masterful *Women in Love.* Formal stories are usually presented in this manner, although Baz Luhrmann achieved the exact opposite with his stylistic, informal *Strictly Ballroom* and *William Shakespeare's Romeo and Juliet,* as did Philip Kaufman with *The Unbearable Lightness of Being* and *The Right Stuff.* The same applies to Terence Malick's *Days of Heaven* and *Badlands.*

A director can also choose to jump forwards and backwards in time, as Anthony Minghella does so skilfully in *The English Patient.* In this way, he conveys his protagonist's state of mind as his thoughts wander from one incident to the next, not necessarily in chronological order. Some directors choose to start in the middle or the end of a story. Action films, especially *James Bond* films, often begin midway through a daring escape or other action before moving on to the rest of the story. Others, like *Out of Africa* and *Another Country,* start at the end with a dying woman reliving the past or a journalist extracting information from a reluctant interviewee and sharing her observations with us.

Directors often permit their films to follow threads and themes which eventually have nothing to do with the final outcome. These little strands of plot seem to be there merely to pad or fill in empty spaces. In *Metro,* Eddie Murphy's character loves gambling, but in the end this has no relevance to the main plot, its resolution or the characterisation.

Sometimes a director may use an erratic, almost incomprehensible structure, as in Adrian Lyne's superb *Jacob's Ladder,* George Roy Hill's *Slaughterhouse-Five,* as well as Robert Altman's loosely constructed *Prêt-à-Porter.* Peter Greenaway is another highly individualistic director well known for the loose structure of his films, which often fluctuate in style and time. Examples are *The Pillow Book, The Draughtsman's Contract* and *The Belly of an Architect.* The same applies to Emir Kusturica's *Time of the Gypsies* and *Underground.*

Ken Russell is often accused of overstepping the boundaries of good taste and cinematic discipline with his wildly irrational exercises in films like *Mahler, The Music Lovers, The Devils* and *Tommy.* Nobody expected him to choose the direction he has ventured into after his magnificent *Women in Love. Whore* is perhaps the final nail in his coffin.

A director can also choose to introduce surrealism into his films, as

Luis Bunuel does in *The Discreet Charm of the Bourgeoisie* or David Lynch in *Blue Velvet* and *Lost Highway*, or Peter Jackson in *Heavenly Creatures*.

Other directors allow several stories or events to occur simultaneously which are then juxtaposed for effect, as occurs in Peter Jackson's *The Frighteners* or Roman Polanski's *Bitter Moon*. In these films the stories in the past and present complement each other in a weird, almost surrealistic way.

Some directors, such as Anthony Minghella, like multi-textured styles, as *Truly Madly Deeply* and *The English Patient* illustrate. Krzysztof Kiešlowski does the same with his *Three Colours* trilogy. Other directors prefer a no-nonsense, straightforward style supported by extreme realism – Mike Leigh's *Secrets and Lies* being a good example. Many directors like to use visual pictures to tell the main story (Kiešlowski, Lynch), while others (Woody Allen and *The Shawshank Redemption's* Frank Darabont) prefer using words.

GENRE AND DIRECTOR'S STYLE

One may sometimes ask whether a film is intended as a non-genre film (also called an "art film"), as described by Thomas and Vivian Sobchack in *An introduction to film* (1987), or whether it forms part of a general group of films. For instance, films like *Farinelli* by Gerard Corbiau and *Funny Bones* by Peter Chelsom can hardly be categorised into a specific genre, while others such as the brilliant *Godfather* trilogy by Francis Ford Coppola, *Body Heat* by Lawrence Kasdan and *Breakdown* by Jonathan Mostow are part of an identifiable genre.

A comprehensive discussion of genres in cinema falls outside the scope of this book. Suffice it to say that there are several genres which need careful analysis and examination, notably *film noir*, the western, the horror and slasher film, science fiction, surrealism, the musical, the gangster and crime film, drama, melodrama, comedy (including slapstick comedy, screwball comedy and black comedy), as well as comic strip cinema and gay and lesbian cinema to name a few.

EXERCISES

1. What is meant by a director's style?
2. Should we always know a great deal about a director and his background before analysing his films? Discuss.
3. Examine the difference in style between directors like Joel Coen, Stanley Kubrick, David Lynch and Alan Parker.
4. What is meant by a subjective and an objective style? Discuss each by giving examples.
5. Do you think Kathryn Bigelow fell in love with her own visual flair and excess in *Strange Days*, or did her style suit the thriller genre and give it a dash of *film noir*?

6. Compare the way a director like Mike Newell portrays the Mafia in *Donnie Brasco* with Francis Ford Coppola's treatment of a similar subject in *The Godfather Trilogy*.
7. When the director of *Titanic* (James Cameron) omitted some of the heart-rending true stories related to this disaster, would you say that it resulted in the fictional love story having been over emphasised to the detriment of the more dramatic real-life tragedy?
8. *A Life Less Ordinary* was torn to pieces by the critics. Was it really a bad film, or were critics and the public expecting another *Shallow Grave* or *Trainspotting*? Discuss the similarity/difference between these three films, focusing especially on Danny Boyle's style.

10

Additional elements

Up to this point we have taken the jigsaw puzzle apart and studied each segment separately. The question now is what happens when we have analysed the separate pieces and we start putting them all together again.

Once we have studied the completed or semi-completed pictures, new questions arise, or we may become aware of other, often subliminal messages which may not always be that obvious. How do we explore and discover these, once we have made a complete study of the technical elements, as well as the story and the underlying motives? As stated before, one should be absolutely sure of what the director is trying to say, and that we have examined every clue he gives us to gain access to his message. Here, finally, are the last clues to ascertaining a director's motives.

SUBTEXT

Subtext is that which lies between the lines or behind the dialogue. Consciously or subconsciously, a director often makes statements that are not directly obvious in the dialogue, but are implied in other ways.

Take the example of a scene in which a man and a woman are discussing the relationship between their best friends and what has gone wrong in that particular marriage. On the surface, they are discussing the marital problems experienced by friends, but on studying the dialogue and analysing their reasons for the discussion, it becomes clear that they are actually talking about their own problems "through" other people, without addressing their problems directly because they are scared of a direct confrontation.

For instance, people often say "I love you" without really using those words, or by talking about a completely different subject. The Cher/Nicolas Cage relationship in *Moonstruck* is a perfect example of where a couple's conversation functions on one level (as understood by them), but in reality they are admitting that they are crazy about each other without saying it in so many words.

In *Heavenly Creatures* two girls are having tea with a woman. She is the mother of one of the girls who plans to murder her after tea. As the mother contemplates whether she should be having a piece of cake (she is watching her figure), her daughter urges her to have it, to "spoil herself", knowing that this is going to be the last pleasure she is ever going to experience. From the mother's point of view having a piece of cake is a transgression, since she is probably on a diet. Our (and the girls') understanding is that it is her last piece of cake before being brutally slaughtered, and that this is a kind of sick, demented "farewell" – the last act of kindness permitted her by her killers. The subtext is: "Have this piece of cake, mother, it is going to be your last. I actually do have some kind of belated feeling towards you, but I have to go through with this to free myself and my friend from you. And we haven't got much time, we should be going."

In a film's subtext we may discover many statements which the characters, director or writer make on a subconscious level, which is often why directors admit that they were not aware that they were making certain statements which students later discover. Ultimately though, most of them agree that that was what they meant without being conscious of it.

IRONY

Irony is the use of words or images to imply the opposite of what they normally mean. In dramatic situations, it is the difference between what is expected and what actually is. Irony links opposites and adds a new dimension to certain situations. It can be dramatic, humorous or tragic and occurs in various forms.

Dramatic irony

A character often lacks the knowledge that the audience has. The character understands the situation in a straightforward way, as in the *Heavenly Creatures* scene discussed earlier. Or a girl may walk into a dark room and call: "Is anybody there?" This applies to the scene in which the Veronica Cartwright character goes in search of the cat in the spaceship in *Alien*. We know that a monster (or a murderer) is lurking in the shadows, and we know that she is probably going to be killed. However, she is completely oblivious of this threat and continues to search for the cat.

84.
Jim Carrey learns how to be a proper father to his son Max (Justin Cooper) by not lying, in the comedy *Liar Liar*. (Copyright © 1997 by Universal Studios, Inc. Courtesy of MCA Publishing Rights, a division of Universal Studios, Inc. All rights reserved.)

Irony of situation With this type of irony a scene turns out differently from what we expected. A character may have good intentions upon entering a restaurant, but the situation may become chaotic when something unexpectedly goes wrong. Just refer to Meg Ryan's famous orgasm scene in *When Harry met Sally*.

In *Edward Scissorhands* the loveable, eccentric character played by Johnny Depp wants to caress or touch the people he likes with his hands, but his fingers consist of blades. The moment he touches people he hurts them, which is not his intention.

Irony frequently occurs in Tom Shadyac's hilarious *Liar, Liar,* in which a father, who has been used to lying or telling little white lies all his life, suddenly cannot tell a lie and lands in all kinds of difficult and extremely funny situations as a result. His intention was to tell a lie in court and win the case, but because of his son's wish, he cannot do this and the scene turns out differently: he exposes his own client's hypocrisy, but in the process reveals the truth due to a technical point.

Irony of character Irony of character means that a character possesses opposing emotions which often clash. He may want to be good, but his darker side often emerges unexpectedly and is far stronger than his good side. *Dr Jekyll and Mr Hyde* (recently remade from another character's point of view as *Mary Reilly*) is a classic example. During his experiments the kind, loving Dr Jekyll turns into the devil incarnate in the form of the evil Mr Hyde who symbolises his dark alter ego. He maims and kills people at night without reason and returns to the laboratory in order to turn into the harmless Dr Jekyll again.

The same applies to *The Shadow* (Alec Baldwin), in which the main character is fully aware of his bad, shadowy side, but is forced to commit himself to helping his fellowman because he knows "what evil lurks in the hearts of men". Because of his personal knowledge of evil, he knows how to fight it, but will always be a prisoner of its power.

Another example is the Clark Kent character in the *Superman* series, in which one body accommodates both a nerd (Kent) and a hero (Superman). The irony is that Lois Lane, Kent's reporter friend, thinks she is in love with the hero-saviour, but actually she loves the nerd more. The professor in *The Nutty Professor* by Tom Shadyac is both the obnoxious, arrogant playboy and the fat, helpless nerd in the person of Eddie Murphy.

Irony of character may also mean that a character behaves differently from what we may expect, for instance, the helpless Kevin Spacey cripple who turns out to be the evil monster, Keyser Soze, in *The Usual Suspects.* The same applies to the Edward Norton character in *Primal Fear* whose schizophrenic tendencies are misread by us – we think that there are two sides to him, a good and an evil. In the end it turns out that he has fooled everybody, and that he has only an evil, vindictive side which he uses to deceive the court and even his lawyer, played by Richard Gere.

In the excellent thriller *Breakdown*, Kurt Russell initially gives the impression of being a weakling, especially in the way he treats the thugs at the petrol station. However, he soon proves to be their match as he frees his wife from their clutches and outmanoeuvres them. A man who appeared to be a nerd, proves to be a hero with extreme courage.

Ed Wood, in the film with the same name, has both an idealistic, masculine side to him and a romantic, feminine side when he dresses up in women's clothes. He feels free and human only when he dresses in angora sweaters and frocks.

Irony of setting

This occurs when an event takes place in a setting where we do not expect it.

In *Bad Lieutenant* by Abel Ferrara, a nun is viciously raped on an altar in the church – the very last place one would expect such a vile act to take place. So too the rape of the nuns in Ken Russell's *The Devils*, and actor Rupert Everett copulating with corpses in a graveyard in *Dellamore, Dellamorte*, also known as *Cemetery Man.*

In *The Shawshank Redemption*, a man who has been wrongfully jailed remains free in spirit – his soul is the one thing the corrupt authorities cannot imprison. He therefore has "freedom in prison", not the place where one would expect to find freedom.

Irony of tone

Irony of tone has already been discussed in the chapter on dialogue and sound (Chapter 5). An example of this type of irony is the joyful "Happy Heart" song at the end of *Shallow Grave*, in which a friendship is brutally destroyed by greed and the characters have no reason whatsoever to be happy. The words to the song mean the opposite of what is happening on the screen, but on evaluating the situation, certain phrases can very well be applied to the characters on a different level from that originally intended by the song.

In *Ordinary People* Mary Tyler Moore, as a cold and distant mother, holds her son (Timothy Hutton) responsible for the death of his brother. When, on occasion, she speaks to him (for instance, when he surprises her in his brother's room), she appears to be friendly but in reality she is deeply resentful towards him, a feeling she hides in her congenial, almost neutral tone.

SYMBOLISM

Symbolism means using something (an object, person or event) to represent something else. It may also refer to an object representing something abstract. In *The Unbearable Lightness of Being*, Sabina's hat symbolises decadence and carefree, erotic love without commitment (the lightness of Tomas's life). The hat plays an important part in her arousing and seducing Tomas and represents the sexual games which are about to start – but Tomas always leaves after the encounters. He never commits, he never stays: he is like the hat which can be taken off or put on at will.

In our everyday lives there are several symbols which we take for granted because we have been conditioned by them or have become accustomed to them. For instance, if somebody is waving a red flag in the road, we expect danger ahead. A blue flashing light symbolises the police; green normally signifies that all is clear and safe. In the same way, we associate the desert with heat and death, while ice symbolises extreme coldness. Night may symbolise danger because we cannot see as clearly as during the day, while water may symbolise life.

In the same way, one associates crows and vultures with death. The scythe in Ingmar Bergman's *The Seventh Seal* symbolises death – the reaping of a life, while a Venus flytrap in the hothouse in *Suddenly Last Summer* may symbolise the carnivorous nature of its owner (played by Katharine Hepburn) who literally loves her son to death. It may also symbolise the scene of cannibalism which exposes the truth behind the mental state of the Elizabeth Taylor character.

In *The Shawshank Redemption*, the prison symbolises a restrictive, corrupt regime. A Bible usually represents salvation, religion or pureness of spirit, but seen in context in Frank Darabont's film it acquires an ironic meaning once the sadistic prison warder abuses his powers and humiliates and tortures the inmates with the Bible clasped in his hands. It now assumes a completely new and different meaning from the one we know: it represents the repressive order of the perverted regime. Moreover, the Bible is abused by the authorities who hide behind what it is supposed to mean; they use it to cover up their loathsome deeds. Right at the end the Bible brings about the downfall of the corrupt prison authorities. Its new symbolic meaning is further enhanced by its other function: it literally becomes a place for concealing the tools which the Tim Robbins character uses to escape and expose the corruption of the authorities.

In *Sirens*, where a conservative, sexually repressed minister and his wife are confronted by their own forbidden desires, most of the objects in the garden have a symbolic meaning, especially the snake which continues to slither in and out of the picture. It may symbolise the decadence (even evil) hiding among the luscious plants, fountains and statues which turn this setting into a garden of Eden. Because the snake is not really threatening, it may also symbolise evil as being deceptively gracious and beautiful, or it may be a warning to us that all is not well in paradise and that something may lead to the downfall of the prudish main characters, played by Tara Fitzgerald and Hugh Grant.

There are several other examples of popular symbols used in films. In many films the American flag symbolises patriotism, while it acquires a twisted, very different meaning in some Vietnam films. The bottle represents the root of the problems in Beth's household in *Once Were Warriors*; it is the reason why her husband has turned into a monster, and it provides the grounds for their separation.

Even in an average movie like *Liar, Liar* the boy's birthday cake represents broken promises to him, as his father (Jim Carrey) does not arrive to help him cut it. The sumptuous food in *Like Water for Chocolate* symbolises Tita's love for Pedro, whom she cannot have because he is married to her sister. She prepares each dish as if she is making love to him, and he tastes it with orgasmic pleasure. The food becomes symbolic of their forbidden relationship.

ALLEGORY

With allegory the apparent intention of a scene or the role of a character acquires a higher meaning, even a spiritual one. Every person or object is symbolic of a certain philosophy or way of thinking. Each symbolic meaning tells a separate story on a fantasy level. One of the best examples is *The Last Supper*, where every guest represents a certain level of society. They exemplify a way of thinking or a certain mentality. The problem is that the guests are not always convincing as people, but appear rather to be mouthpieces for the director's views.

LEITMOTIF

A leitmotif is something which is often repeated in order for it to take on a symbolic or higher meaning. Sometimes it becomes a trade mark of a particular character.

Sabina's hat in *The Unbearable Lightness of Being* and Charlie Chaplin's cane and bowler hat are two examples. "The claw" in *Liar, Liar* is also a kind of recurrent theme which establishes the father and son's relationship with each other. The moment another character tries to imitate "the claw", that is, the shape in which Jim Carrey forms his hand to tickle and play with his son, the routine collapses.

A specific phrase may also serve as a leitmotif, for instance "Smokin'!" in *The Mask,* or the word "dude" in the *Bill and Ted* series, or phrases ending on the word "not" in the *Wayne's World* series, for example: "I like you. Not."

Other phrases or sentences which are used only once or twice in films may also become a trade mark of a certain character or actor. For instance Clint Eastwood's Dirty Harry is forever associated with the phrase: "Make my day!", while Arnold Schwarzenegger's "Hasta la vista, Baby!" and "I'll be back" are synonymous with him. Also note Dianne Wiest's hilarious "Don't speak!" in *Bullets over Broadway.*

CONTEXTUAL DISSONANCE

This means the representation of something (a person, event or object) in a time period in which it would not normally exist. For example, one would not expect to find a piece of ice in the middle of a scorching desert, or a greasy hamburger with ketchup on the Queen of England's dinner table.

In *The English Patient* a Santa Claus dressed for the North Pole, walking around in the stifling Cairo heat during the Christmas lunch, is a contextual anachronism. The irony is heightened because the British are completely out of place in the stark desert, and Geoffrey Clifton (played by Colin Firth) also does not belong in this scene where the two doomed lovers are about to make love right under his nose.

SURREALISM

This topic belongs with a discussion of genres, but since there is a movement promoting this particular genre in modern-day films, a short explanation is needed here.

Surrealism originated in the early twenties, stressing Freudian and Marxist ideas. It means tapping into the subconscious and dream world and exploring that which reality denies us but fiction or cinema can fully explore. Surrealism functions on an unreal and irrational level. It usually aims to shock the audience and rejects conservatism.

We would all like to control our own dreams, and that is what surrealism is: a controlled dream or nightmare, at which we can marvel from the comfort of our cinema seats. It brings us into contact with the forces in our own subconscious minds and often awakens the monsters which slumber there while still allowing us to maintain some kind of control.

Surrealists refuse to separate the dream from so-called "reality", *Lost Highway* by David Lynch being a case in point. Lynch and other directors who favour surrealism as a means of expression stimulate our imaginations with possibilities, but do not necessarily supply the answers. This is why *Lost Highway* has frustrated so many viewers who demand explanations – there are none. Lynch's films take place in never-never land, but we still recognise that world as close to our perceptions of "reality".

Lost Highway is about fear. Chris Rodley explains the Pete Dayton character, played by Balthazar Getty, in *Sight and Sound* (1996: 8) as "trying to make sense of why his own life has become so strangely unfamiliar. He feels that he seems to know her [the strange woman, played by Patricia Arquette, who turns up at the garage where he works]. However, he's severely disoriented, stumbling through what seems to be a nightmare of someone else's making. It's just possible (in Lynchland) that he is actually part of a highly organised hallucination: Madison's (the Bill Pullman character) mental creation." In the same magazine the following explanation appears on the opening page of the script: "[*Lost Highway*] is a 21st century noir horror film. A graphic investigation into parallel identity crises. A world where time is dangerously out of control. A terrifying ride down the lost highway."

Lost Highway is about hallucinations, about getting caught in the mind of an obsessed narrator. He introduces us to different versions of the same character. Patricia Arquette is both Rene and Alice, although by Arquette's own admission the blonde Alice could be a hallucination, because Rene, the other woman she resembles, has been murdered. Arquette continues: "I play two different interpretations of the same woman. I think it's about a man trying to recreate a relationship with the woman he loves so that it ends up better. Fred (Pullman) recreates himself as Pete (Getty), but the element of distrust in him is so strong that even his fantasy turns into a nightmare" (*Sight and Sound*, 1996: 18).

This film is all about the workings of the subconscious, about dreams being part of a demented reality. Lynch shows us the flipside of reality. He shows us where our dreams and the hallucinations of the characters come from, and how our fears manifest in surrealist dream images which can still be related to reality. Lynch takes even the simplest scene and through his imaginative use of camera work, dark lighting, dreamy, eerie songs and strange, unexpected camera angles, he turns what may appear to be insignificant events (like a woman getting out of a car or a man answering his intercom in a house) into something far more profound.

Lynch does not want to answer any of our questions. He is simply interested in creating a compelling cinematic journey into the subconscious. Where he previously explored middle-class values (*Blue Velvet, Wild at Heart* and to a certain extent the inferior *Twin Peaks: Fire walk with me*), he now explores the rich upper class, bored with their perfectly symmetrical lives in technically perfect surroundings. The house looks like a cube, the dull bedroom consists of brown walls and black sheets, while the living room is a cold, desolate place. These people live in slow motion, they do not communicate and are surrounded by fear and uncertainty. Their own dreams are their worst enemies. Lynch seems to be saying that reason must acknowledge the existence of the imagination and must accommodate hallucination. In other words: don't be a slave to realism or logic, allow your imagination to roam free if you want to understand Lynchland.

Surrealism is more about image and instinct than reason. It turns our way of feeling and thinking upside down, as directors Bunuel, Fellini,

85.
Balthazar Getty is one of the most promising new talents of the younger generation actors, here in a scene from *Lost Highway*. (Courtesy of Ciby 2000)

David Cronenberg and David Lynch do. Examples of films with surrealist influences are *After Hours* (Martin Scorsese); several Fellini films, especially *Fellini Roma, Fellini Satyricon* and *And the Ship Sails on; Barton Fink* (Joel and Ethan Coen); *Carrie* (Brian De Palma); *The Company of Wolves* (Neil Jordan); *Kiss of the Spider Woman* (Hector Babenco); *Naked Lunch, Videodrome* and *Scanners* (Cronenberg); *Don't Look Now* (Nicolas Roeg); *Pink Floyd: The Wall* (Alan Parker); *The Tin Drum* (Volker Schlöndorff) and especially *Delicatessen* (Jean-Pierre Jeunet and Marc Caro).

PARODY

In parody the style of the original artist is imitated in a humorous way. It can be seen as a send-up or a thumbing of the nose, but in the process, the greatness of the original artist is usually acknowledged. We are forced to look at an existing work of art or a well-known story or film through new eyes and to explore its meaning outside the normal artistic borders.

Andy Warhol (and with him Paul Morrissey, the director of many of his avant-garde, experimental, underground films such as *Trash, Heat* and *Lonesome Cowboys*) usually attacks the middle-class values of the consumer society. Take note of Warhol's famous symbol of consumer mentality, the soup can painting and Marilyn Monroe. Parody is all about imitation (which can also be the sincerest form of flattery), and about exploring the banal in the everyday.

Mel Brooks is famous for parodying genres in his comedies. He takes the best-known scenes from famous films, and gives them his own, personal, satirical touch. He reinterprets them by sending up the original in an often flattering or even "respectful" way – thus acknowledging the impact or status of the original. In *High Anxiety* he spoofs many Hitchcock classics, specifically *Vertigo*. In *Blazing Saddles* he sends up the western, and in *Young Frankenstein* he parodies the Mary Shelley novel and original film version of *Frankenstein*. Also remember his mockery of the Robin Hood legend in films like *Robin Hood, Men in Tights*. Other famous spoofs by Brooks include *The Producers, To be or not to be, Silent Movie* and *Life Stinks*.

Other films by various directors which parody the originals include *Airplane!* (the *Airport* series); *Mars Attacks!* (science fiction films of the fifties, especially *The War of the Worlds*); *The Brady Bunch Movie* and its sequel; *Earth Girls are Easy; So I married an Axe Murderer; Hot Shots!* and its sequel; *Last Action Hero* (a commercially unsuccessful send-up of the Arnold Schwarzenegger films, but critically one of his better films); the *Naked Gun* series; *The Rocky Horror Picture Show* (which parodies the Frankenstein legend, as well as science fiction films of the fifties); the entire *Monty Python* series; *Love at first Bite* (the Dracula films); *Lust in the Dust* (forties melodramas); *Freeway* (the Little Red Riding Hood fable); *Scream* (horror films); and *Down Periscope*.

EXERCISES

1. What is meant by irony? What different kinds of irony are there? Discuss with examples.
2. A director often communicates with his audience through subtext. Explain what subtext is by referring to *The English Patient*, *Heavenly Creatures*, and *Ordinary People* by Robert Redford.
3. What does parody mean? Give examples.

11

Writing an analysis

PREPARATION

In preparing an analysis or a paper, the following points should be taken into consideration.

1. Always know what you want to write before you start writing. If possible, your ideas should firstly be written down on a piece of paper and then organised, so that once you start writing the style and form are concise and to the point. In other words, know what you want to say when you put pen to paper or finger to keyboard. If you do not know what more to say, do not "pad" by repeating the same idea over and over in different forms.

2. Always know what the director is trying to say and analyse how he says it. Then analyse whether he has achieved his goal, which techniques he has used and whether these techniques have been applied successfully.

3. Do not relate the whole story. Give a brief version, for example:

   > *Dead Poets Society* concerns an unorthodox teacher (superbly played by Robin Williams) and the profound impact he has on a conservative school, where he teaches the boys to explore their own potential. He clashes with the rigid school system and is opposed by the parents, which ultimately leads to tragedy.

   Do not go into detail by explaining what happens in every scene, except when you analyse what is happening and why it is happening (for instance, by referring to the suicide scene and the way it was shot).

4. One expects the acting to be good in a professional film. Do not waste too much space by heaping praise on the actors. Comment only on the acting when an actor gives an exceptionally complex or interesting reading of a part, for example:

> Edward Norton presents a new slant on the traditionally clichéd part of the psychopath in *Primal Fear*. His performance shows a full understanding of the complexity of the sly, demented character. He is initially scarred by sexual abuse, but is also clever enough to get back at the system by fooling both the law and the psychologists. These opposing characteristics are conveyed by his portrayal of a totally believable wide-eyed innocent as opposed to the monstrous murderer who exposes his true identity only in the final confrontation.

Refer also to Norman Galloway's criticism of Ralph Fiennes's performance in *The English Patient,* in Chapter 8. Be sure you are able to explain why a performance is good or bad.

You should apply the same approach to the cinematography, editing and directing. Simply to say that the photography is breathtaking is not enough, for instance, as in *The English Patient*. Explain why Minghella shot his film on such an epic scale and whether this complements the story or overpowers its more intimate elements.

Use the same approach again for Kenneth Branagh's epic vision of *Hamlet*. Why did he film the famous "To be or not to be" soliloquy in front of a mirror? What effect is achieved by the raining confetti in the marriage scene and its epic presentation?

86. Kenneth Branagh starred as Hamlet in the film version of Shakespeare's immortal drama. He also directed this screen version in 70 mm. (Courtesy of Castle Rock; Photographer: Rolf Konow)

5. Always follow a logical pattern of thought. Analyse each theme or element separately if need be, and later demonstrate how they all fit in together to enhance or illustrate the director's point. Do not jump around, but keep to the point.

6. If writing for a newspaper or student publication, and you need to use examples, do not quote an obscure film which you know your public may not have seen. Your examples should be reasonably accessible.

7. Unless a film is really beyond redemption (as *Carpool* is – but that may also be a subjective view) do not use personal or offending and overly sarcastic language. There are, of course, exceptions such as the famous Libby Gelman-Waxner essays on film which appear in *Premiere* magazine and which themselves are parodies of the original film. This writer usually sends up a film with compassion and often with respect.

   When preparing a paper, do not overindulge in clever or sarcastic comments, unless the particular paper, article or review aims to entertain a television audience, for instance. Even then strong comments should only be made in exceptional circumstances.

8. Always try to be as objective as possible. If a movie like *Kids* offends your religious or moral beliefs, stick to a formal analysis of why the film may offend certain viewers or why the director used particularly offensive images.

   Do not turn your essay into a sermon and do not preach to your audience or force your opinion on them. Also remember that the critic is not the superstar or the focal point. The film is. Always stay as sober in your analysis as is humanly possible. Be careful of demanding that a film should be banned. Besides infringing on the artist's right to freedom of expression, the reader may not be interested in your own moral view, but in the artistic quality of the film. Suggesting that a film be banned, does not remove it nor its statement from existence. Your viewer has the right to decide for himself, so do not try to decide for him.

9. Always check the spelling of the names of directors, films, actors, etcetera. Note, for example, that the classic 1952 musical is called *Singin' in the Rain* and not *Singing in the Rain.* The title of *sex, lies, and videotape* does not have capital letters. The full title of *E.T.* is *E.T.: The Extra-Terrestrial* (with proper punctuation). The title of *48 Hrs* is not spelt *Forty Eight Hours.* Other often incorrectly quoted titles are *Jungle 2 Jungle, $* (the Warren Beatty film) and **batteries not included* (not *Batteries not Included).* Some press notes spell the title of *Seven* as *Se7en,* but mostly as *Seven.* Also check your grammar and general spelling.

   Be sure also to give foreign films or films with more than one title their correct names. For instance *Leon* was called *The Professional* in

South Africa. Explain this in your essay by referring to this film as: *The Professional,* also known as *Leon.*

10. Always enjoy what you are doing, whether you are watching your six thousandth film or writing you umpteenth review. There should always be a new way of looking at a subject or a new way of writing about it. Do not fall into a predictable, monotonous style of writing, even if you are writing about the worst film ever made. Remember your reader must still be stimulated to read what you have written, whether it be your teacher, lecturer, an audience or newspaper readers.

11. Do not copy other people's reviews or ideas. With the invention of *Cinemania* and the Internet, the whole world's reviews are suddenly at your fingertips, which has tempted some people to rewrite a particular review in their own words or even plagiarise the original. Avoid doing this at all costs. Your lecturer, teacher or audience is interested in your own views, and somebody else's view will soon turn your paper or review into a mess, as your thoughts may become muddled. Furthermore your reader may have read that review already and your plagiarism will quickly be exposed.

    You may, of course, refer to what other critics have said, which can start a whole new debate. For instance you may write: "*The Ghost and the Darkness* has been attacked as being un-South African, completely implausible and laughably unoriginal, as John Smith says in his review in *The Sunday News.*" Always credit the original writer and your source.

12. Try to avoid clichés and meaningless phrases, especially terms like "this is a not-to-be-missed film", "it is definitely Oscar material" and "what a wonderful experience!"

    If you do have to use such statements when writing for a very general audience, especially a vast television audience, or when you are writing for a commercial magazine or newspaper and the editor specifically instructs you to keep your intended audience's requirements in mind, keep them to the minimum or try to find a new way of saying the same thing. This does not mean you may never use words like "stunning" or "beautiful", but explain why you use them and do so economically.

    Try to avoid meaningless words like "nice" or "sweet". If you do refer to "the haunting musical score", or "breathtaking photography", define and explain why you use those words, as Norman Galloway does in his essay on *The Mission* in this chapter.

13. Write economically. An extended sentence such as:

    > There are several factors which make Alan J. Pakula's film *The Devil's Own* an overt exercise in sheer manipulation, glamorisation and exploitation which eventually has a numbing effect on the audience's perceptions of the main theme.

could read:

> In *The Devil's Own,* Alan J. Pakula glamorises the Irish civil war and exploits it for commercial reasons.

Most critics and students are guilty of overwriting, because we are often so swept up by a film or the effect it has had on us that we cannot cut down on unnecessary words or descriptions. Try to avoid this.

14. Be aware of your audience. The style of an influential and highly respected publication like *Sight and Sound* will obviously differ and be more sophisticated, even more complicated than that of a family magazine.

    Sights and Sound's audience usually consists of cinema-literate people, academics and students. One communicates with them on a different level and accepts that their knowledge of cinema terms and trends is far above that of the average person, hence there is no need to explain so much.

15. Your introductory paragraph usually sets the tone for the rest of your review or sums up what the film is about. Take time to construct a coherent, logical opening paragraph which may motivate your readers to continue reading your review.

    Your concluding paragraph often complements your opening paragraph or brings it to a logical conclusion. Make a specific statement with that paragraph, so that your readers know exactly what you were trying to say. If the film warrants it, answer all the questions you have posed.

16. Before or after you see a film about a subject about which you know very little, try to read up on the subject. If a film deals with a civil war in a rather obscure country (*Before the Rain,* for example), try at least to obtain some information about the causes of the conflict, which may make the film easier to understand. Do not read reviews beforehand – they could influence you subconsciously!

17. If you have to take notes during a film, make those notes concise and only write down an idea when absolutely necessary. Writing a note should not distract your attention, especially when the film has subtitles. By looking away from the screen, you jerk yourself out of its atmosphere and line of vision momentarily. As we cannot all see a film twice, it is often necessary to write down keywords, but do not write a whole essay while watching the film.

    Notes such as "incredibly beautiful and striking photography" are unnecessary. If you are watching *Hamlet* or *The English Patient* and the photography strikes you from the beginning, you are not likely to forget it. Other elements may be more important, and notes like "Fiennes bland" or "blandness unmotivated" could lead you to analyse the reasons for his performance. "Pitt too glamorous" or "casting manipulative" is enough to enable you to write about a wrong choice of role or to evoke our sympathy for a negative character. For *Lost Highway* you would simply need to write: "Colours subdued" or "surrealistic dream" or "questions don't need answers" or "Arq. different sides, one woman?"

EXAMPLES OF FILM ANALYSIS

The two contributors to this book, Norman Galloway and Tascoe Luc de Reuck, were given the following assignment: Write a cryptic review on a film of your choice, concentrating on the statement the director is trying to make in his film. Does he succeed in conveying his message? How does he communicate with his audience? Ultimately, is this particular film good or are there elements which detract from the overall impact? Write as concisely and economically as possible.

The Basketball Diaries – Tascoe Luc de Reuck

From the diaries of renowned author, Jim Carroll, comes this surrealistic glimpse into the madness created by substance abuse. *The Basketball Diaries* is an exploration into the soul of every young kid who is unable to make sense of it all. It is a shocking revelation of what can happen when misguided pranks begin to spin out of control. In this true story, the character of Jim is brought to life in spectacular fashion by Leonardo DiCaprio. The young actor sizzles from beginning to end, drawing the viewer into the mind of his character and leaving him shocked and exhausted.

At the beginning of the film, Jim is much like an average teenager, a character with whom many of us can probably associate. Trying to escape the suffocating formality of his Catholic upbringing, Jim submerges himself in the world of basketball and writing. After a friend of his dies, however, he begins to question the purpose of his life and is confronted with issues that he is incapable of dealing with. He becomes involved in a nightmare world of crime and drug abuse, a habit which spins out of control until eventually his mother (Lorraine Bracco) throws him out. Jim finds himself locked out of a world he had once embraced, and so begins a journey that spirals downwards towards self-destruction. In order to support his habit, he is forced to do unspeakable things which threaten to destroy his grasp on reality.

Through his diaries, Jim reveals his inner emotions to us, his desire to break out of the shackles that one creates for oneself. He describes his life as a four-hour movie that nobody seems to understand. In his writing, he almost acknowledges the fact that he is lost, but is not yet in the position to deal with it. At one point in the film, he sees one of his old basketball friends on television, and is overcome when he has a vision of what he could have become. He realises in one pure defining moment that he has become his own worst nightmare, someone he promised himself he would never become.

The surrealism which the director attempts to create is effective in depicting the state of mind of someone caught in the nightmarish world of drug abuse.

"After four deep whiffs
We were sailing some place else,
Bells ringing through my ears,
And little lights flashing through my eyes ..."

These are words from the film that seem to epitomise what it must be like to get lost in a hell that seemingly has no way out. Through the eyes of Jim Carroll, director Scott Kalvert reveals to us how quickly things can get out of control, forcing us to deal with many difficult and emotional issues. He draws us into the film, allowing us a glimpse into the heart of madness and despair. This is an epic story of self-destruction, a journey from the apparent innocence of youth to the wisdom that comes through experience.

The Basketball Diaries is a film with a social conscience, a film that warns one at every turn about the fears, dangers and temptations associated with growing up in our modern world.

87. The multi-talented Leonardo DiCaprio in *The Basketball Diaries*. (Courtesy of PolyGram)

The Mission – Norman Galloway

The Mission attempts to immortalise those who lost their lives while fighting for what they believed to be justice. In this case, the film documents the true events which occurred in the jungles of South America during the eighteenth century. The struggle is between the interests of the church, represented by the Jesuit order, and the Spanish and Portuguese nations. The object of the conflict is the native Indians who inhabit the jungles. One group wants their souls, the other wishes to take their territory and enslave their bodies.

The film centres around the lesser of the two evils – the mission of the Jesuit priests to introduce the Indians to the law as prescribed by their Christian God. Jeremy Irons plays Gabriel, a Jesuit priest who enters the jungle in the hope of creating a new mission station for those natives who are still untouched by foreign influence. In an exquisitely photographed location, and accompanied by an excellent score by Ennio Morricone which comfortably moves from elation to defeat, Gabriel begins his work. Along the way he succeeds in converting a slave trader, Mendoza (Robert De Niro), into a God-fearing Jesuit priest.

This film has the potential to be a masterpiece: powerful cast, breathtaking photography, an appropriately haunting musical score, and a dramatic and controversial true story as subject matter. The conflicts are monumental and complicated.

The protagonist is difficult to identify. The obvious solution is to see the Jesuit priests as being on the side of good. But the film does allude, however briefly, to the fact that if the church had never decided to blunder blindly into the jungle, the Indians would have been able to continue their existence in peace. The antagonists are not that difficult to identify, and there are plenty of them – from the bloodthirsty slave traders to the equally brutal Portuguese armies.

The director, Roland Joffe, uses the musical score both to support the emotion within scenes, as well as for characterisation. One of our first impressions of Gabriel is that of him "subduing" the Indians by playing the flute. It is a beautiful piece, which suggests innocence and purity. Later this same piece is warped into a disturbing, almost chaotic sound, which accompanies the slave trader Mendoza. This is an excellent example of how music can support characterisation. The problem is that, at times, Joffe relies too heavily on the score, and the music alone becomes the medium which evokes the required emotional response. A more effective approach would have been firstly to have ensured that the scenes work without music (through the editing technique), and only then to have added the music if required.

The photography of Chris Menges (also director of photography for *The Killing Fields*) captures the exotic and mystical feelings of the natural surroundings. He makes use of wide-angle lenses to emphasise the magnificence and sheer size of the jungle. A good example is the opening sequence where a Jesuit priest is crucified by the Indians, and is sent down the river to plunge over what must be the largest waterfall ever photographed. This same wide-angle technique is used with good effect in juxtaposing Gabriel with the same waterfall, a visual metaphor for his monumental struggle.

One of the shortcomings of the film is that we never know enough about any of the characters to be able to identify with them or their struggle. Hence the deaths of Gabriel and Mendoza have little emotional impact. We are not provided with enough of an insight into what drives and motivates them. It seems that Joffe tried to tackle too many issues in the film, without really making a point about any one of them, except that hope survives everything.

An interesting quirk in the film is the single shot placed after the closing credits: that of an official sitting at his desk. He looks up sharply into the camera. The look seems to be half remorseful and half challenging, as if Joffe is challenging the audience to find the greater truth in the film (which I believe to be that the priests had no place in the jungle in the first place).

On the whole, the film is a good piece of work. The cast portrays the numerous characters with passable historical accuracy. The visuals and music stand out as the real achievements of the film, as it tries to reveal the plight of the Indians who had the unfortunate "pleasure" of being saved from their own barbaric selves. This theme alone demands a great deal of respect for the film.

* * *

Here is an analysis of a commercial film, *Breakdown*, written for a newspaper with the specific purpose of informing readers whether they should spend their money on the film or not. I was also asked to analyse the reason for the film's appeal or lack thereof.

Breakdown – Leon van Nierop

Breakdown is about survival. It uncovers the lengths an everyman would go to to preserve his comfortable existence. It is about the tension between civilisation as represented by a yuppie couple and the savage shrewdness of a rural, backward community which has been excluded from such comforts. The film also scrapes away the thin veneer which hides man's primitive instincts. We are living on the edge of chaos, and one wrong step (like leaving your Jeep's hood open) could plunge one into unspeakable terror.

As a metaphor for this message, the film's promising first-time director, Jonathan Mostow, uses an ordinary couple with whom the audience can identify. Like Hitchcock, Mostow separates them from their comfortable surroundings and plunges them into unusual circumstances they cannot deal with. Civilisation has made them too self-assured, too used to talking themselves out of difficult situations. Man has become a soldier of war. He has lost none of his primitive skills though. When called upon, these instincts surface in unexpected forms to ensure his survival.

An ordinary couple (Kurt Russell and Kathleen Quinlan) drive through a desolate wasteland in America's Southwest. When their jeep breaks down, a truck driver (J.T. Walsh) offers Amy (Quinlan) a lift. Uneasy music and an edgy atmosphere created by unusual camera angles and a restless camera already anticipate danger. Amy vanishes and Jeff (Russell) tries to find her.

There are hints of *The Vanishing* and *Duel* in this scenario. Those films skilfully tapped into our fear of the unknown. We never see *Duel's* driver, and the woman's fate in *The Vanishing* (the Dutch version) is so horrifying we prefer not to have known. In *Breakdown* we identify the perpetrators early in the film, but they form such a formidable and evil combination while still being convincing as people, that they pose a much bigger threat than the aliens in *Independence Day* ever could have.

The baby-faced Jack Noseworthy as Billy is perfectly cast in this respect. He fools us by appearing to be innocent, which proves that the fiercest evil often comes in the handsomest packages. *Breakdown* is not only a tautly directed action film about a search and urban terror, but it also highlights the vulnerability of man who has become so civilised that he fails to heed danger signs. He trusts people too easily and he is too self-assured.

It is as if rural America is taking revenge on corporate, over-saturated urban America. Mostow skilfully explores this tension through aggressive editing which speeds up as the film progresses. He juxtaposes violent aggression with quiet horror in scenes in the bar, especially when a patron plays a practical joke on Jeff. This makes us even more aware of the unpredictability of thugs – Jeff could just as well have walked into a morgue. The characters are openly hostile, they look as if they have the same parents and they despise Jeff's good looks, manners and friendliness.

At this point Mostow puts the film into neutral as he reverts to a camera which glides over the townsfolk. They do not speak to one another and resemble living statues. Mostow evokes an uneasy feeling of terror and uncertainty which prompts our imaginations to leap to scenarios even worse than the actual outcome.

While in the main storyline Jeff asks the owner of the bar if he has seen his wife, in the subtext the townsfolk despise the breath of clean-cut civilisation he brings with him into their stale existence. The same applies in the scene in which the camera picks up a noticeboard at an ill-equipped police station where the personnel are not much different from the patrons in the bar. The board is filled with missing persons. Their names look like engravings on tombstones and the director implies that Amy is now only a statistic to the police, no longer a person.

Mostow later again reverts to Hitchcock's technique of terrorising the audience with the unusual in the everyday: he makes an innocent man look guilty in the eyes of the law, as in the scene in which the sheriff takes the side of the truck driver and almost arrests Jeff. We identify with Jeff's frustration. How often have we found ourselves wrongly accused or clashing with bureaucratic indifference?

Unfortunately *Breakdown* succumbs to an audience-friendly ending. The terror would have been heightened had Amy never been found. There are only two scenes where Mostow reverts to the current trend to blow an audience away with an explosive climax.

The story is quite simple. The terror the film evokes through an almost unobtrusive, eerie musical score, a quick-moving narrative structure and frequent close-ups which imprison the characters somehow fades where it should have haunted us.

The over-the-top bridge-hanging sequence and Jeff's struggle under the truck which he boards in mid-flight may be exciting, but they harm the film's credibility. The scene in which the vehicle drifts down a raging river is also tense, but loses credibility when the jeep is retrieved without much trouble. According to the previous scene the jeep had washed much further down the river and would have been inaccessible to the thugs. Furthermore, it is retrieved unscathed despite having hit rocks and other obstacles.

Breakdown is like a mixture of *Straw Dogs* and *Deliverance*. It builds towards unbearable tension which never lets up. It terrifies us because most of the action is plausible and the director hypnotises us with fear of the unknown which appears superficially calm but hides violent chaos.

Breakdown is a great thriller in the Hitchcock tradition, aimed at audiences who are tired of the exaggeration offered them by junk food movies like *Con Air* and *Speed 2: Cruise Control*. It is a terrifying rollercoaster ride of the imagination which touches the raw nerves of many an urbanised yuppie who thinks survival only means keeping your job and putting food on the table.

88.
The climactic confrontation between good and evil in the final scenes from *Breakdown*, an above-average thriller by Jonathan Mostow. (Spelling Films)

BIBLIOGRAPHY

Boggs, Joseph M. 1996. *The art of watching films,* 4th ed. Mountain View, CA: Mayfield.

Brewer, Ebenezer Cobham. 1995. *Brewer's cinema.* Wellington House, London: Cassel.

Case, Christopher. 1996. *The ultimate movie thesaurus.* New York: Henry Holt.

Cinemania 97. Microsoft Windows 95.

Ebert, Roger. 1996. Roger Ebert's column "Video Companion" in the *Chicago Sun-Times* on Internet http://www.suntimes.com/ebert/ebert/htm/.

Empire Edition. 1994. Issue 64.

Empire Magazine. 1996. Issue 85, July.

Giannetti, Louis. 1993. *Understanding movies,* 6th ed. Englewood Cliffs, NJ: Prentice Hall.

Kael, Pauline. 1985, 1986, 1987, 1988, 1989. *Hooked.* 2 Park Avenue, New York: E. Dutton.

Kael, Pauline. 1975, 1976, 1977, 1978, 1979, 1980. *When the lights go down.* 383 Madison Avenue, New York: Holt, Rinehart & Winston.

Kaleta, Kenneth C. 1993. *David Lynch.* 866 Third Avenue, New York: Twayne.

Matthews, J.H. *Surrealism and film.* 1971. Canada: University of Michigan Press.

Reisz, Karel & Millar, Gavin. 1984. *The technique of film editing.* London/Boston: Focal Press.

Sight and Sound. 1996. 6(7): 8 & 18, July.

Sobchack, Thomas & Sobchack, Vivian. 1987. *An introduction to film,* 2nd ed. Boston/Toronto: Little Brown.

Stok, Danusia. *Kieślowski on Kieślowski.* 1995. 3 Queen Square, London: Faber & Faber.

FILMOGRAPHY – A SELECTION

2001: A Space Odyssey
UK (1968): Science Fiction
139 min

Producer	Stanley Kubrick
Director	Stanley Kubrick
Screenwriter	Stanley Kubrick
	Arthur C. Clarke

Based on the short story "The Sentinel" by Clarke

A Clockwork Orange
US (1971): Science Fiction
137 min

Producer	Stanley Kubrick
Director	Stanley Kubrick
Screenwriter	Stanley Kubrick

Based on the novel by Anthony Burgess

Alien
US (1979): Science Fiction/Horror
117 min

Producer	Gordon Carroll
	David Giler
	Walter Hill
Director	Ridley Scott
Screenwriter	Dan O'Bannon

Based on a story by O'Bannon and Ronald Shusett

All That Jazz
US (1979): Musical/Dance
123 min

Producer	Robert Alan Aurthur
Director	Bob Fosse
Screenwriter	Robert Alan Aurthur
	Bob Fosse

Amadeus
US (1984): Musical/Biography
158 min

Producer	Saul Zaentz
Director	Miloš Forman
Screenwriter	Peter Shaffer

Based on the play by Shaffer

Another Country
UK (1984): Drama
90 min

Producer	Alan Marshall
Director	Marek Kanievska
Screenwriter	Julian Mitchell

Based on Mitchell's novel

Antonia's Line
Belgium-Netherlands-UK (1995): Drama/Comedy
102 min

Producer	Gerard Cornelisse
	Judy Counihan (co-producer)
	Hans De Weers
	Antonino Lombardo (co-producer)
	Bert Nijdam (line)
	Wim Ode (co-producer)
	Hans de Wolf
Director	Marleen Gorris
Screenwriter	Marleen Gorris

Barton Fink
US (1991): Drama/Comedy
117 min

Producer	Ethan Coen
Director	Joel Coen
Screenwriter	Ethan Coen
	Joel Coen

Being There
US (1979): Comedy
130 min

Producer	Andrew Braunsberg
Director	Hal Ashby
Screenwriter	Jerzy Kosinski

Based on his novel

Blue Velvet
US (1986): Mystery
120 min

Producer	Fred Caruso
Director	David Lynch
Screenwriter	David Lynch

Born on the Fourth of July
US (1989): War / Drama / Biography
144 min

Producer	A. Kitman Ho Oliver Stone
Director	Oliver Stone
Screenwriter	Oliver Stone Ron Kovic

Based on his autobiography

Breakdown
USA (1996): Thriller
96 min

Producer	
Director	Jonathan Mostow
Screenwriter	Jonathan Mostow and Sam Montgommery

Cabaret
US (1972): Musical / Drama / Dance
128 min

Producer	Cy Feuer
Director	Bob Fosse
Screenwriter	Jay Presson Allen

Based on the stage play by Joe Masteroff, the stage play "I Am a Camera" by John van Druten, and the writings of Christopher Isherwood

Chariots of Fire
UK (1981): Sports / Biography
123 min

Producer	David Puttnam
Director	Hugh Hudson
Screenwriter	Colin Welland

Citizen Kane
US (1941): Drama
119 min

Producer	Orson Welles
Director	Orson Welles
Screenwriter	Herman J. Mankiewicz Orson Welles

Citizen X
US (1995)
103 min

Producer	Timothy Marx
Director	Chris Gerolmo
Screenwriter	Chris Gerolmo

Based on the novel by Robert Cullen

Das Boot/The Boat
Germany (1981): War
145 min

Producer	Gunter Rohrbach Michael Bittins
Director	Wolfgang Petersen
Screenwriter	Wolfgang Petersen

Based on the novel by Lothar-Guenther Buchheim

Diva
France (1982): Romance / Crime
123 min

Producer	Irene Silberman
Director	Jean-Jacques Beineix
Screenwriter	Jean-Jacques Beineix Jean Van Hamme

Based on a novel by Delacorta

Don't Look Now
UK (1973): Mystery
110 min

Producer	Peter Katz
Director	Nicolas Roeg
Screenwriter	Allan Scott Chris Bryant

Based on a short story by Daphne du Maurier

E.T.: The Extra-Terrestrial
US (1982): Science Fiction
115 min

Producer	Steven Spielberg Kathleen Kennedy
Director	Steven Spielberg
Screenwriter	Melissa Mathison

Fargo
US (1996): Thriller / Crime
97 min

Producer	Ethan Coen
Director	Joel Coen

Screenwriter	William Richert Joel Coen Ethan Coen

Forrest Gump

US (1994): Drama/Comedy
142 min

Producer	Wendy Finerman Steve Tisch Steve Starkey
Director	Robert Zemeckis
Screenwriter	Eric Roth

Based on the novel by Winston Groom

Hamlet

US (1996)
238 min

Producer	David Barron
Director	Kenneth Branagh
Screenwriter	Kenneth Branagh

Based on the play by William Shakespeare

if ...

UK (1968): Drama
111 min

Producer	Michael Medwin Lindsay Anderson
Director	Lindsay Anderson
Screenwriter	David Sherwin

Based on a script by Sherwin and John Howlett, entitled "The Crusaders"

It's a Wonderful Life

US (1946): Drama
129 min

Producer	Frank Capra
Director	Frank Capra
Screenwriter	Frances Goodrich Albert Hackett Frank Capra Jo Swerling

Based on the story "The Greatest Gift" by Philip Van Doren Stern

Lost Highway

US (1997) : Mystery
135 min

Produced by	Deepak Nayar Tom Sternberg Mary Sweeney
Directed by	David Lynch
Written by	(in credits order) David Lynch & Barry Gifford

Naked

UK (1993): Drama
126 min

Producer	Simon Channing-Williams
Director	Mike Leigh
Screenwriter	Mike Leigh

Natural Born Killers

US (1994): Drama/Crime/Comedy
119 min

Producer	Jane Hamsher Don Murphy Clayton Townsend
Director	Oliver Stone
Screenwriter	David Veloz Richard Rutowski Oliver Stone

From a story by Quentin Tarantino

Once Were Warriors

New Zealand (1994): Drama
103 min

Producer	Robin Scholes
Director	Lee Tamahori
Screenwriter	Riwia Brown

Ordinary People

US (1980): Drama
123 min

Producer	Ronald L. Schwary
Director	Robert Redford
Screenwriter	Alvin Sargent

Based on the novel by Judith Guest

Philadelphia

US (1993): Drama
119 min

Producer	Edward Saxon Jonathan Demme
Associate producer	Kristi Zea
Director	Jonathan Demme
Second unit director	Kristi Zea
Screenwriter	Ron Nyswaner

Picnic at Hanging Rock

Australia (1975): Drama
110 min

Producer	Jim McElroy Hal McElroy

Director	Peter Weir
Screenwriter	Cliff Green

Based on the novel by Joan Lindsay

Platoon

US (1986): War
120 min

Producer	Arnold Kopelson
Executive producer	John Daly
	Derek Gibson
Director	Oliver Stone
Screenwriter	Oliver Stone

Psycho

US (1960): Thriller / Horror
109 min

Producer	Alfred Hitchcock
Director	Alfred Hitchcock
Screenwriter	Joseph Stefano

Based on the novel by Robert Bloch

Pulp Fiction

US (1994): Drama / Crime / Comedy
154 min

Producer	Lawrence Bender
Director	Quentin Tarantino
Screenwriter	Quentin Tarantino
	Roger Avary

Based on stories by Tarantino and Avary

Reservoir Dogs

US (1992): Crime / Drama
99 min

Producer	Lawrence Bender
Director	Quentin Tarantino
Screenwriter	Quentin Tarantino

Schindler's List

US (1993): War / Historical / Drama
195 min

Producer	Steven Spielberg
	Gerald R. Molen
	Branko Lustig
Director	Steven Spielberg
Screenwriter	Steven Zaillian

From the novel "Schindler's List" by Thomas Keneally

Secrets and Lies

UK (1996)
142 min

Producer	Simon Channing-Williams
Director	Mike Leigh
Screenwriter	Mike Leigh

Seven

US (1995): Thriller / Drama / Crime
127 min

Producer	Arnold Kopelson
	Phyllis Caryle
Director	David Fincher
Screenwriter	Andrew Kevin Walker

Shallow Grave

Scotland (1994): Thriller
94 min

Producer	Andrew MacDonald
Director	Danny Boyle
Screenwriter	John Hodge

Shine

Australia (1996)
104 min

Producer	Jane Scott
Director	Scott Hicks
Screenwriter	Scott Hicks
	Jan Sardi

Sophie's Choice

US (1982): Drama
157 min

Producer	Alan J. Pakula
	Keith Barish
Director	Alan J. Pakula
Screenwriter	Alan J. Pakula

Based on the novel by William Styron

Strictly Ballroom

Australia (1992): Comedy
93 min

Producer	Tristam Miall
Director	Baz Luhrmann

The Basketball Diaries

US (1995): Drama / Biography
100 min

Producer	Liz Heller
Director	Scott Kalvert
Screenwriter	Bryan Goluboff

The Battle of Algiers

Algeria-Italy (1965): War
123 min

Producer	Antonio Musu
	Yacef Saadi
Director	Gillo Pontecorvo
Screenwriter	Gillo Pontecorvo
	Franco Solinas

The Crying Game

UK (1992): Drama
112 min

Producer	Stephen Woolley
Director	Neil Jordan
Screenwriter	Neil Jordan

The English Patient

US (1996) : Drama
162 min

Produced by	Steve E. Andrews (associate)
	Scott Greenstein (executive)
	Bob Weinstein (executive)
	Harvey Weinstein (executive)
	Saul Zaentz
	Alessandro von Norman (line)
Directed by	Anthony Minghella
Written by	Anthony Minghella
	Michael Ondaatje (novel)

The Go-Between

UK (1971): Drama
116 min

Producer	John Heyman
	Norman Priggen
Director	Joseph Losey
Screenwriter	Harold Pinter

Based on the novel by L.P. Hartley

The Graduate

US (1967): Drama / Comedy
105 min

Producer	Lawrence Turman
Director	Mike Nichols
Screenwriter	Calder Willingham
	Buck Henry

Based on the novel by Charles Webb

The Mission

UK (1986): Drama
125 min

Producer	Fernando Ghia
	David Puttnam
Director	Roland Joffe
Screenwriter	Robert Bolt

The Name of the Rose

France–Germany–Italy (1986): Mystery / Historical
130 min

Producer	Bernd Eichinger
Director	Jean-Jacques Annaud
Screenwriter	Alain Godard
	Andrew Birkin
	Gérard Brach
	Howard Franklin

The Other Side of Sunday

Norway (1996) : Drama
103 min

Produced by	Grete Rypdal
	Oddvar Bull Tuhus
Directed by	Berit Nesheim
Written by	Lasse Glomm
	Berit Nesheim
	Reidun Nortvedt (Novel Søndag)

The Searchers

US (1956): Western
119 min

Producer	Merian C. Cooper
	C.V. Whitney
Director	John Ford
Screenwriter	Frank S. Nugent

Based on the novel by Alan LeMay

The Shawshank Redemption

US (1994): Prison / Drama
142 min

Producer	Niki Marvin
Director	Frank Darabont
Screenwriter	Frank Darabont

Based on the short story Rita Hayworth and the "Shawshank Redemption" by Stephen King

The Shining

US (1980): Horror
142 min

Producer	Jan Harlan
	Stanley Kubrick
Director	Stanley Kubrick
Screenwriter	Diane Johnson
	Stanley Kubrick

Based on the novel by Stephen King

The Silence of the Lambs

US (1991): Thriller/Mystery
118 min

Producer	Edward Saxon
	Kenneth Utt
	Ron Bozman
Director	Jonathan Demme
Screenwriter	Ted Tally

From the novel by Thomas Harris

The Unbearable Lightness of Being

US (1988): War/Romance
171 min

Producer	Saul Zaentz
Director	Philip Kaufman
Screenwriter	Jean-Claude Carrière
	Philip Kaufman

Based on the novel by Milan Kundera

The Usual Suspects

US (1995): Thriller/Mystery/Crime
105 min

Producer	Michael McDonnell
	Bryan Singer
Director	Bryan Singer
Screenwriter	Christopher McQuarrie

The Wild Bunch

US (1969): Western
144 min

Producer	Phil Feldman
Director	Sam Peckinpah
Screenwriter	Walon Green
	Sam Peckinpah

Based on a story by Green and Roy N. Sickner

Thelma and Louise

US (1991): Drama/Comedy/Adventure
128 min

Producer	Ridley Scott
	Mimi Polk
Co-producer	Callie Khouri
Director	Ridley Scott
Screenplay	Callie Khouri

Three Colours: Blue

France-Poland-Switzerland (1993): Drama
100 min

Producer	Marin Karmitz
Director	Krzysztof Kieślowski
Screenwriter	Krzysztof Piesiewicz
Co-screenwriter	Krzysztof Kieślowski

Three Colours: Red

France-Poland-Switzerland (1994): Drama
99 min

Producer	Marin Karmitz
	Gerard Ruey
Director	Krzysztof Kieślowski
Screenwriter	Krzysztof Piesiewicz
Co-screenwriter	Krzysztof Kieślowski

Three Colours: White

France (1994): Drama
92 min

Producer	Marin Karmitz
Director	Krzysztof Kieślowski
Screenwriter	Krzysztof Piesiewicz
	Agnieszka Holland
	Edward Zebrowski
Co-screenwriter	Krzysztof Kieślowski

Titanic

US (1997) : Romance
195 min

Produced by	James Cameron
	Pamela Easley (associate)
	Al Giddings (co-producer)
	Grant Hill (co-producer)
	Jon Landau
	Sharon Mann (co-producer)
	Rae Sanchini (executive)
Directed by	James Cameron
Written by	James Cameron

To Kill a Mockingbird

US (1962): Drama
129 min

Producer	Alan J. Pakula
Director	Robert Mulligan
Screenwriter	Horton Foote

Based on the novel by Harper Lee

Trainspotting

UK (1995)
93 min

Producer	Christopher Figg
	Andrew MacDonald
Director	Danny Boyle
Screenwriter	John Hodge

Based on the novel by Irvine Welsh

Unforgiven

US (1992): Western
127 min

Producer	Clint Eastwood
Director	Clint Eastwood
Screenwriter	David Webb Peoples

William Shakespeare's Romeo & Juliet

US (1996)
120 min

Producer	Jill Bilcock (associate) Martin Brown (II) (co-producer) Baz Luhrmann Catherine Martin (associate) Gabriella Martinelli
Director	Baz Luhrmann
Screenwriter	Baz Luhrmann Craig Pearce

Based on the play by William Shakespeare

Witness

US (1985): Crime
112 min

Producer	Edward S. Feldman
Director	Peter Weir
Screenwriter	Earl W. Wallace William Kelley

Based on a story by William Kelley, Earl W. Wallace and Pamela Wallace

Women in Love

UK (1969): Drama
129 min

Producer	Larry Kramer
Director	Ken Russell
Screenwriter	Larry Kramer

Based on the novel by D.H. Lawrence

Source: Cinemania '97

NAME INDEX

A page number followed by a "p" indicates a reference to a photograph on that page. The bold "**p**" refers to a colour photograph.

C

D

N

O

P

T

U